Michael Musto

CARROLL & GRAF PUBLISHERS
NEW YORK

La Dolce Musto
Writings by the World's Most Outrageous Columnist

Carroll & Graf Publishers
An Imprint of Avalon Publishing Group, Inc.
245 West 17th Street, 11th Floor
New York, NY 10011

AVALON
publishing group incorporated

Library of Congress Cataloging-in-Publication Data is available.

ISBN-13: 978-0-78671-879-5
ISBN-10: 0-7867-1879-X

9 8 7 6 5 4 3 2 1

Interior design by Maria Fernandez
Printed in the United States of America
Distributed by Publishers Group West

To anyone who can still manage
to exude glamour with mud dripping down his or her face

Contents

Acknowledgments

Endless gratitude goes to Carroll & Graf and specifically my wonderful editor, Don Weise, for making this project seem so effortless, along with creative director Linda Kosarin, senior publicity director Karen Auerbach, and publicist Betsy Steve. I'm also indebted to the *Village Voice* and the editors there who've encouraged and liberated me through the years (including Karen Durbin, Vince Aletti, David Schneiderman, Scott Malcolmson, Barbara Odair, Donald Forst, Charles McNulty, Ward Harkavy, Jorge Morales, and David Blum) and Catherine McGann, who for years adorned the column with her zesty photos. I have to thank my parents Anna and Ciro for all the love and support and for helping make me so adorably, excitingly twisted that reaching this point was inevitable. And I'm deeply grateful to everyone who's ever taken the time to gossip with me, thereby helping give me both a life and a livelihood (Beauregard Houston-Montgomery, Bill Love, Anita Sarko, Patrick McMullan, Mickey Boardman, Angelo Pitillo, Lee Kimble, Cathay Che, Richard Turley, Michelangelo Signorile, Lynn Yaeger, Michael Ellis, Ann Ellwood, Stephen Schaefer, Colin Shanley, Chuck Attix, Stephen Saban, Patrick McMullan, Amy Lumet, Thomas Bober, and Susan Anton, as well as my freelance employers over at *Out* and *Ocean Drive* magazines and the crew over at *Countdown* with Keith Olbermann). Finally, thanks to the gossip community for, not only giving me constant must-reads, but for making me feel so well reported on (Richard Johnson, Cindy Adams, Liz Smith, Rush & Molloy, Lloyd Grove, Ben Widdicombe, Jessica Coen, Perez Hilton, and anyone else who cares more about Lindsay Lohan than seems logical).

Introduction

In 1984, Big Brother was watching over me, but apparently only to make sure I got a job where I could watch over other people: writing "La Dolce Musto," a regular column for the alternative weekly the *VillageVoice* about whatever I freakin' felt like. You know, Dr. Seuss musicals, private s&m clubs, unspeakably sick gossip, gay culture, sample sales, sex with strap-ons, myself. What's more, I could curse, I could out celebrities, and I could hobnob with the world's most insanely riveting people, and then write anything that struck me about it all. And get paid!

This was especially intoxicating because, as a freelance writer, I was used to getting strict instructions as to how to format and style every single article. I was also used to getting kill fees. But here was a chance to let loose, to go too far, to have my work published. And so, after stumbling around in print for a few months, overwhelmed with the possibilities, I found my gay, snarky footing. Sensing that there was more than enough fluffy celebrity journalism out there, I realized I could whoosh the other way, armed with a raised eyebrow and a libel lawyer. I come from a fan mentality and in fact had to study English lit at Columbia only because they didn't offer a major in Cher, but like everyone else, I do adore the chance to bring celebs down a peg when they deserve it (and conveniently enough, they do, they do). Having nothing to lose, I could use my column to vent at the biz, and I could do so in an ultrapersonal way based on actually leaving the house. While the dailies have to rely on secondhand sources and publicists' hokum ("*Basic Instinct 2* promises to be another feather in the cap for Hollywood grand dame Sharon Stone . . ."), I had the luxury of going on a madcap trolley ride through Gotham's twilight zone every night and reporting my first-person thoughts—sometimes even favorable ones—in a trashy, man-about-town whirl that was part Proust, part garbage pail.

Gossip, movies, and bad taste had gotten me through my early years, and now I was finally cashing in on that lowbrow expertise. I grew up sitting on the front stoop and bitching out the neighbors in between going to the local dollar theater to see various Liz Taylor flicks (*Boom, Secret Ceremony*) that had crashed and burned, and to me it was all entertainment—cathartic, escapist fun to help relieve my borough boredom. I had no idea those movies were bad, just like I'd never learned to be suffocated by good taste, probably because most of my family's Brooklyn home was covered in plastic and featured fascinatingly practical kitsch items like mama's miniature replica of the Pietá, which doubled as an invaluable holder for Barbie dolls.

And now, no matter how classless and clueless, I had the chance to become a midlevel media player. As one of the first gossip snarksters of the modern age, I learned to perform a delicate tightwire act whereby I'm devilishly nasty and dubious, but not so much so that they cut me off the guest lists. There were the dark years when I was relegated to the Nick at Nite roster—I did countless interviews with the likes of David Cassidy and Karen Valentine, who were delightfully available—but a '95 New York magazine cover story on the city's top gossip purverors deemed me OK, so I was back on track, buffet plate in one hand, crumpled note paper in the other.

I was also the world's first gay, partly because I knew that in being out, I wouldn't be hypocritical in dissecting public figures' sexuality. (A closeted columnist can't comfortably scream, "How dare you, Clay Aiken?") Besides, I couldn't exactly pass for straight. And so I gayed it up like crazy, mocking all the bold-faced liars, screaming at anyone who held back the fight against AIDS, and relentlessly promoting gay talent, from drag queens to porn stars, while wearing a fetching assortment of my own braids and boas. I was stunned that the queer community didn't instantly crown me queen. But being a little too in touch with my feminine side, I wasn't the kind of gay the queers always love to promote. When I was hired, the now-defunct New York Native basically wrote "Who cares?" and a short time after that, author Dennis Cooper hyperbolically complained to an interviewer that I only write about people with punk hairdos. (Well, HIS favorite topic—the hacking up of young boys—was already taken.) But fueled by my friendship with outing pioneer Michelangelo Signorile, I kept tackling gay issues and mixing frivolity with furor. One fateful day in '87, I walked into an ACT UP meeting, where my head spun from the way the individual rage was being funneled into awesome communal strength. I'd never seen gay men and lesbians in the same room before, let alone agreeing on something. Still seething two years later, I egged Signorile on to throw butter at artist Mark Kostabi—who'd just given moronically homophobic comments to *Vanity Fair*—and I even encouraged him to call the incident in to Page Six. The cholesterol content alone was very damaging.

And I kept on raging. I outed Ellen DeGeneres when the rest of the press was saying she and Anne Heche were just close friends. I called upon Rosie O'Donnell to stop pretending she was an ambiguous single mom who loved Tom Cruise, and she later responded by calling me a "gay Nazi" (though by that point, she'd come out, with rainbow bells on). And as I ragged on other celebrities for any number of reasons, Whoopi Goldberg told me to get a life, Gwyneth Paltrow said she admired my rage, Fiona Apple looked deeply wounded, and Vincent Gallo left me a message berating me as "Miss Musto." It's Ms., motherfucker!

Sometimes I had to configure my gossip info into blind item form—not because I didn't think it was true, but because I didn't necessarily have the backup evidence to show in court if sued—you know, the handcuffs, the gerbil X rays, or the chopped penises. But that makes the items even more perversely appealing to readers, who generally froth at the mouth while begging for the answers. Silly them. The answer is always Courtney Love.

For me, the answer all these years has been constantly running back to clubland, forging a schizo life that's zig-zagged between protest marches and club kid pageants. Ever since I came of age in the ultimate glitz palace, Studio 54, clubs have been my safest haven, my most seductive home base. They're sparkly, eye-popping, and accepting (once you get in) and their endearingly attention-seeking denizens quickly became the alternate family I always dreamed of. None of us was loved enough as children, but with each other, we're validated and instantly sprout into fabulousness. In clubland, no one says anything bad about your outfit. They don't even NOTICE your outfit as they're too busy swinging from a chandelier and showing off their own.

Of course there's a dark side to the glitter dome. My biggest blind item in '96 detailed the hammer, Drano injections, pillow, and chopping and river-tossing of drug dealer Angel Melendez's body. (I was dangerously verging on Dennis Cooper territory here.) Never did I pray so hard for an item of mine to not be true, but it was sadly on the money. The killers—Michael Alig and his roommate Freeze—were eventually incarcerated and club life died, further clobbered by Giuliani's campaign to turn New York into an overpriced Disneyland.

It took years—and lots of tacky people springing for bottle service—before it came back, but it did, despite constant raids and regulations geared to make New York safe for real estate owners who USED to go to clubs. Meanwhile, I was dealing with dramatic changes in the other direction, as gossip reporting got trashier and more loose-limbed. By this point, bloggers had changed the dishing landscape, posting virtually anything they wanted because there were no apparent repercussions. Print journalists were horrified and threatened, calling the bloggers wildly inaccurate. (Yeah, but not nearly as much as the print journalists.) But I was big enough to welcome the fresh energy and admit that the blogs had pushed things forward to the point where EVERYONE had to be more immediate in their reporting, not to mention wilder and less squeamish about celebrity sexuality speculation.

Now, it seems, everyone's snarky and everything's gay, so I'm fighting more tenaciously for my place in the gossip-sphere and on the overcrowded red carpet. These days, I'm generally called either "legendary" or "verging on obsolete," but I'm more visible than ever, thanks to TV exposure, so my nerves are usually calm enough. (That prescription didn't hurt either.) I spent several years trying to navigate some integrity while veering between shows like *The Incredible Life of Britney* and *Britney's Horrible Existence,* and I can't say I hated the taste of midlevel celebrity it conferred. But my column has turned out to be my truest constant. MY incredible life? It's as surreally enchanted as ever, and to commemorate the fact that I've survived almost as long as a Sondheim song about survival, I've compiled my favorite columns, snippets of columns, and features for your "dolce" delectation. And apparently, I get paid again!

SCARY JUNKETS AND OTHER INSPIRING PERSONAL ADVENTURES

Reagan redux:
What presidential balls!

January 29, 1985

My last memory of New York was the almost dignified Myrna Loy tribute, during which my almost transsexual date loudly exclaimed, "This panty line is cutting right through my dress. I might complete my sex change right here in Carnegie Hall."

Well, spontaneity like that went right out the window the second I beamed myself to Washington, D.C., a town of such little sexual ambiguity that the men are definitely men and the women are, too. This is the city that never sleeps, or at least never snores, so as not to wake up the dead in nearby Arlington. They have grievances.

My credentials admitted me to one of nine inaugural balls, which I'd been told amounted to a one-way ticket to one of the nine circles of hell, Washington style. I must say the advance signs were not good as I schlepped by porno stores that sold spiked dildos and magazines like *Dyke Boss* a mere block away from the gala $125-a-head event. Once inside the Convention Center, I wasn't sure whether things

3

had gotten more or less respectable. To someone used to just *simple* excess, the room assaulted the senses with all the extremeness of something even later-period Elvis might have sneered at. The cavernous hall was done from top to bottom in insidious shades of red, white, and brown, or at least it seemed that way once the stampede of social and mountain climbers was let in to pose in front of huge inaugural emblems and say, "Love you, lunch." These gaudy purveyors of off-the-rack chic could make you want to scream, "Tacky old ladies don't die, they go to inaugural balls"—or just scream, period. It was either the most spectacular or most appalling scene I've ever witnessed.

Two big bands competed with each other from opposite ends of the room in an even more insipid entertainment battle than Saturday night's televised gala ("Do you think they're getting paid?" remarked someone who must have read some newspapers lately), but the show didn't climax until a hyper bunch of whitebreads lip-synched through songs from *Shenandoah* providing what may be the best argument for vigilante violence yet. "They're cute," said a matron from Dallas. "Sort of like Up with People."

Admission entitled you to cash bar and supposedly to some heinous fruit-and-nut concoction called Shuttlemix. Let me tell you, the road to hell may be paved with cash bar, but the road to Washington must be paved with Shuttlemix. It's so heinous it never even arrived. All that money also gave you the chance to jostle and jab for the best standing position (but not too hard—that could be your future congressman you're slamming into).

"Talk to the people who actually paid," advised Page 6's Susan Malcahy, an old pro at this. I was furious that she seemed so happy. "This ball's much better than the last one," she gushed. "In '81, they gave me grief for wearing a jumpsuit." There was also the excitement—or terror—of a new regime, which this time had been transmuted into a sort of dull complacency. In '81 festivities cost $15.5 million, but this year's only hit $12 million. That means that $3.5 million worth of Shuttlemix is missing.

An investigation was in order, but I was too busy worrying about terrorist threats, and especially about all the celebs who might have chosen to go to Jesse Jackson's prayer vigil for the poor instead. They certainly weren't here at this prayerless vigil for the rich, except for one civil rights leader's widow (Coretta King) and one *Playboy* magnate's ex-girlfriend (Barbie Benton), who grimaced for the cameras, then split.

I'm not paranoid, but I was convinced that half the people at the ball were laughing at me. The other half probably hadn't noticed me yet because I was spending much of the evening in the men's room, where I gnawed feverishly at a crust of bread left over from the Holiday Inn. This wasn't meant to be a political act, it was strictly a matter of survival. Wearing the only bell-bottomed tux left on the Eastern Seaboard was a political act.

Men's room talk centered on such inaugural issues as the Super Bowl and the weather, but I swayed it to the subject at hand. "Men *like* him," one local biggie told me about Reagan, "because he's a real man's man, and women like him because he has a certain elegance." (I guess that put him in the same league with that almost-transsexual friend of mine.) "I abhor the man," said a lawyer who'd paid, "but it's a hell of a party" (I couldn't have agreed more—and less). Press scurried around photographing one another and wondering if there were "any recognizable people from New Jersey" for God knows what reason. One reporter swore he'd almost definitely maybe seen Tom Selleck, who'd almost definitely maybe go to the opening of a fluffernutter sandwich. He knew nothing of Barbie Benton and I wasn't going to tell him either. Pulitzers have been given out for smaller coups than that.

"They're here," shouted the head of inaugural press, and a cameraman jumped up and said, "Who? Reggie-poo? No, that's the next band." Silly boy—it was indeed the president, and she'd brought her husband Ronnie, too. Nancy looked glittering in her Galanos gown and so proud to be an American. He looked living. I looked half-dead, but so proud to be a Democrat.

"I understand this is sort of New York," said Ronnie ("Yeah," answered the crowd in a unison Southern accent). "You know, the first inaugural ball was held in New York, one week after George Washington became president. I always like to add that his wife was in Virginia packing. His favorite dance was the minuet, and don't let that give you any ideas. I've forgotten all the steps." Some reassuring remarks about the economy, then Ron and Nancy danced to "Tenderly" while we fought our way back to the pay bar for some White Russians. A few stayed up front to shoot the Reagans; security had let all those Kodaks go through.

I now knew what D.C. socialite Jayne Ikard meant when she said the inaugural weekend was "50 per cent historical and 50 per cent hysterical." Except I was 100 percent hysterical. It was bedtime for Bonzo, and time to call the party off for four more years.

Carnaval cruising

March 8, 1988

In Brazilian hell, the joke goes, you're forced to swim in excrement as guards make sure you stay there—but it's not so bad because the guards are usually on strike. Our version of Brazilian hell came as we were forced to swim in mudslides, dodging the people carrying goats for umbrellas as they evacuated down the hill. All right, I exaggerate. There was a drizzle, a few peasants, and maybe one goat. But in our delirium, this procession was as big and horrific as any samba parade. We'd been shipped by entrepreneur Chico Recarrey and socialite Anna Maria Tornaghi, who managed to exude glamour even in the neckbrace she wore to combat tension. At Carnaval time, a neckbrace is just another accessory.

We quickly learned all the salient points about Rio: Guys rub their balls in public. No one stops at red lights because if you do your car gets stolen. "Shhh" means "Come here," so as you're telling some nightmare to shut up, they actually come sit on your lap.

A muscled 18-year-old driver was assigned to writer

Michelangelo Signorile (who made history for buying a Coke at a samba ball—yes, a Coke—for $59.70) and myself. His name was Luiz (pronounced Loueesh) and it was just a matter of time before several people wanted Luiz on a leash. To further taunt the tourists, Luis produced a twin brother, Fernando, and both wore more cheap cologne and less clothing with each passing day. They drove everyone—crazy. There's a long story about how another driver agreed to show his uncut *pau* for $10. He was bargained down to five. Pau wow.

But about Carnaval. It's insane, with the line between convincing drag queens and mustachioed women shrinking per samba. Everyone's naked and out for fun with a psychotic vengeance. They stampede into tie balls at Scala, where the musicians only break if they're having heart attacks and it's so hot your sweat becomes a separate person. All the time you think, "Why am I here?" but you can't stop dancing. Even as fat, surly security men push you down flights of stairs for no reason, you can't stop dancing. I stopped only when a drag queen lactated into a champagne glass and made me drink it. In Brazil you're allowed to nurse in public.

Two nights are spent at the Sambadrome, where thousands obsess till 10 A.M.—gotta have that fix—over the amazing parade of samba schools, Harvard not among them. Not only do they stay, but they dance in place nonstop; apparently they're shot if they stop moving. Each school features 3,500 people in staggering sequins and feathers, singing about how they're trapped in their *favelas*, maybe because of those unwieldy headdresses. Some strange juxtapositions are carried off in the name of excess—a girl dressed as Carol Channing in *Dolly!*

danced spreadeagle on the float about Princess Isabel—but hey, it's all in fun. As several thousand people in flamingo heads went by, Patrick McMullan didn't photograph them, though a few days later at lunch he asked us if we wanted a shot of the meat.

In between the parades, handicapped people spin around in wheelchairs, and I swear some drag queens pretend to be crippled to get into the photo op. The biggest pretender there, though, was a crazed Brazilian Addison de Witless who'd been poisoned against us by a lump of human caca who used to throw parties at Studio 54 (First name: Carmen). The guy tried to throw me out, upon which I tripped him, McMullan hid his shoes, and Signorile locked him into the balcony. The next night, he was slapping Stephen Saban, but in better spirits. The unflappable Anna Maria explained all this by saying he wasn't throwing me out, he was saying, "Hi. How are you?" in Portuguese.

The Roman-style twilight gallery Caligola was our nightly rendezvous place. We missed only one meal there, but God was with us; it was the night Merv Griffin and Eva Gabor happened in. We took two side trips. The first was to plastic surgeon Dr. Ivo Pitanguy's island ("Ilha dos Porcos Grandes," or Big Pigs), where famous people come to recuperate from their surgery. You expect to see Cher taking nature walks in bandages. What you do see are herds of bizarre animals à la Dr. Dolittle, and then at lunchtime you see them on your plate. But wait—were the Chers transformed into these animals à la Dr. *Moreau?* This sick thought prompted us to go up to the critters and say, "Who did you used to be, little pig?" Pitanguy, who fixed Anna Maria's nose when it was split open in a stampede of Julio Iglesias fans (another long story), told Saban his nose was okay—oh, really? As we left, colorful arara birds screamed "arara" at us, which has been adopted here as the word for colorful. If they screamed "shit," would *that* be the word for colorful?

The second side trip was to Salvador in Bahia, though I think they took us to El Salvador by mistake. Mayor Mario Kertesz wants to restore the old sector, make Salvador fab again, and become president. In a private meeting, he served us coconut phlegm and plied us with gifts, lunch, and a slide show. Then, Gilberto Gil, the secretary of culture and a huge recording star, came out and said *he* wants to be mayor, à la Sonny Bono. "Any questions?" Gil asked after serious statements about the restoration. "When are you going to play S.O.B.'s?" wondered Saban. We wished him well in the election and the Grammys and went back to the wicker-and-macramé sensory deprivation island resort of Itaparica, which was mostly for the araras.

Traumatized by the sun, I swear I got trapped on the beach dangling from a slate wall with weasels popping out of holes as high tide jumped at my neck. The next day I was in bed with Itaparica's revenge, just to have something to do. And besides, Anita Sarko had gotten so much attention with food poisoning, McMullan with a horseback riding injury, Anna Maria's sister Titila with a mysterious swollen foot, and The Post's Richard Johnson with a nervous stomach due to his paper's then-uncertain fate. But Anna Maria had taken off the neckbrace— our cue to leave. When I got back to New York, there was a three-alarm fire blaring on my block. Mudslide anyone?

I get my kicks above the waistline, sunshine

February 13, 1990

My primary knowledge of Bangkok was from two films—*The King and I* and *Emmanuelle*—so on my recent trip there, I naturally expected a bald king to ask me to dance, and some creep to rape me in an opium den. Neither happened, though the second one came pretty close.

In this bawdy, gaudy, naughty town (to which I and some other press were sent by Mars's owner Toshiaki Umeda for the opening of Mars-Bangkok), everyone and everything's for sale, including Percodan, which you can get over the counter, and should. The anything-goes spirit is liberating but ultimately works your nerves so badly you shake from the sleaze. Someone you used to respect grabs your crotch and says, "You fuckee me now, poppy?" Walking into what you think is a simple nightclub, you find a woman onstage viciously shooting ping-pong balls out of her vagina. Most of your time is spent either dodging ping-pong balls or shooting them back with your dick.

We stayed at Novotel, where—the only touch of class in

town—a string quintet plays "My Way" in the lobby as you down five daiquiris your way. Rather than wait for "New York, New York," we took a boat ride on the Chao Phraya River, whose waters are used by the shanty residents to assist a variety of contradictory bodily functions ("Never shit where you eat," my mother always said). We ended up at the King's Palace, which—surrounded by phallic temple after jewel-encrusted phallic temple—is like everything on the Home Shopping Club all thrown together and melted.

But fake phalli are not what bring people to Bangkok. What draws them is the buying: of food, clothes, and human sacrifice. The food is tasty, mouth-numbingly spicy stuff with names like spaghetti sometime, pork throat, mussel in earthen pot, and chicken hidden in pandanus bush (typical).

The shopping is amazing, too, from the outdoor flea markets, where Fanta is sold in a colostomy bag, to the department stores, where knockoffs are so cheap and nego-tiable you can get a top "designer" shirt for 500 baht (about $20). Rumor has it the real designers have come here to license their names, only to find they've been taken already. Who cares? Fauxtier, Fauxji, and Matpseudo are good enough labels for me.

Above all, and very real, is the sex—onstage, in bathtubs, and sometimes even in beds. Mars's Rudolf went out for a simple massage and got unexpectedly straddled by the girl ("The s&m is better in Cambodia," he advises). A similar thing happened to the *News's* Nancy Stedman and the *Post's* Beth Landman and Pat Wadsley, who went as a threesome to an all-female massage parlor that, to their chagrin, turned out to be more than a massage parlor. At least one of them ran screaming toward the exit in a towel.

At a place called Barbeiry, the live show on the bar has boys fucking covered with soap suds, fucking in leather, and fucking with hot candle wax on them. I think I even saw one of them fucking with a condom on—a real novelty act. Between shows, they dance about with numbers around their necks like racehorses. You pick one and go to an upstairs cubicle with the guy, as some geek checks the number off on a big chart on the wall. One afternoon, someone from our group was "licked from head to toe" by #37, who was conspicuously absent from the club that night—a breakdown?

Super Girls lives up to its name; its stars shoot darts from their vaginas, blow out candles with them, and even use them for the normal activity—the ping-pong trick. One of them, ignoring warnings to not drink the water, emptied a bottle of the stuff between her legs and poured it out brown—that time of the month? Later, a guy passionlessly banged a girl on a motorcycle. And then it was the audience's turn.

At Johnny's, guys penetrate each other in a pyramid formation. And at Ciro's, where that "fuckee me" incident occurred in the bathroom (I passed), the quaint Copameets-Maxim's decor of glitter balls and crepe curtains masks the fact that anything here (even the busboys) can be baht and sold in any formation. As "Electric Youth" plows its levels of irony into your eardrums, you witness the parade of teen boys working the paunchy Americans to bang-kok for as low as $3.60. On one typical night, an old clone was having his eyeball sucked on by a short Thai boy, and a hustler who couldn't have been more than 12 was being unzipped by someone acting out *The Queen and I*. The next night, I got an exclusive interview with the 12-year-old. "I ugly. I from Laos. No one sleep with me," he whined—his shtick, apparently (each boy has one). I didn't disagree, so he suddenly became a pimp—these guys are versatile—bringing over other boys and telling me, "My friend thinks you're handsome." A lot of them thought I was handsome—they wanted my baht.

The place is down the alley from Harry's, which attracts the same crowd, only earlier, and whose Playgirl revue features drag queens and musclemen who later on, at Giro's, turn out to be hustlers. One night, Susanne Bartsch happened to be there and stole the show in an egret feather skullcap and not much else. She terrorized the whole town, especially the shopping mall.

Oh, and then there's Mars. Four floors and a roof, like in New York, it's kitschily decorated by Benjamin Liu, and spiritually correct, since 10 monks performed a blessing on it opening day. Only drinks are for sale—amazing on a block with places called Pussy Alive and Pussy Galore. New York DJ John Suliga was flown over to play the opening but slept until 90 minutes into it (though that day he was right on time for his lunch date with writer Kiki Mason, who he sees constantly in New York).

The other big drama was *Details*'s, Stephen Saban writing

an anonymous postcard to the trip's controversial publicist Bruce Lynn saying, "Dear pitiful, ugly, excuse for a woman . . ." and going on from there. Bruce then sent a letter to everyone saying whoever wrote the postcard was a "raging asshole" who needs to see a shrink. Finding out it was Saban, whom he desperately needs careerwise, he's been groveling ever since.

Moscow does not believe in queers

October 3, 1993

I can't totally take credit for the civil war going on in Russia, but it's impossible to rule out *some* cause and effect. After storming the place last week with a bunch of crass New Yorkers in search of the hedonistic thrills associated with capitalism, it made perfect sense for them to try to throw Yeltsin out and bring back the Commies.

We were shipped over by Manhattan Express, a New York–style boîte in Moscow run by Club USA codirectors David Rabin and Will Regan, who'd sent a block of red cement—a red square, as it were—as the year's heaviest invite. It was an offer we couldn't (put in the) refuse. The motley junket crew they assembled included giggly models, surly press, and a woman who stood out glaringly in a captain's cap and a jacket made from loudly clashing patterns of fake fur. It turned out to be Gael Greene, arbiter of taste. For once I was going to be the "normal" one.

Being on the verge, we were ready for Russia on the brink. The country we found was comparable to gold rush

California, a pandemonium-laden, moolah-grubbing Wild West movie wherein money-making schemes run rampant, nightclubs have gun checks, and anyone with a car can be a cabdriver. There are slot machines in the airport, and all over town people thrust purchasable goods at you, from fur hats to those famous wooden-dolls-within-wooden-dolls that give birth to each other like inbred gnomes.

Because of ruble instability, the dollar is king to the point where some establishments will accept only American currency (imagine going to a club in New York and being greeted with, "Rubles only, please"). They crave our economy so much they've even started marketing a mutation called New Yorkskaya vodka, "a taste of liberty." Drink a batch and go to GUM—a vast, glass-domed department store, where dozens of shops hawk more of those damned dolls. As you're buying one, nonemployees come up to you and try to countersell ("I have political—Yeltsin inside Gorby"), and it's completely allowed. But the country hasn't fully caught up with capitalistic hauteur. At McDonald's, when my friend didn't have enough rubles to pay for his meal, they simply smiled and said, "That's OK," a Twilight Zone–ski moment I'm still pinching myself over.

For din-din, our tour bus took us to a bathhouse-turned-restaurant that resembled the Harmonia Gardens crossed with the old Continental Baths. As they brought out chicken Kiev after a five-course meal, hotelier Andre Balazs murmured, "The decadence of this is so delicious." He ended up smuggling more caviar out of the country than you can fit in Orca's ass. In the midst of dinner, Gael Greene stood up to ask how many people wanted to go with her to a flea market the next morning. She quizzed each person—"yes or no?"—getting enough of them to agree to go to commandeer use of the bus.

Desperately leaving the group behind, my friend and I found the Underground, the first real gay bar in Russia (the others have been floating, as opposed to drowning), which is located in a dark alleyway across from a pizza restaurant. It has a quaint, coffeehouse feeling to it—it's like Pop Tate's Choklit Shoppe in Archie comics—but is rife with repression, as everyone slow-dances to dour music like "This Used to Be My Playground" and various Elton John dirges. Things are much better than in the precoup days, when limp wrists were practically shot on sight, but it still isn't any great jubilee to write home about. When the Moscow Tribune announced, "Gaidar returns," they meant the famed economist, not the art of spotting other queens.

Straight sex is more easily procured. At Nightflight, a prostie bar, a naive tourist was heard to ask one of the gals, "Where do you work?" "Here," she deadpanned. Less knowingly, models there said they'd noticed the ripped up Lenin statues all over town and were wondering where Paul, George, and Ringo were commemorated, tee-hee.

The next day, Gael and entourage made their pilgrimage to that flea market and a pricey lunch at the Metropole Hotel, as the rest of us waited for almost an hour for the scheduled use of the bus to tour Moscow. On the way back from the Pushkin Museum, she asked if anyone wanted to stop and buy an orange. No one answered—you could have heard a

Pushkin drop—but she got the vehicle to screech to a halt anyway. Just as well; we scarfed up 35-cent Cokes that cost five bucks in the hotel.

And then came the Manhattan Express 'do, which started with bologna sandwiches and caviar in a rare cockroach-free suite at the Rossiya. Gael wasn't there at first, having nabbed a limo to Estée Lauder. But new mystery people had flown in, like a *Beverly Hills, 90210* writer, who simply said, "Forgive me," and two "dancers," who were there, apparently, to pleasure the Russian mobsters (a taste of liberty). They weren't from the Bolshoi.

The club turned out to be a sleek, medium-sized box with Woody Allen's *Manhattan* on video screens buffeted by state-of-the-art sound and lasers. It was nice, but rather minimal, if intentionally so; where did the 2 million smackers go? "Bribes," said an informed source. It wasn't a total joke; an AP reporter claimed that most other recent clubs there had closed after a week because they couldn't keep up with the extortion payments.

In any case, they attracted the hoped-for crowd of overnight millionaires in suits, but while some of them asked for the music to be softer, others wanted *more* from the place. *The Moscow Times* suggested that the hype had backfired and quoted Rabin as saying ominously he didn't know who the main owner was. Which makes it hard to know who to ask for the extortion payments.

When we awoke again, the Manhattan express moved on to the Kremlin, which we instantly redubbed the Kreplach. "Is the bus going back at 5:10?" asked Gael. "I have to get back to the hotel and go to the ballet." Frantically, we were all assembled on time, and then she took a cab anyway.

Final stops included Arkadin restaurant, where a jazz combo played "Michelle," the theme from *The Sting*, and other Russkie folk songs. And then there was an artsy house party, where I got to meet Vladik Monroe, Russia's premier drag queen—as opposed to Russia's drag-queen premier. Vladik showed me holograms of himself as Marilyn Monroe and Hitler, as well as a picture he made of Gorby in earrings and makeup (Russia's drag-queen premier). "After that," he said, "my commander in the army put me in a mental hospital for four months." Now, in the thrill-ready frenzy of the new Russia, he's a star.

By the end of the trip, I was ready for a mental hospital from Gael, but I sort of liked her and understood her insecure, grasping need to constantly have a full plate. And unlike *L.A. Weekly*'s Belissa Cohen, who terrorized the '90 junket to Kyoto, at least she was friendly in between her little machinations. I say they should get rid of the two-president situation—which, by the way, reminds me of the time when Pete Hamill stormed in and tried to seize the *Post* back from Abe Hirschfeld—and let Gael Greene kick the country into shape. But not in that jacket.

SoBe it!

October 25, 1994

To do Miami Beach properly, you must draw in your cheeks as if sucking on an onion, raise your pretty head higher than the nearest blimp, and walk—heel, ball, toe—down Ocean Drive like it was the world's toniest runway, convinced that all the professional oglers stationed in the outdoor cafés are simply gagging over your supernatural beauty. Never—repeat, *never*—turn around or you may notice them all laughing their heads off.

Only the beautiful or pretend-beautiful have a place in South Beach, but fortunately there's an awful lot of uglies running around hoping it'll rub off. And though the town reeks of superficiality and a distinct lack of real culture, it's still an idyllic resort with natural and architectural loveliness to surpass the presumed perfection of the fashion-victimized faux-models slaving behind the notions counter.

I was sent down by the Shore Club, a new gay resort hotel that promises to be the quintessential hangout for the pecs-and-sex crowd, though it wasn't quite ready because for two weeks it had rained on their pride parade (and construction). There was only occasional hot water, no working elevators, and a verdant color scheme I'm absolutely certain can't be final. The walls in the rooms are mint green, the carpets are emerald green, the bedsheets are kelly green, and suddenly one prayed even for teal.

Mysterious alarms kept going off in the middle of the night, and—though I was desperate for an excuse to run from the greenness—I stayed put, convinced that it was just another endearing glitch. During the day, by the pool, lascivious queens were filing in, and I felt like Rosie O'Donnell in *Exit to Eden*: "We're the only people on this island without handcuffs!" The cocktail waiter informed us that he was also an escort—don't give up your day job—and handed us a card that cryptically offered "three-for-one" (three what for one what? Blowjobs for a dollar?). His specialty, he added, was "the ass," which raised yet more questions, like, um, his or mine? And what *was* this place anyway—an institution of learning or a teenage brothel? To add to the confusion, we noticed a giant clamshell positioned in the middle of the pool, and a neon-studded, goldfish-shaped drapery on the side. And I thought the Dada Ball wasn't until days later.

Weirdness continued the next day as Martha Wash was found unexpectedly singing on the balcony over the pool area and urging us to yell "Ow! Ow!" But Sunday, it all came together when the place was packed for a ditsy array of poolside entertainment that raised my red lantern. Two *Absolutely Fabulous* drag queens, still dressed up from a Comedy Central party the night before, lip-synched "Rock Lobster" and promptly jumped into the pool. Then, after diving medal-ists performed slightly more graceful exhibitions, Mother Kibble—the drag who, legend has it, does the entire Judy at Carnegie Hall concert, "but makes it her own"—ripped off her wig and followed them in. Ow! Ow! Finally, at the climax of a swimwear fashion show, the clamshell opened and a swimsuited male model in pearls sultrily emerged amid pink balloons. Now it all made sense—except for the neon goldfish.

Elsewhere in town, there was a Caribbean parade, a hip-hop convention, and dinner at Bang with Alice Cooper ("I'm not worthy!"), who was on his way to Orlando—not to go on the *Backdraft* ride, mind you, but to shoot some eso-teric yet edifying program for VH-1. Alice admitted that he has all the *AbFab* shows on tape and said his favorite movie this year was *Romeo Is Bleeding* because "Lena Olin made me an instant fan. She was so violent—I was laughing my head off." Charmed, I'm sure.

I was in for another thrill on learning that Porcel—the Latin American Benny Hill, who regularly does drag in his riotous (if unintelligible to me) comedy sketches—now has a Miami Beach restaurant called A La Pasta With Porcel, a takeoff on his old TV show's title, *A La Cama Con Porcel*. Pos-sessed with offbeat-star worship, I waltzed in and demanded to see the guy, upon which the maitre d' pointed to the cor-pulent comic, dining at a window table, and generously said, "Sit down and have dinner with him!" So it's that easy? Alas, Porcel was busy on his cellular phone and I was afraid he was calling the police to have me dragged out, so I ran.

Back in New York came the real Dada Ball at Webster Hall, an attempt to re-create the Blindman's Ball, held in this very same place in 1917 (and which, I recall, was quite marvelous). While the original Dada—which defied definition, by the way—began as a reaction against the carnage of World War I, the new Dada nostalgia has risen up in response to the death toll on the AIDS battlefield (this event benefited Housing Works and Visual AIDS). The intention is playful irreverence to delight and provoke, a lavish attempt to create our own nihilistic reality, but a lovely, loopy one. Performances, costumed revelers, displays, and body-painted go-go dancers all melded into a perfectly sensical nonsensical whole. "This is a gathering of bizarre human beings," as someone with silver tubes coming out of his head and a 15-foot feather boa, but apparently no sense of irony, remarked.

For the first two hours, we enjoyed "Dada's Just Desserts," fattening displays courtesy of notable restaurants, as assembled by artists into tasty museum pieces. A lemon sorbet extravaganza was topped with a Jesus statue wearing Mouse-ka-ears. Another exhibit consisted of caramelized apple desserts that you had to push your hand through gauze to seize ("It's interactive art," insisted the presenter). In between chowing down, you caught the performances, which—for better or worse—left many in the audience with caramelized apple falling out of their open mouths. Dancer Robert LaFosse had two studly guys in blindfolds and jock-straps holding a toilet as he stumbled around in a straitjacket. Bill T. Jones struck poses over a screaming soundtrack, then chanted, "Lick me where it hurts, baby." Upstairs, a monitor showed a 1949 *Dating Do's and Dont's* flick, which was more delightfully irrelevant than ever. And all over the place there were more freaks, more nuts, more apples.

My heart belonged to Dada, but not everyone was happy, like the jaded attendee who was heard to murmur, "I thought bad art stopped when you left art school." "No," answered his friend, "that's when it begins."

Perhaps it's just a penchant for playful irreverence that's kept Mariah Carey from approving for release the video she and Luther Vandross shot for their duet of "Endless Love" (the clip only came out in Europe). This must be especially galling to Luther, who's been quite vocal about his desperation for a No. 1 song, especially since "Love," videoless, went all the way up to No. 2, then dropped. As the record company isn't talking, we can only speculate that Mariah's not anxious to promote this project for some reason having to do with the recording, the video, or her costar. And we can only walk away—heel, ball, toe—and, serve our blinding beauty elsewhere.

Seizure's Palace

December 9, 1997

Promise me you'll never get sick, people. Not because of the horrible pain, suffering, and disintegration—that's all fine. But the bureaucratic nightmare you'll be thrust into while trying to seek help is truly unbearable. Trust me. Let's start at the very beginning. Over three weeks ago, at a party for that HBO movie about Don King, I suddenly felt disoriented, then blacked out, unwittingly causing the biggest excitement of the entire evening. Apparently, I had turned periwinkle blue, convulsed like an anaconda, and almost swallowed my tongue in lieu of my buffet sampling. The next thing I knew, various emergency personnel and my friend were urging me to get my ass into an awaiting ambulance, and after yelling at them in dazed confusion for a while, I decided to go along with this plan. Who knew that, while the seizure hadn't killed me, the red tape ahead would come close to strangling me?

At New York Hospital, perfectly nice doctors asked me routine questions, then shoved me up a CAT scan machine—that tube you hope they don't forget to eventually get you out of.

They didn't and mercifully found nothing in the way of bad brain goings-on. But they apparently had no idea what I did have (aside from Oxford coverage). They sent me home, instructing me to call a certain neurologist—we'll call him Dr. John—the next day to immediately get an EEG, which I think is that test whereby they attach electrodes to your head, but at least don't shove you up a tube. I was all too willing.

Day 2: Weak and stunned, I spent the day making the battery of business calls necessary in the midst of a hideous health scare. It's just what you feel like doing when you're half-dead. I called Oxford—which is currently being investigated by the New York Attorney General's office—to let them know of my emergency visit because if you don't do this right away, you're on your own, honey. I also called Dr. John, but horrifyingly enough, the earliest date he could offer was nine days away! I explained in frantic tones that this was an emergency situation, and he finally conceded to see me a mere three days away. This was still iffy—every seizureless second was a gift—but I wasn't feeling up to calling oodles of other neuros to check out their availability. I did, however, make sure to phone my primary-care man, Dr. Allen, to get a referral for the Dr. John visit because in Oxford land, no one can even let you peruse the *Highlights* in the waiting room unless they have that miracle piece of paper.

Day 5: I dragged my poor mother through a storm to Dr. John's office, gaily thinking, "I'll finally get my EEG!" I never thought I'd be so happy to have electrodes strapped to my head. Think again. The attendant looked completely dumbstruck when we announced ourselves. She was only a temp, but even she knew that Dr. John had gone off to Phoenix for some reason (probably just to avoid this visit). She said Dr. John couldn't have done the EEG that day anyway—that has to be done in the hospital—but I guessed he could have probably conducted some kind of examination. She suggested we go to the fairly nearby Dr. Nancy, who was covering for Dr. John, and after we weighed all our fabulous options for about five seconds, we found ourselves panting at Nancy's door. She also didn't find anything wrong with me, plus when I asked her what to do if that dreadful preblackout feeling recurred, she said "Sit down"—but she was nice, she was there, and she made an EEG booking for the following Monday, so my nerves adored her.

Day 7: Dr. Allen's referral for Dr. John came in the mail. Yay! If he ever returns from the desert, maybe I can use it!

Day 8: I called Oxford again to make extra sure they had a record of my emergency room visit. Call me paranoid Pete. Sure enough, the human voice I got after a 10-minute wait couldn't find any trace of my tragedy in the system. "Maybe it just hasn't shown up yet," she said, assuring me they'd take care of it. I had other things on my mind anyway, and damned if I wasn't going to find out what they were. I dragged Mom up to New York Hospital for the long-awaited exam that would surely render all past aggravation irrelevant. We got there, all pleased with ourselves and ready to be strapped in. Well, apparently I had more chance of being cast as Rizzo in *Grease!* After filling out papers, we were told that they simply couldn't do the test because they hadn't gotten—everyone now—a referral. "Silly me! Well, let's get one, shall we?" I chirped, on the verge of the world's biggest breakdown. The attendant promptly called Dr. Nancy and asked her to fax one over, but she either wouldn't or couldn't. The other freak, natch, was still in Phoenix. And Dr. Allen might as well have been, because the attendant's repeated entreaties to his office were also coming up as barren as a British town without a maypole.

In a desperate move, I hobbled to a pay phone to call Allen's office myself, and amazingly enough, they said they'd been trying to fax us the whole time, but the line was busy (no doubt with other people's referrals). They added that the attendant should have taken their word that she'd get to it, and it was inhumane for me to be denied care in this way. I couldn't have agreed more or known what to do less. I limped back to the attendant, who now said that, as an hour had elapsed, the hospital couldn't allot me any more time, even if a referral did magically arrive! Cripes! Forget the EEG—now I probably needed cardioplasty. Crushed, Mom and I headed toward the elevator, where we ran into one of my original emergency room doctors, who sweetly offered to do the EEG. Sometimes so suddenly there is God. Alas, after I pathetically explained the referral situation, he muttered, "Oh, Oxford," and walked away in defeat. I was too weak to cry—and I didn't have a referral to do so anyway. Zombielike, Mom and I schlepped way downtown to Dr. Allen's office to nab that fucking referral in person. Now I had to get another EEG appointment so I could use it.

Day 9: I called the hospital first thing, hoping to get an appointment for the next day. Wrong again. The attendant now said they didn't have anything until December 3! More than two weeks away—and my birthday yet! When I started my now well-rehearsed freakout routine, she intriguingly offered December 1. I accepted, then called Dr. Nancy's office, begging them to use their clout to get me an earlier date. The girl actually said, "I doubt it—and by the way, we don't have a referral [from Dr. Allen] to take care of your last week's visit here!" Heeelp! My head was pounding so hard I was sure that if they shoved me up that CAT scan again they'd find something now. I told the girl I had a referral from Allen for John, but she explained that it had to be for Nancy. I grabbed Ma and we went right back to Allen's, where I pleaded for a referral for Nancy. We got it and mailed it, overcome with history's most pitiful sense of triumph. Now I was all set. My EEG was 12 whole days away, but hey, if I had another seizure before then, I could always sit down!

While I counted the moments in terror, everyone in town weighed in with well-meaning advice ("Drink water," "Pray") except for that Don King fete's publicist, who never so much as checked to see if I was alive—or at least to thank me for having the spasm that ensured her event Page Six coverage. To get my (convulsing) mind off stuff like that, I went to see *The Rainmaker* but quickly realized it's about a sadistic insurance company that screws over a patient and writes his mom, "You must be stupid, stupid, stupid." "Fuck you, fuck you, fuck you!" I yelled at the screen, my head throbbing harder than ever. Refer this.

Author's note: Tests eventually revealed that a previous head injury had been acting up again. Now, thanks to medication, I only flop around when I want to.

Confessions of a Sound Bite whore

July 29, 2003

Hello, my name is Michael and I am a sound bite whore. I'm one of those talking heads you see on cable TV giving college-educated opinions about Winona Ryder's meltdown, Britney Spears's lost virginity, and the Hilton Sisters' flair for tabletop dancing. I help grease the wheels of the entertainment-television industry, providing innumerable free quotes that allow them to fill endless hours of eternally repeatable, low-budget airtime. In exchange, I get to promote myself and my paper and become vaguely familiar to the millions who care about Donald Trump's comb-over or J.Lo's ass. The modest celebrity fallout from spewing these nonstop dicta is less amazing than amusing. People regularly chase me down the street to say stuff like, "Hey, aren't you that guy from *VH1 All Access: Awesomely Bad Girls?*" or, more likely, "I've seen you somewhere. Didn't you once fix my clogged toilet or something?"

The joys and sorrows of being a windup nattering head in medium demand? Well, the live shows are the most fun to do because they're blissfully immediate and, satisfyingly enough, every single word you say gets on. But with pre-tapings, you leave the outcome to editing and chance, so a 90-minute interview can result in just three chopped-up sound bites, airing aeons later. (It's happened. Try to find me on MTV's *Celebrity Love Affairs*.) Still, you have to act as if each taping is your star opportunity and sparkle like Kelly Ripa on crack. You must look directly at the interviewer, incorporate the question into the answer ("Sean Penn is belligerent because . . ."), and make your reply short and unbelievably pithy. (An involved story will be axed or shredded.) What's more, don't come in wearing something that strobes, and never let your hairline look shiny; leave the strobing and shining to your short, impeccably worded answers to questions like "Is the disco glitter ball an American icon?" and "Why Demi Moore now?"

For all the ego gratification they supply, the live shows have their own demands—in fact, you're generally made to cartwheel through fiery hoops to do these people the favor of a free appearance. First, you're routinely pre-interviewed by an assistant producer who grills you for 25 minutes for a segment on which you'll probably get to say two things. This is their big moment—they've got you captive and are suddenly playing with themselves and fantasizing that they're the hosts. But their even bigger moment comes when you call back later to confirm and they bouncily announce, "Sorry, we're going with someone else. We'll call you again." Little regard is paid to your scheduling concerns; once you're on their whore roster, they know they've got you by the balls. Typically, Bill O'Reilly's show recently wanted me to discuss the tawdry state of MTV (the levels of irony here are pretty enormous), then told me the segment was canceled, though I watched the show that night and found out it wasn't—they'd just dumped me for an angrier guest. Worse, no fewer than three other gabfests this year booked me, then ended up murmuring, "Sorry, we're using Gloria Allred instead." Even a gag order can't stop *that* woman from chatting up a lens.

If Gloria's somehow tied up (literally) and her fellow pundits Alan Light and Emil Wilbekin are suddenly abducted, you might actually get on. If so, you should know that panels are the worst—you have to lift a rifle just to get a word in—especially when you're debating right-wing nightmares. (Use humor; they'll never know what hit them.) And whoever you're on with, live shows have entirely *different* rules: Smile at the camera as you're introduced, even if the topic is "Remembering the Titanic." Have a first statement ready, no matter what the question is, so you don't start off by going "Ummmm." Use specifics (say "Kerry Kennedy Cuomo," not "the wife"), don't bob your head or flail your hands, and don't pause for effect; on talk TV, silence equals death. Also—there's more—never say "as I said before"; that's unpardonably boring. And be sure to save your best zinger for last; people will remember you fondly. But most of all, just relax and be yourself, honey!

I was doing so well with this formula that Greta Van Susteren had me on seven times in a row last year, until the D.C. snipers and the war annoyingly eclipsed talk about Rosie O'Donnell and *American Idol*. (Stunningly, I never met Greta, though. Even when you're in the same studio, they put you in a separate room where you chirpily talk to a blank screen. This gives a more international feel.) Since she dumped me, I've gone on other shows, *any* other shows, and blabbed about nudity in videos, Lisa Marie Presley's marriages, and Hollywood catfights. I even agreed to discuss the pros and cons of a 12-year-old model on MSNBC's *Scarborough Country*, hosted by an arch-Republican. "But he won't interrupt you," a producer assured me. Well, he interrupted the very first thing I said—though he ended up being surprisingly inoffensive. Was I getting so hooked on cable exposure that anyone who gave me a chance to be glib for a mass audience was suddenly my best friend and fame dealer? (If you want to answer that, by the way, please do it succinctly and without strobing.)

There are limits, of course. I turned down a show called *Love Chain: Tom Cruise*—I just won't go there. But I gladly did an *E! True Hollywood Story* about Anna Kournikova, barely knowing what sport she's in; after some astute Web surfing, I was the world's pithiest expert on . . . what was it, tennis? Whenever that one airs, I'll be tangentially, disposably visible for one more lovely hour. *People will notice me*—as I said before.

Before I'm replaced here by Gloria Allred, let me return to my job of columnist—you know, going out and getting *other* people's sound bites. There was an opening-night event for Shakespeare in the Park's big-shticked *Henry V*, which is so long that by the end, it's *Henry VI*—though there are innovative flourishes and Liev Schreiber is superb. Anna Wintour had bolted by Act II, furthering the Wintour of our discontent. But at the after-party at Belvedere Castle, Alec Baldwin told me he loved the show, and he also loves that he's off to do a Scorsese flick, *The Aviator*. But what happened to the movie of *The Devil and Daniel Webster* that Alec directed and starred in? "Federal prosecutors just indicted two of the investors for fraud," he told me. "My name's off the picture." Don't you hate when that happens?

Indictable for their bad habits, nasty nuns get their come-uppance in *The Magdalene Sisters*, which is especially fun when aping those old women-in-prison flicks, down to the loony-bin punishment, the hair shaving, and the confrontation with the warden, I mean Mother Superior. At a dinner for the potent film at the Plaza Athenee, Nora-Jane Noone—who yells at the head penguin, "Let go, you fucking twisted bitch!"—turned out to be a sweet young thing who'd just tasted our country's culture at its finest by visiting the Mall of America. But guest Marisa Tomei was still in shock from the movie, moaning, "I'm wrecked!" That was good—short, sweet, and very effective. But she strobed!

I'm not a failure,
I just play one on TV

August 30, 2005

TV appearances are my crack cocaine—point a camera and I'll sparkle—but I've been craving a return to more reliable television gigs, particularly the kind that actually send some coinage afterward. I'll still do absolutely anything, mind you, but I'm a little weary of the piecemeal jobs, the ones that bump your scheduled segment because there's a late-breaking story about a seven-year-old midwife. (That actually happened to me once, and I still want to take that freakin' kid and . . . no, she's a doll.)

So for years I've been pitching my wares to the big guys by doing more pilots than a horny flight attendant. I've auditioned, begged, prostituted, and performed a soft-shoe routine on my knees. As you can imagine, that can be even more dispiriting than the piecemeal lifestyle.

My sad saga? Well, about four years ago I shot my very first pilot—a house party kind of show hosted by a wan model who asked the guests for the meaning of life before cutting to various card tricks and music videos. I was there to spice things up by reciting blind items to a pretend socialite who'd feign drunkenness and keel over when I whispered the answers in her ear. She wasn't picked up. Neither was the pilot.

Then a lovebug over at Al Roker's production company decided I was the shit and pitched a show with me leading a sort of titillating yet civilized dinner party conversation. Alas, at the same time, another channel picked up a show with Jon Favreau leading a sort of titillating yet civilized, etc., etc. My hopes for a regular meal ticket were suddenly flushed into the Gowanus. (And it turned out neither of those channels was exactly begging for me anyway.)

But five minutes later some hope nouveau came ringin' on my wind chimes. Al Roker himself—a genuinely nice guy—had me and IFC's Alison Bailes join him in a pilot for a movie show, a sort of cinephile's E.T. as hosted by the Mod Squad. Having just met, we had to summon more instant chemistry than a Lionel Richie tour band, but the world failed to reward us for it. I was crushed that the show wasn't picked up, even as I ran around crowing, "I worked with Al Roker!"

But I wasn't ready for the glue factory just yet. I dusted off and auditioned for *Queer Eye for the Straight Guy*, finding the idea for the show such a stereotype that I simply had to be part of it. Gay TV is where I belonged—or so I tragically thought as I practiced my carefully tousled hair and dangerous wrists. At the audition, we were shown a video of a straight person who supposedly needed a makeover, complete with his friends' rudely dismissive comments. So when it came time for me to impress the producers, I came on like gay gangbusters, screeching, "That guy needs more work than Asbury Park! What a hideous, orange-alert mess!" I bombed bigger than a suicidal terrorist, and I never even got to back-track, since one of the other auditioners in my group dom-inated the whole session with prerehearsed, windy speeches and boring platitudes. He hadn't listened when they said they were looking for team players. I hadn't listened when they described the show as "*Extreme Makeover* with heart." Both of us were sent back to the Meat Rack.

But there were other op'nin's and other shows, and next time I would surely try to listen a little. I seized the offer to meet a top tube exec and truly heard him when he assured me, "Doing this channel without you would be like MTV without Madonna" (i.e., you're really old but indispensable). Well, he's not in the same position there anymore, and now I guess they *are* doing the channel without me (though, interestingly, MTV still uses Madonna).

'Ho Springs Eternal

I was ready to shoot my agent, but I was suddenly thrown a brand-new chance at superficial wholeness. A producer I'd once worked with wanted me to cohost a showbiz-related program he was excitedly winding his arm to pitch. It was more than a pitch, actually—this was the surest bet since Tori Spelling auditioned for her father. See, he had already schmoozed the intended channel's development guy, so we had the kind of in that people sell their fetuses for. And we had an actual meeting set up! Reeking of gift-bag scents, we swaggered into the big man's sanctum, determined to play tough and not sign any old contract on the spot. But as it turned out, devastation was on the menu once again, with stale croutons. In fact, we deflated like fake titties in a car accident when we noticed that Mr. Man was avoiding any mention whatsoever of our proposed show, going on instead about his messy personal problems! WTF? Either he was ingeniously testing our chat skills or he was the most self-absorbed little kook in Christendom. A possible third scenario was that we sucked big-time, as witnessed by the fact that after the meeting he never returned my producer friend's calls, even to say, "Thanks for the therapy"! I was back to doing Canadian public-access satellite Internet dinner theater!

Stumbling back onto my feet, I did a fun pilot for a Richard Belzer-hosted show about conspiracies, which had me debating with Johnny Rotten and G. Gordon Liddy about whether or not Princess Di was murdered. It aired and I even got paid, but somehow—everybody now—the series wasn't picked up. (Killed by paparazzi or by the royal family?) Regrouping, I did a satirical segment for a *Smoking Gun TV* special, which ran and got a good review from the *Post*'s Linda Stasi. Again, I actually got some dough, and what's more, *Smoking Gun TV* was renewed as a series. But I was replaced by bobble-head dolls! I am not shitting you! I now hate them more than that freakin' seven-year-old!

I Am Woman, Hear Me Whore

But just as the gun was edging toward my own mouth, that thing called hope repositioned its li'l head through my half-opened door. A high-level producer decided to assemble a syndicated talk show for women starring gay men—sort of *The View* meets *Queer Eye*. Well, *The View* didn't want me (except maybe as a prospective husband), and *Queer Eye* had already shown me the window, but this little baby craved me, with fringe on. Here was my chance to finally cash in on the Latin boom, I mean gay boom, that had taken over every industry believer who'd drunk the pink Kool-Aid. I'd been a one-man gay boom for years, but now instead of bristling against shrieks of "Tone it down!" I was suddenly trying to keep up with the frantic calls of "Flame it up!"

"Gays are hot right now!" one of the show's creators exclaimed, luring me aboard as I glossed my lips and danced the Bump. The program's premise was that gay men are a lot like women—don't look at *me*—but a production assistant assured, "Of course, it won't be all mammograms and mascara." Too bad—I'd *love* to star in a show just about mammograms and mascara. Anyway, we went on to make a pilot, for which we obediently acted as "gay" as possible as we did everything from group-singing a Diana Ross hit to somberly discussing children's car safety. It got tons of press, the people were swell, and more importantly, I got paid, but guess what, girl? The show hasn't become any more airborne than Aretha Franklin (though if you believe in fairies, please applaud and it will live). Suddenly I was thinking of turning straight.

But I canceled the electroshock—I was still in the game, honey. That same producer now wanted to pitch a reality show about my fabulous life to the one channel I actually hadn't bothered yet. This seemed maybe sorta wildly promising—until it turned out they already had enough reality shows, thank you. And so *Growing Up Musto* stayed as grounded as the dodo bird.

There were other doomed pilots that were less nibbled-on than an Olsen Twins breakfast buffet, but finally I hit gay-dirt this year when along came a gay game show that actually wanted me! At last, a real job. In a professional setting. Which would make me part of the gay boom. Tons of people craved gigs like this. And I always wanted to be on a game show. I came alive at the run-through. I adored the people. I felt at home. I turned it down.

See, it required being in L.A. more than I'd hoped, and when push came to shove, I nervously stayed put. Could there be anything sadder or more irony-drenched? My life is hell. Still, I'm willing to sparkle again for a camera, any camera. Here I am, world. Anyone want to do a pilot about mammograms and mascara? With bobble heads?

Sex with the proper stranger

April 4, 2006

I recently wrote about the sharp rise in my sexploits in the wake of an emotional crisis and described how my new-found accessibility and craving for human contact had me suddenly swatting off guys like drosophila. People responded to the write-up with bravos, warnings, and condoms, while begging for a richly detailed follow-up.

Well, it's time for one because that was just the tip of the ding-dong, honey. I already discussed the three-way in the chapel of Avalon, but let me remind you that it all started when a photographer coaxed a handsome man to unleash his trouser pipe, leading to much (safe) cavorting and mayhem—and I helped!

I thought that was a fluke, but it was actually just an opening ceremony. Running around clubs with an open approach—and fly—not to mention a Neurontin prescription, I was suddenly getting attention and picking up on it rather than trying to find ways to make a chastity belt look chic, like back in the crotch-rot days. Not long after the

Avalon incident, I found myself at Happy Valley in a me sandwich flanked by two *other* appealing slices of gentleman toast. One—a tall guy with a sweet face and a nose ring—was smashed and all over me like a sample-sale suit. The other one—a cute, wispy thing—kept buying me Cokes and flattering my jacket, a Thriller-type '80s number that demanded to be noticed. Suddenly I was backed into the wall by the tonsil hockey skills of this Olympic-caliber duo, and though I felt a little like Jodie Foster in *The Accused*, you can't exactly rape the willing, can you?

Later that night, the wispy one was so insistent we stay in touch that he wrote his number on my hand, where it still happens to be carved. The other one kept tonguing me in between pleading, "I love you! Please don't hurt me, Michael!" *Me* hurt *him*? He'd ended up with his arm tightly wound around my neck, and I felt as if I were going to be strangled by the wrong Mr. Right. I gently released myself and slipped out the door, intoxicated by the experience but not about to take things to the next, messy level.

Trinidad and Toboggan

How could this be happening? Maybe because, thanks to Vitamin E oil, I read younger than I really am? "And it's dark in clubs," as a friend so nicely suggested. Whatever the case, I must have still been sporting a scarlet letter D for "Doable" because the next week at Duvet, a pretty Caribbean queen impulsively joined me on the dance floor, rubbing his leg up and down mine like a dog, so I could feel his hanging penis. It made the above-mentioned appendage seem like a spaghetti strap by comparison. At one point, the dude playfully put his cap on my head, obviously so he could later say, "Let's trade. You give me back my hat and I'll give you my number." And he did—though it turned out the business card he handed me was actually someone else's! Oh, well, I needed a humbling experience—and maybe the guy whose card it was wanted some action, right?

In the meantime, there was plenty more a-comin'—in fact, when it rains, it whores. At Happy Valley again, my striped outfit got noticed by an exotically handsome guy—the clothes-as-icebreaker gambit works every time—so we bonded and danced, in between him purchasing me some very fizzy sodas. He strangely introduced me to his "boyfriend," but that was all forgotten when he boldly reached into my pants and exclaimed, "Come on, let's go home! You're so hot!" I was flattered but was still afraid of intimacy and terrified that someone who thinks I'm attractive must be ready for a series of lobotomy needles. Once again, I snuck out, albeit on a cloud made of vaporized ego juice.

Clearly I was enjoying all the attention and the playing around for an audience, while wanting to protect myself from anything too real like actually having relations. But there were ramifications to this skittish-Casanova routine. When I ran into the exotically handsome guy two nights later at Duvet, he was friendly but I could swear he looked a tiny bit wounded. So now I, the troll of ages, was actually a gigantic heartbreaker? Fantastic! I must admit that knowing I suddenly had the power to hurt people gave me a distinct rise. Maybe I could finally get back at menfolk one by one for all those years when I was rejected? Alas, I'd probably be punishing myself in the process.

So I kept seeking thrills, and back at the Kurfew party at Avalon, a shirtless clubbie did an unsolicited lapdance for me, his ass smack up in my face as I gasped for air. Once I made it to freedom, I was introduced to a cute guy with green hair, whom I naturally asked, "Are you a top or bottom?" "A bottom," he blithely responded. "Guys fuck me for hours and it's so annoying. It's like, 'Come already!'" Bummer. We ended up corresponding by e-mail—he seemed like a literate enough type—and we were going to meet up at Happy Valley, but the dork canceled, saying he needed to work on his career instead. Maybe he was afraid I'd be a delayed ejaculator. Maybe he didn't realize I like to be the one doing the rejecting nowadays.

Kiss Kiss Bang Bang?
But for every misstep, a slut gets handed a giant plum, and sure enough things clicked again back at Duvet, where I met a young Michael Hutchence look-alike who'd just moved here, obviously via spaceship. He was sprawled out on a bed, beaming from God knows how much booger sugar and booze. The new, friendlier me said "hi" and he immediately responded, "I want to make out with you." We were truly skipping all the boring stuff now—you know, time wasters like "What's your name?" and "Where am I?" Quickly enough, his tongue was so far down my oral cavity it was almost cleaning out my kneecaps—for three straight hours. *How was this happening?* I don't know, but per usual, I left the

guy at the proverbial altar, pretty sure he wouldn't remember one second of it all by daybreak.

By now, I was making such frequent public spectacles that I thought the townspeople would stone me like Monica Bellucci in *Maléna*. But I had miraculously acquired some mojo and I was determined to work it to full release. Too bad the magic didn't last nearly as long as my hard-on. On the phone, the wispy guy from the me sandwich apologized for having been so drunk that night, which I took to mean that he had since awakened into sanity. Back at Happy Valley, my Caribbean queen was now enveloped in his *real* love; the Hutchence guy was admitting he's a starfucker and by the way he's fantasized about killing me; and the striped-outfit admirer was back with the "boyfriend." I'd lost my touchy-feely touch. I'd cockteased away all my hot chances and now they'd returned to the safety of each other. I'd had nine potential boyfriends and somehow ended up alone!

Undaunted, I took my equipment to an uptown dinner party, where I met an Italian guy with a puppy dog face who moaned that gay nightlife isn't what it used to be. I vehemently disagreed and offered to show him around, handing him my number with a bold smile. I'd gotten so shockingly confident. The only problem is he never called. And back at Duvet, even toothless troglodytes with three heads were taking a pass. Maybe word had gotten out that I'm an indiscriminate slut—oh yeah, I'd written that myself. And maybe I was getting too slick and not projecting the raw yearning that had attracted guys in the first place. I needed to throw away the Neurontin and have another breakdown.

Meanwhile, my only hope—short of that guy on the business card—was the trouser pipe hottie from that Avalon three-way. He'd called me repeatedly since then, but I'd played hard to get, stupidly wanting to move on to the next flavored jellybean before coming back for seconds. I was a mess, remember? But now I was anxious for someone to hold on to and maybe even develop a semi-quasi-relationship with. I might even consider taking him home this time. I nobly left the guy a message, offering him his choice of any club night-out he wanted. I was cocksure he'd come a-crawling with his tongue out. But shockingly enough, he didn't call back! I was devastated by the dis, retching from the taste of my own medicine. I'd gone from a sizzling stud back to a lonely letch in just two months. "Oh, good," I consoled myself. "This kind of utter collapse is just what you need to get action again." And then he called. Help!

No, wait, we made a date, then he never followed through! I was horrified again. How many of these ups and downs could a simple girl handle? But in the meantime I met a really sweet Hungarian guy who's cuckoo-crazy about me. Help!

STARS AND BARS

Pianist envy:
A visit with Liberace

April 9, 1985

"This is just temporary because it's too small," said Liberace, apologetically escorting me into his new Trump Tower co-op, resplendent with mirrors and flowers and antiques. Already I noticed that the couch alone was the size of my whole apartment. "There are two bedrooms and two and a half bathrooms," he whimpered, heartbroken. "I'll have to move into something bigger."

Torn between his problems and Afghanistan's, I'd have to side with Afghanistan. But if pressed to choose someone to sit and gab with (i.e., listen to), I'd go with Lee, the darlingest bundle of bad taste, a man so conspicuously tacky he's his own *Night of 100 Stars* every night of the week. The 40-year show biz veteran is not coy about his wealth; his press kit includes a list of his belongings—nine cars, 300 miniature pianos, over $700,000 worth of furs, and so on. "But I've attained these things through years of endeavor," he explained. "Everything I've acquired is something that's been part of the fantasy of my show biz life. And I share it with the public." He has many charities, as well as three houses, a shopping center, a museum, and a restaurant.

And a video—yes, a video—in which he flaunts his wealth for the 11-to-29 crowd. "You can be dripping in diamonds," he said, "but if you make fun of it, people will accept it." MTV had so much fun with it, they've made him April's guest veejay. And for the next 18 days he'll tinkle and dazzle at Radio City, pausing to dance with the Rockettes in a musical salute to New York. Can he kick under the weight of all those jewels? "We'll see, we'll see."

Lee's half Grandpa Munster and half Lorelei Lee. He talks in a nasal voice, smiles a nasal smile, and oozes simple, down-home Las Vegas charm. He aims to please, telling you anything and everything: how he bought a $3 thrift-shop handbag for Barbra Streisand; how the first four rows in Pittsburgh are always nuns; how one should do everything in moderation, "but who knows what moderation is?" He says this wearing a ring *bigger* than the couch. "Some have said that if I came out looking austere, I'd be like a beautiful present that wasn't wrapped. People would feel cheated. I was very disappointed the first time I saw Boy George without the gear. He looked so ordinary. He was just a person. Cyndi Lauper, she's talented. She's no kid—she's 31. And you know what, if you try to buy these so-called rags she wears, they're very expensive."

I wasn't really talking to Liberace about Cyndi Lauper. Surely this was a bauble-induced hallucination. "My favorite house is the one in Palm Springs," he went on. "It's like a friend I saved from dying, because it was going to be a parking lot and I made it a historical preservation. Every time I go in, the house talks to me. It says, 'Thanks for saving my life.' I have a Valentino Room, a Napoleon Room, a Gloria Vanderbilt Room, a William Randolph Hearst Room. . . ." I smiled wanly; I only have a Larry "Bud" Melman Room.

I posed no questions about his former chauffeur's unsuccessful palimony lawsuit (a case of pianist envy, I'm sure) or other personal matters, only because that's that Rupert Pupkin of journalism, Alan W. Petrucelli's turf. When Alan asked Lee who he sleeps with, he cryptically answered, "Them." Our conversation was more tasteful, centering on highway hookers, crotch shots, and a transvestite Lee knew who had "a schlong down to her knees," a big surprise to one of her dates. "She must have felt rejected," I said, always the one to sympathize with a drag queen. "I don't think she *was* rejected," said Lee, dissolving into expensive laughter.

Lee had gone so far beyond the call of social duty, I wanted to give him money. "And all after only one drink," he giggled. "I'm a cheap date." When we left him, he was reeling off the names of people whose Radio City box office records he'd just broken. "We beat Barry Manilow!" he exulted. "We beat Diana Ross!" "Take care, Lee. You're really a trip." "We beat Bette Midler! We beat Menudo! . . ."

High tea with
James fucking Woods

September 24, 1985

Six years ago, James Woods was an angry young man whose idea of small talk was to tell me about "all these fucking movie mogul bozos talking about how Donna Summer would be great for Lady Macbeth" and how "You mention *Swann's Way* to these people and they think it's a street in Brentwood." I loved him. Now, he says, "I'm just a Hollywood guy who drives a Porsche and hopes some day to do *Terminator 6* with Schwarzenegger. I was young then and sort of an artist. Now I'm a big commercial fatso. I live in L.A.— a good place to pick up a drink and put it back down and you're 85. It's better than dying in a subway, I suppose."

Woods, the world's most employed non-movie star (*The Onion Field, Against All Odds*), hasn't really changed at all, even though he now gets central roles that aren't murderers, in films like his latest, *Joshua Then and Now*. The Mouth still works overtime ("I only do this for you"), smacking its lips on everything from "New scum Coke" to bad nouvelle cuisine "that looks like Totie Fields's face" to one of his favorite actresses whom he taught liar's poker "and was honored, because anybody who was fucking Elvis Presley at age six, or whatever she was doing, has got to be pretty hep." Am I the only person who finds this man charming? Six years ago he offered me "a $30 danish" and I declined. Now I sip tea as he sits, dressed like a young Republican, eating "a goyishe chicken sandwich" in a fancy-schmancy hotel. He used to beat up winos and take their clothes, he says, "but now I sell my car so I can buy some socks at Charivari." That only makes his foot more color-coordinated as I force it gently into the Mouth.

This year, Woods tells me, "there were 48,000 movies about kids getting laid in the back seat of a Chevy for the first time. That's why it's your moral obligation to like *Joshua.*" Actually, I did like the first half a lot, but he says everyone prefers the second half. I hated the second half. No one in either half gets laid in a Chevy, though there is some delicious vulgarity in it and a softer, less maniacal Woods. "I still have an edge, even though I don't kill anybody," he says. "If I ever lost my edge, there'd be nothing left but dust and a pair of shoes." Guccis, no doubt. He proves he still has the edge by lacing into the chicken sandwich as if there's no tomorrow. Is he mad at it? No, he's mad at near-stardom and the tricks it's playing on his masculine ego. "All of a sudden it's 'Oh, you're James Woods' and I can't put my moves on the chicks anymore because they're overwhelmed and it's cheating, it's like having an advantage. I want them to do it in a phone booth with me because I'm sexy, not because I'm James Woods. So now I gotta talk them into thinking I'm not really a box office star, and when you think about it I'm not special, so can we go down the hallway and do it?"

The Mouth does know when to draw the line—Woods won't badmouth any of his movies, mainly because if he didn't believe in them, he wouldn't be doing them, and that's why I love the guy. He even made up with Faye Dunaway, "and everything I said came true anyway." He only gets mad when someone like Woody Allen, whom he loves, squirms at Elaine's as if he assumes Woods's friend is craning her neck to look at him, "when the truth is, she was looking at the TV and he was kind of blocking the view. It was no big deal that he was sitting at the next table is the point of that story."

What gets Woods really worked up, though, is any mention of the bitterly vicious and uncalled-for magazine story written about him in which he came off like Attila the Hun and the writer came off far worse. It made Bette Davis's daughter's book look like an act of good faith. "The story actually helped me," he says, "because people realized the author was a degenerate scum-sucking pig who instead of sucking dicks on Eighth Avenue, which is where she'll probably end up making her living at two dollars a pop when she's still getting overpaid, was only setting me up for a muckraking job. . . . She's a fucking pile of unmitigated pus ripped from the ass of a dead dog. I'll let her hang herself by her three tits." He grins and wipes mayo out of the corner of his mouth. "Anyway, I'm not like this anymore."

Once bitten, "Twice" high

November 5, 1985

"Pose with John Forsythe," one of my contingent suggested to Boy George at a Regine's dinner for yet another *Dynasty* cologne. "No. He's homophobic," said George irritably, making me kind of irritable because it's the character who's homophobic, not the man in real life. But then it hit me—*Dynasty* is real life.

Proudly wearing my Carrington cologne, I sashayed Moldavia-style to a very chic Regency Hotel dinner for *Twice in a Lifetime*, a schmaltzy, beautifully acted divorce movie I liked so much I can't wait to have a relationship so I can get divorced. The dinner was appropriately schmaltzy/beautiful, the first party of the year where they actually underinvited and yet practically all the film's stars were there. And what stars! Ellen Burstyn, who stoically gained 15 pounds (her secret? "Living") so she could lose them in the course of the film and appear more glamorous after the divorce. Ann-Margret, my second biggest childhood idol (after Ann-Margrock from *The Flintstones*), who plays the other woman and said, "I didn't break up that home. That marriage started to disintegrate long before me," going into a lengthy self-defense as if this were real life (*Dynasty*'s real life, this is just a movie). Gene Hackman, an actor's actor who's unfortunately not an interview subject's interview subject, and who actually said the movie was "a once-in-a-lifetime experience." "I'm sorry I'm kind of dry," he added, after apologizing for a string of "boring adjectives." That's okay, Gene. I'll still remember your more eloquent moments, like your "Mush, Miss Teschmacher, mush" scene in *Superman II*.

I sat with Christine Lahti, Michelle Lee, and Superman himself, Chris Reeve, a fun guy who was grinning when he crept up behind me and said, "Making up quotes? What's the lag time between the time they say something and the time you write it down?" As a matter of fact, I write the quotes in advance, then match them up with the celebrities later. "Airline food," the appallingly fabulous William Friedkin kvetched at the top of his lungs about the glazed duck, before pulling down my dark glasses and asking me what I was on. This is the guy who didn't want to sit down with me unless he was sure it was going to be a serious interview. No wonder—his casting director Bob Weiner had talked me up to him as a sort of new wave Joey Adams. I asked Billy if it's true that he said the *Voice* is about "quiche and fags" and he laughed and said, "No, I never use the word 'fags.' I said 'cheese and homosexuals.' Every time I open the paper there's a cheeseboard. *L.A. Weekly*'s surpassed you. They write about Nicaragua." They probably write about Friedkin, too.

Richard Brandt from the AFI made a speech introducing the film's director-producer Bud Yorkin, and Friedkin stood up. Yorkin introduced someone else, and Friedkin stood up. "This is the best cast ever put together," said Yorkin, the best morale captain ever to make a movie. "I don't care what happens with this picture. I'm a happy Jew." He thanked Sally Struthers for coming and she sarcastically screamed, "Thank you for putting me in the movie!" ("That's my line," murmured Chris Reeve.) "Hey Bud, who *didn't* you like in the film?" yelled Friedkin, who must have mistaken this for *his* party. The janitor, said Bud.

I went back to Ann-Margret, a ravishing kitten, whip or no whip, and asked her the tackiest question of all: How would she react if *her* husband (Roger Smith) had an affair? She gulped and turned mildly greenish. "I don't deal in those kinds of if situations," she said. I gasped. I crawled. I was back with Billy Friedkin. By now he had appropriated my pad and was writing my column for me ("Tonight I had the . . . unspeakable thrill of meeting William Friedkin"), nobly giving me permission to call his *To Live and Die in L.A.* "the *Citizen Kane* of drek movies." I told him I liked the film, at which point he took back his facetious offer of lunch and a hustler ("Why buy him lunch—he liked the movie"). For lunch and a hustler I could have *loved* the movie.

"What'd I tell you—isn't he crazy?" said Weiner, who was wearing a T-shirt that said, "Evil, wicked, mean and nasty." How did he get hold of my shirt?

Deck the Hall
with boughs of folly

August 5, 1986

Anthony Michael Hall—the kind of dude who uses words like "cat" and "man" in all seriousness—entered his *Out of Bounds* premiere party drenched in some bodily secretion or other as he weaved around throwing flowers at angry photographers' lenses, playing with a finger puppet, turning up the music box he brought to drown out his own gurgling, and generally acting in the I-used-to-be-a-geek-now-I'm-a-Hollywood-star fashion that we all thought died with John Belushi. I must say I admire this tyke's spirit but wouldn't want to clean up after him.

An army of publicists from Columbia Pictures and PMK who'd promised indentured servitude suddenly abandoned me the moment their slobbering star entered. "Get Michael Musto away for five minutes," one of them shouted. But wait—I'm the King of New York. I did corner the film's producer, John Tarnoff, and asked what it was like working with this hell-bent idiot. "On the record?" he asked. Yes, it was. "Oh, he's very talented and he's great in the movie." Hey, stop the presses! He added that the guy's kind of "headstrong," but everything ended up peachy-keeny—a lovely little uplift that momentarily took me away from the pandemonium at hand. Bouncers were pushing me toward the vile buffet in the back. A lynch mob of riffraff was pushing me back to the front. Disturbed camera crews were getting incoherent footage of Anthony that publicists would later plead with them not to use. Anthony was making out with some girl and carrying on *Out of Bounds.* As I feigned a swoon, club denizen Mojo turned up and said, "I had a dream like this once. I woke up drowning in a bowl of cereal." Frosted flakes, no doubt.

Warhol sendoff: To die for

April 14, 1987

The very last death knell for the '70s (not to mention the '60s and the East 30s) was sounded at the memorial service for Andy Warhol at Saint Patrick's, which became a veritable cathedral of sinners as party people filed into church for the first time since the Limelight opened. It was 9:30 A.M. and everyone looked like hell. Some threatened to melt—it was their first experience of sunlight—but that would have messed up their outfits, so they didn't. And what appalling grandeur! They paraded in the long way, to be seen; regardless of religion, they lined up to take communion just to be near Don Johnson; and some idiots even stood in the back handing out invites to the Tunnel. Outside, a woman was screaming, "The monster's dead! The monster's finally dead!" It was enough to make you flag the next plane to Tibet.

But can I tell you it was fabulous? Can a memorial service really be fabulous? For Andy Warhol, it had better be, and it was. Celebs were in obscene abundance—Liza Minnelli, smiling and waving at strangers; Bianca Jagger, looking gamine and saying, "Andy was one of those great . . . figures"; Yoko Ono and Timothy Leary comparing notes on being " '60s people"; and Grace Jones, greeting camera crews with real, genuine, I-swear-to-God-I'm-crying tears. The entire art, design, and drag queen worlds were there, and for once they weren't being artful, designing, or a drag. And the speakers played along, shrewdly painting Andy as an unbesmirchable Christian saint, a martyr, not a manipulator. What the hell, we believed it for a day. They told about "lemmings" who latched on to him (that screaming woman must have been a disgruntled lemming) and how Andy loved the idea of being reincarnated as a gigantic ring on Elizabeth Taylor's finger. Liz didn't show, but I have a feeling Bianca had borrowed the ring and Andy was sitting on her hand, listening to every word.

Everyone was dressed sedately. I was dressed like a 14th Street hooker. Outside, I asked departing celebs what they missed most about Andy. John Waters said, "The thought that he's not going to make another movie. I ran away from Baltimore to go to the world premiere of *Chelsea Girls*." Irene Worth (Irene Worth?) said, "That incredible smile." (That incredible smile?) Lou Christie said, "The parties."

But there *was* one coming—well, a wake, anyway—which (Is this too cheap?) was undeniably the most glittering event of the year so far. Held at Steve Rubell and Brian McNally's upcoming, as-yet-unnamed restaurant in the Paramount Century hotel, it had just the right mix of trashiness and taste for an April Fools' Day memorial lunch. You followed a trail of *Interview* covers to a gilded, silvery room that was like the magazine come to life, plus buffets. Everywhere you looked, incredible, incongruous combos of people were chatting glamorously—Mary McFadden and Fran Lebowitz, Ono and Richard Gere. This was too exciting, and it wasn't even noon yet. Andy would have loved it—it redefined "to die."

Gere, nicer with each passing bomb, patted me on the hat and asked what the hell it was. Peter Allen gushed about his *Legs Diamond* workshop, though he refrained from handing out invites. Claus Von Bülow made bosomy gestures and talked profoundly about "boobs" while—wow, synchronicity—DJ Johnny Dynell said he was wearing "the titty connection," a Vivienne Westwood shirt one has to see to be appalled by. And schlepping all through the place was a cheery gaggle of Instamatic-toting bag ladies everyone assumed would be flung out momentarily.

Posing for them as a goof, I soon learned they were Andy's family from Pittsburgh. They were fab! How much money did Andy leave you, I asked one of these shabby-coated ragamuffins, a cousin named Eugenia King, knowing full well how much. "None. Was he supposed to?" she said, daffily.

By now a whole new bevy of celebs was there to say what they miss about Andy. Lou Reed: "Andy." Timothy Leary: "New York without Andy is like L.A. without Swifty Lazar." Richard Gere (even nicer by now): "I miss him saying 'Great' and 'Fab.' " Keith Haring: "Saturday afternoons when we'd talk on the phone and decide what to do Saturday night." Tama Janowitz: "I miss that sarcastic look, like, 'Oh, Tama, what have you done this time?' " Steve Rubell: "I'm not good at answers. Bullshit, yes. Answers, no." Three more people said his smile, four more said his saying "fab." Then Tama invited a bunch of us to her house for barbecued beef. We couldn't go—we'd feel like lemmings—and the invite wasn't for that day anyway. Besides, this event had been drainingly monumental—a kaleidoscopic tribute of tributes. Let's hope no one else has to end up on Liz Taylor's overcrowded hand before we get another one.

Mother Eartha

June 2, 1987

What Eartha Kitt needs is to be left alone before a show, as I learned at the Ballroom, where I foolishly ventured backstage moments before opening night curtain. Looking like the statue in *One Touch of Venal*, Eartha was understandably tense as she toyed with her precious poodles while someone teased her hair, nyah-nyah. I thanked her for letting me in. "It's very rare," she said, and everyone in the room laughed before realizing she wasn't kidding. "I know you're not going to ask any questions," she added. Well, just one, actually. "Well, ask it," she snapped, "and get it over with." The dogs recoiled in horror. Okay, is it true you're playing a madam in two Golan-Globus films? The dogs winced. "Get that from my publicist," she ordered. "I'm a different person now." Yes, madam. As I crawled out, I heard a bark, then realized it was Eartha.

By showtime, her mood had swung and she was exuberant and grinning, exquisitely singing about her lust for Cadillacs and Piper Heidsieck. She taunted the audience ("Too bad you can't afford me"), reworked "I'm Still Here" ("I was a new face in '52/Now I'm much older, but so are you"), and asked a cute guy in the front row for his card, reaching capitalist nirvana when he handed her his American Express Gold Card. By the end, everyone was crying, and I think Eartha had forgiven me and maybe even Lady Bird.

Susan Anton
didn't get the memo

March 29, 1988

Rossellini restaurant threw a party for Susan Anton, but unfortunately the singer/actress didn't know it was her party; she was just having a dinner reunion there with her old Hurlyburly costars. How curious it was, then, when swarms of press turned up, and were seated at tables near Anton so we could observe her as if she were the result of a biopsy. "What?" she exclaimed. "It's my party? Does that mean I'm paying for it?" No, just that wily publicists were turning her dinner with friends into a major PR affair, and she could cry if she wanted to.

But it didn't turn out to be her party anyway. Midway through, photographer Aubrey "My Wife Thinks I'm in the Library" Reuben got his new escort (as in service), Jessica Hahn, to show up, and the paparazzi *really* went hurly-burly, as Anton seemed to avert her head like Anna Magnani when Marilyn suddenly became the toast of Rome. Hahn went from table to table speculating on who could play her in the miniseries. "I could play myself *after* the PTL," she said. "Or a girl on *Days of Our Lives*, I can't think of her name, could play me. Or Valerie Bertinelli." Or maybe Madonna. "Donna who?" she said. Never mind. Or Hahn could play Tammy. "What! I never even met the woman!" Well, then, Hahn could play Jim. "You guys!" she shrieked. "Why are we talking about this?" And she was off. As the last frenzied flashbulb died down, Anton was asked if she appreciated Hahn being there. "Oh, I didn't know she was here," she said, blithely. Everybody now—I'm just wild about Harrah's. . . .

Snap out of it, Oscar!

April 16, 1988

Pre-Oscar L.A.—a walking petri dish of hype and hoopla. The whole town crawled with celebs making their very last rounds of self-promotion, even though the voting was long over (it didn't matter—most of them weren't nominated anyway). And everywhere you went, even blue-haired old ladies sat around debating whether *Au Revoir Les Enfants* would win best original screenplay. Come on now—these people haven't seen a movie since *Gigi*.

Suddenly it was Oscar day and everyone converged outside the Shrine Civic Auditorium, a Rupert Pupkin wet dream come true. In the sweltering late afternoon sun, hundreds of screaming solophobes (people with a morbid fear of being alone) stood in bleachers, losing it over the cavalcade of celebrity arrivals. The screams were continual, and you could never be sure if they were for the person arriving or the person being interviewed by Army Archerd (who was situated like a bowling pin at the end of the red velvet runway), though Edy Williams seemed to think it was for her on all three entrances. It's appropriately barbaric and superficial, so Nina Foch barely registered a five on the applause meter, while Rob Lowe almost broke the machine. The sun makes you think strange thoughts: Did a guy named Lasse really make a picture called *My Life as a Dog?*

Little Richard, who's becoming essential to any awards show, pranced by and announced, "I'm gonna knock 'em down and pick 'em up and pull it out," as he got down with his bad self and got back up again. Sally Kirkland, recovering from a yoga accident that had her sending her mother to parties as a sub, got her neck in gear in time to show up in person and reallyreallyreally want to win. Someone was incongruously screaming at Dudley Moore's wife, "Who made your dress?" as someone else yelled, "Who paid for it?" Ice goddess Sean Young flitted by twirling an ever-so-coy parasol, preparing to present Best Editing—somebody's idea of a sick joke because she was veritably shredded out of *Wall Street* (but then remember Marlee Matlin presented Best Sound last year). And one-time pregnant Oscar winner Eva Marie Saint was told by Army, "Glenn Close is very expectant," to which Eva responded, "That's right. She's close." The crowd screamed at her wit—Proustian by today's standards.

As throngs scurried to their seats, Ann Sothern (30 on the meter) hobbled in like a sequined Jabba the Hut and raised cane to the crowd. And about 15 minutes after the show had started, when almost all hope was gone, Cher (100) made the entrance of death. I think she did that so that someone else could have their 15 minutes. From then on it was all about Miss Sarkisian LaPiere Bono Allman Bagelmaker LaLanne

Naveldiva Oscarmama. Say that 10 times backward and it comes out just "Cher."

Inside the press (i.e., circus) tent backstage, a sumptuous watermelon buffet welcomed us, but we didn't greet it back. As publicists frantically handed out freshly typed versions of the acceptance speeches, we watched the show on monitors via headphones, stopping only to interview the triumphant winners and drag them back down to reality. It's all very efficiently done, but too much is left to chance. You have the headphones on for an awful musical number, but in the background you hear everyone guffawing over something Jack Lemmon said in the tent (presenters are also brought in as a sideshow, if they want to be, and they all—except Eddie Murphy and Audrey Hepburn—wanted to be). You pull off the headphones, but no one will tell you what Lemmon said. Meanwhile you've just missed something brilliant on the telecast. It's a no-win situation, but not boring.

The lesser award winners are so ignored that one victorious guy, besieged by no questions, started singing "Moon River." The major winners, meanwhile, incite pandemonium without even opening their mouths. There's such an air of frenetic confusion that when asked if he had a lot of offers right now, a baffled Patrick Swayze replied, "A lot of ovaries right now?" and Jennifer Grey chimed in, "I have two. Two ovaries." Only two? It must be a slow month. The *Inner-space* winner talked glowingly about that movie ("Obviously it just didn't do very well. It just failed."), and the Documentary Short Subject twosome impressed us with their upcoming ovaries ("We certainly are available!"). Olympia, the Best Supporting Dukakis, announced, "It's the year of the Dukakii," and Billy Wilder discussed how Gloria Swanson wasn't "an old hag" when she made *Sunset Boulevard*—just a young hag? "My first experience?" said Wilder, misunderstanding a question. "My French experience? My first French experience?" Oh, never mind.

By now the *Last Emperor* sweep had reared its first broomstick, and everyone decided it was because the film puts trashy elements—remember the turd-smelling?—into prestige surroundings, allowing you to appreciate art in an LCD format that's not intimidating. It's the cinematic equivalent of Laurie Anderson. I personally failed to see the second half of the film because, to paraphrase Jerry Lewis about another longie, the kid in front of me grew up.

Predictable as it was turning out, no one could stop the show and let us go home. The winners just kept on coming and suddenly there were two kinds of melon. Sean Connery had beaten Albert Brooks, whom we love even though *Broadcast News* made him into a bite-free cuddly bear of the type homogenized enough to be up for awards. Connery went the opposite route, starting out in whimsy like *Darby O'Gill and the Little People* and ending up in dark, creepy work. The message here is that any career change merits an Oscar nomination, but if you've done it longer, you get the trophy.

"*Last Emperor* just won best editing," announced Billy Crystal. "It also just passed Michael Dukakis in the New York State primary." But it didn't win Best Song ("Turd-Smelling Blues" wasn't even *nominated*), leaving an award-toss to *Dirty Dancing*, the winners of which exclaimed how this was all "beyond the dream"—beyond the nightmare even. John Patrick Shanley—who looks William Hurtish and sounds like someone who was thrown out of Cardinal Spellman High School—picked up his original screenplay award for *Moonstruck* and tawked about his fave writer dudes. "Shakespeare, Shaw," he grinned. "They're pretty good." Now that *Moon* has struck gold, Shanley's not exactly about to change course and write about Maori mating rites. His next play—a stretch?—is called *Italian-American Reconciliation*.

Rob Lowe, mother in tow, discussed *his* upcoming ovaries and said, "I'm waiting for something as good as *Masquerade*." Time's up. "He's dating *me*," screeched Sean Young—yeah, in your dreams, girl. Best Actor Michael Douglas said dad Kirk was not there because he was "too nervous." Huh? The most chilling moment of the telecast, by the way, was Evita-like Diandra Douglas's triumphant expression when Michael copped the bronze—no way is she letting that man go. But none of this mattered as we were quickly treated to a seminar on how Marlee Matlin's been working on her "muscle groups."

Meanwhile, the *Last Emperor* winners kept on keeping on, getting more and more statistic-oriented and faux-poetical (the costume designer told how he made 9,500 costumes for 19,000 people and concluded with, "Thank you, the city of the angels. You are, you are").

Finally, the climax—Cher, the feelgood winner from the feelgood movie, entered the tent saying, "I feel I've given my first born to get this dress" and added that Theda Bara would have been proud of her look. "I don't think you can see anything," she said, surveying her outfit. "I'll tell you, there's not much to see, if you could." But let's get to the serious issues: Cher, did you like the way you looked in *Mask?* "I thought my nose was too big," she squawked. And now, I'll tell you, there's not much to see, if you could.

No bitches were allowed to read an Eve Harringtonish "I beat you, Meryl" into Cher's acceptance speech—this was a feelgood win, remember? But there were some bad vibes about her thanking her hairdressers and not Norman Jewison or Shanley (she later compensated for this with a three-page ad in *Hollywood Reporter*, commending *everyone* in her career) and sounding a little like she was doing another gym commercial (she thanked "everyone I worked *on*"). Besides, this Extremely Serious Actress will soon be playing Atlantic City to the tune of mucho moolah after pooing on the idea of returning to Vegas (same difference). But knocking Cher is like spitting on the Blarney Stone. She's conquered every entertainment form except voguing (no, *including* voguing) and deserves to make a mint off the clam-sucking crowd if she wants to.

Finally—the resolution—Bertolucci came in to talk about how he condensed 6,000 years into a mere 5,000 hours of moviemaking, or something like that. He explained his "Hollywood is the Big Nipple" metaphor with, "Nine nominations is a big suck for me—the milk of gratification." And nine wins out of nine is a giant slurp on the lactation of life. "Next," he said on leaving, "is to get rid of the Chinese obsession." An hour later, he was probably hungry for more.

We weren't, stuffed to the gills as we were with *three* kinds of melon. As the bedraggled press filed out, a real buffet of hamburgers was ushered in—bad timing, a sensual obsession. By that point, some were heard to echo the immortal words of Tom Selleck to Mickey Mouse, "You got any more of that magic dust?"

Tony! Tony! Tony!

June 21, 1988

Right after winning their Tony awards, Broadway's brightest were ushered in to Sardi's to meet the press and give their greatest performances yet. Best Featured Actor, M. Butterfly's B. D. Wong explained his relatively low profile in the press with, "It's important that all the people who see the show every night are virgins." Best Musical Actor, Phantom's Michael Crawford, said, "Thank God Lon Chaney couldn't sing." Presenter Gregory Hines laughed, "Why am I here?"

Then special guest Kathleen Turner hit the podium, a mass of diva mannerisms ranging from the nervous to the self-assured to the nervously self-assured. Puffing away on a waning cigarette, she grew impatient if the questions stopped for a second ("Just don't leave me hanging!")—endearingly insecure for a woman critics said was the least vulnerable Camille since the Mack truck. During Ron Silver's press conference, she stood around yelling, "Yay, Ron!" like an over-charged cheerleader. Whatever emotion she's doing, I find

Turner mesmerizing, a real Movie Star. It's not *her* fault that *Julia and Julia* is already on video.

Other Tony thoughts: Someone should tell Madonna that *she* wasn't punished by her lack of rehearsal—*we* were. And I do think that now that the mudslinging campaign against Sarah Brightman is over, everyone in New York should send her a personal apology note on especially pretty stationery. The high point at Sardi's was Sarah wailing away on the monitors as Judy Kaye said, "Sing it, Sarah, sing it. Hit that note. It's an E—You can do it." She hit it. It's not *her* fault either that *Julia and Julia* is already on video.

The press was allowed at the Hilton post-Tonys ball for only 20 minutes. I—a late RSVP—was not allowed at all. So it was on to Chita Rivera's Tony party at her restaurant Chita, colorfully done up as a shrine to guess who, replete with Chita dolls, posters, bathrooms labeled "Chito's" and "Chita's," and even a Chita look-alike—her sister Lola— practically dancing a cancan as you enter. Once there, you will never forget where you are.

Chita looked hot, having helicoptered in dressed like a zebra, not a cheetah. Dr. Ruth, impersonating Willow, wore acetate and said, "Everybody's dressed except me!" Nell Carter came in dressed like the Chrysler building and a while later went off with Chita to the real party at the Hilton. We stayed, just for the hell of it.

Ruthie—who in the last few weeks has danced with Zubin Mehta, been kissed by Bruce Springsteen, and got hugged by B. D. Wong (So what? I got semi-smiled at by Celeste Holm)—was now schmoozing with Michael Feinstein. Isn't it romantic? The banned-to-cable doc is going to see M. But-terfly again with Feinstein to try to further figure how a man could sleep with a tranvestite for years without knowing. "I don't understand how someone could be hugging and kissing him without automatically feeling something," she said, adding that maybe John Lithgow's character was gay, and kept it quiet. Or, I figure, maybe M. tucked his penis. Or maybe the Lithgow guy was really a woman and they were lesbians. It's all so confusing.

Debbie's daughter after all

1989

Anyone who loves art, beauty, or, hey, life itself should run to their local bookstore and demand a copy of Touch Me, The Poems of Suzanne Somers, the '73 tome that is being rediscovered thanks to this seminal actress/bard's renaissance on that noir western, She's the Sheriff. Divided into six chapters with names like "Touch Me—I Can Never Be Touched Enough," the collection runs the spectrum from winsomeness ("I wore my green sweater today—and smiled") to more winsomeness ("Once while I cooked for you/I told the brussels sprouts/I knew you loved them") to shock endings ("Sometimes I want to be a little girl—So touch my cheeks lightly. . . . Because I am a little girl"). The italics are mine, but the feelings are deeply, eminently Suzanne. There are photos, too, like one of SuSu crouching amid potted plants for the poem about how her coleus proposed marriage to her. It all begins with a foreward that tells us, "I love this book." It's written, it turns out, by none other than Ms. Somers herself.

An ever brighter literary revelation—and this time I do

mean it—is Carrie Fisher's *Postcards from the Edge*, a semific-
tionalized account of her leap into the void of drugs and
Hollywood romance. This startlingly vivid confessional starts
with the line, "Maybe I shouldn't have given the guy who
pumped my stomach my phone number," and then gets into
the depressing stuff, all with a sharp-tongued realism that
would send Suzanne Somers hiding behind her African vio-
lets ("Their dry leaves cling like withered fingers . . ."—oh,
never mind).

I caught up with Carrie at the Berkshire after she'd already
done every magazine known to modern man, but not
enough to drive her back to drugs. Maybe this was going to
be the one. She'd just come off the phone with a 7 A.M. L.A.
TV show, and thanks to her three-course Coca-Cola breakfast, she sounded alarmingly perky—this is Debbie's
daughter, after all. "I love doing this!" she bubbled, facetiously. "I could promote my thirties away!" Being in her
"cooperative years," Carrie will do practically anything
Simon and Schuster tells her to but admits, "I couldn't say
doing this is my fondest wish. It's tricky because I get interviewed as if I wrote an autobiography, or I didn't and now I
should. They want you to evangelize about drug addiction
or give some new dirt on Debbie and Eddie. I feel like I'm
qualifying for some public office and I have to clear my
name." I always felt she had to atone more for the third *Star
Wars* than for any cocaine problem.

Postcards will be filmed by Mike Nichols, who's helping
Carrie structure the script, but Carrie's toyed with screen-
plays before and says, "I don't think I'm gonna win any

awards for it." She's relentlessly self-aware, which has only made the tour more grueling. One San Francisco interviewer tried to get her to say John Belushi had started her on drugs. "The guy weighed like 300 pounds, and he was saying, 'Why did you do drugs?' and I wanted to say, 'Why do you eat that much? Are you *that* hungry?' " For that matter, why did *Belushi* eat that much? The *Today* show was a particularly disturbing experience, akin to that stomach-pumping event, except no numbers were exchanged. "Nancy Collins was nice enough as a human being," Carrie says, "but then we got on the air and it was *You Bet Your Life.* She never asked me about my book. She asked me about Debbie and Eddie, Belushi and Paul Simon, and Liz Taylor even." I was going to ask Carrie about her book, but I first had to tell her about how Eddie once said I looked like a young him. "That's probably a compliment," she laughed. "I bet *he* wishes he looked like a young him."

Carrie likes to joke that she only did drugs to research the book. What a thorough job she did. "I was just experimenting like some lab animal," she giggles. And now she's experimenting in promotion like an all-too-willing mouse in a Skinner box operated by 300-pound sadists. Always a good Leia, she's now a good writer, too. But why do people get so excited about celeb drug revelations like hers? "Because they're fascinated with foul-ups," says Carrie Fisher. "It's the principle on which Dynasty's based—fuck-ups of the rich and famous."

Who's on Forest?: The Madonna and Sandra show

June 6, 1989

Much like *Speed-the-Plow*, "Don't Bungle the Jungle!"—a concert to benefit Brazilian rainforest conservation groups—
became known immediately as "the Madonna show."
Ultimately, most people who were there to stop the steady
ruination of trees, species, and oxygen were more interested
in seeing whether Madonna was going to wear pumps.

It was that kind of night—a unique BAM mix of preten-
sion, portentousness, high-mindedness, and sequined
bodices. The audience varied according to ticket price:
younger music fans ($25 to $100, for just the show), artsy
BAM types and a few black-tie people ($250 for the pre-
reception, show, and Mars party), celebs ($500 for every-
thing plus dinner at Indochine), and the media (free). The
incongruities came all night. First, the reception, in the upstairs
Lepercq Space, offered mozzarella balls, inflatable iguanas,
and Mary Beth Hurt. Then, the media moved down to the
auditorium for a photo op, where the entire cast was trotted
out onstage, some meeting each other for the first time in

the glare of camera lights. The backdrop was a tree by the benefit's key organizer Kenny Scharf that in other versions said "Save Me," but here was so sad it couldn't even make polite conversation.

Madonna and Sandra Bernhard verbalized for it—suddenly this was the Madonna and Sandra show. They wore identical psychedelic jeans (oh, and spike heels) and were giggling uncontrollably. "Who are *you*?" Madonna wondered at someone who turned out to be the Grateful Dead's Bob Weir. They shook hands, and as the photographers snapped away, she told Keith Haring to come stand next to her. "Grab me," she insisted, adding under her breath, "It's a hetero world." He grabbed her.

"I love you Keith. I love you Kenny," beamed Madonna. "I only *like* you Sandy." Sandra, meanwhile, was giving profile angles as if this were a police lineup. Madonna wanted her to say something because she has "such a way with words," except when Revlon pays for 12 or less. "As you know, Madonna," said Sandra, rolling her eyes, "I don't know anything about this benefit."

"Don't start!" barked Madonna. Already, they were doing an Abbott and Costello routine (Who's on forest?). Sandra was being even more petulant than usual and seemed headed for some kind of public smashup. You'd have to have incredible eye-to-mind control to keep up with the faces she was making. Weir explained some tree-related realities, and she nodded her head facetiously. "Absolutely," she smirked to the assembled media, "give yourselves a round of applause."

Come showtime, everyone marched slowly to their seats, sensing it might be punishment time. The evening turned out to be only intermittently torturous, as the audience streamed in and out in hopes of catching Madonna's appearances and found other things, from the wooden to the sappy to the deeply rooted. No announcer introduced the acts; perhaps the organizers assumed we would all automatically know who Maria McKee was on sight. We did know who Madonna was, especially with her famous innie belly button showing thanks to her sheer, cropped, blue top with halter bra. She slinked out and thanked us "for coming—again and again." People chattered and buzzed, and she grinned, "Excuse me, the spotlight is on me now," as if we were chattering about anything but her. Admitting her original attitude was "Who cares about some trees in South America?" (but Scharf had enlightened her), Madonna explained the greenhouse effect and said it's going to be a very hot summer. One so hot only costumes from her "Express Yourself" video would seem practical—prepare to lick milk. She ended by dedicating the evening to "the first martyr of our cause," assassinated rubber-tapper/activist Chico Mendes. Already, three big-name moviemakers (Robert Redford, David Puttnam, and Peter Guber) are scrambling for the rights to Mendes's story. Let's hope they don't bungle *that* by casting someone wearing lots of Max Factor.

The star performance of the night was given by Bernhard, who entered wrapped in an American flag, holding burning incense, and looking perturbed but still petulant. Backed by a nine-piece tropical/funk band, she sang Joni

Mitchell's "Woodstock," unfolding layers of anger, sarcasm, and idealism that were mesmerizing, all the while clutching that flag. Her voice has gotten incredible—she can even scat—and no longer has to be described as "great, for a comic."

After the song, Bernhard dropped the flag to reveal a floral Rachel London minidress bedecked with black roses—yet a new layer of wryness. In a freewheeling monologue, she roasted Mary Boone (who she says can "pal around with the Schnabels and the Salles, but fuck Sandra Bernhard"), Ralph Lauren ("a/k/a Lipschitz"), and Indian art collector Andy Warhol, who "really understood the concept of potlatch." Claiming she cried into a rug she bought at the Warhol auction and felt desert smells well up in her nose, she said, "I felt like fucking Georgia O'Keeffe walking down the grand canyon of Fifth Avenue."

Changing moods one more time, Bernhard recited a tone poem to the pulse of a bass. It used the failing heartbeat of the jungle as an emblem for all the "beats" we have to keep going, from Gandhi to Liberace, from consciousness to angry righteousness. "Lech Walesa has the beat—a polka beat," she said. "Even Mother Teresa has a lowdown funky beat." Getting more intense, she culminated with a call to fight racism, sexism, homophobia, and to "Act up. Fuck AIDS." This mysteriously—wonderfully—led to a tribute to Sylvester ("creator of the disco beat"), as she whirled into his "Do You Wanna Funk?" and explained how Jim Baker got caught with his finger in the funk, Jesus Christ was tempted by the funk, and we've all got to keep the funk in our lives.

In her brief time onstage, Sandra forged a whole new genre of beat/punk activist musical comedy.

The entire cast came out for bows in groups—by now some of them knew each other—and we thought it was all over, when Abbott and Costello reunited.

"I'm Madonna," said Madonna. "I'm Shashana," said Sandra. "We're a couple of dynamic gals," they sing-songed. Madonna gave some more facts (every year, rainforests the size of New York State are decimated), and Shashana said, "Who the fuck do you think you are, Tracy Chapman?" "No," said Madonna, "I'm not working at a convenience store. But I do like to sneak off to a 7-Eleven at night for some jawbreakers." "The bitch is cold," hissed Sandra. "Funky cold Medina."

They sang "I Got You Babe," Madonna taking the butch, lower-register part, Sandra being Sonny. Again, the layers ranged from satirical to self-parodistic to baldly sweet. Sandra played havoc with the lyrics a bit, grabbing her crotch and singing, "I know we don't have a cock, but at least I'm sure of all the things we got."

"Don't believe the stories," said Madonna, arm in arm with her girlfriend. It's a hetero world. "*Believe* the stories," said Sandra. People started filing out to the dinner at Indochine, and the girls were still singing, even with the curtain down. "Can you believe this shit?" said Madonna, and the curtain went up again.

Urine the money: Tracey the pee girl is a real pisser

1990

Your average, starry-eyed sociopath would probably reach a fever pitch of delirium upon meeting luminaries like Kate Hepburn, Mother Teresa, J. D. Salinger, or even Meg Tilly. These are exemplary choices, clearly worth getting all goofy about. But this little fella's personal icon—and goshers did I crumble when I bumped into her at the Channel J studio (don't ask)—is Tracey Love, the girl from the 970-PEEE commercial who brings such depth and poignance to that immortal line, "The extra *e* is for extra pee." This lovely conduit of probably the most disturbing yet compelling, unwatchable yet irresistible ad in TV history (you're lying if you say you haven't seen it) turned out to be a real water sport and not at all a princess about her pee. With a little prodding, she answered all the obvious questions related to her unquenchable thirst for fame. Like, Is that menacing stream of liquid bounding her way in the commercial really what it's supposed to be? ("No, it's Gatorade mixed with water. But when they show *me* peeing, it's for real.") Does her mother know about the commercial? ("Yeah. She said, 'Can't you do something with your clothes *on*?' ") And does she get recognized a lot—a by-product, as it were, of her having climbed the bladder of success? ("Sometimes. One cabdriver wanted to know if I'd pee on his girlfriend. I declined.") A real lady. Though Tracey's not sure what her future plans are, she does know urine is just a sample of what she can do. That's Tracey with an *e*, by the way. The extra *e*. . . .

Meanwhile, golden shower ads may leave them singin' in the rain, but Manhattan Cable does know when to get pissed off. Last week, they refused to air the *Closet Case Show* featuring a GMHC safe-sex video fairly bursting with condoms and dental dams. Public access TV banning safe sex education? Or banning *anything*? This is not only illegal, it's just plain ill. (Dental) damn these jerks!

Details—changing in September to a piss-elegant men's mag subtitled "Style Matters"—has just banned (i.e., pink-slipped) some staffers, including fashion editor Ronnie Cooke. Nightlife gadabout/associate editor Stephen Saban remains, but Saban's learned he'll now be writing about things like "haircuts, sideburns, and stitching." Whether that means macramé or suturing seems a moot point. A more pressing issue: will deposed editor Annie Flanders start her own *Mirabella*-like mag called *Weinraub* (her maiden name)?

And why did Kathleen Turner—Broadway's steamy, appealing Maggie the Cat, whose hot tin roofs can be found in clubs owned by her hubby, Jay Weiss—tell *Playbill* that today, if Maggie found out Brick had really done it with Skipper, she would probably just leave him? Kathleen, *bubbe*, so many married men have had gay experiences that if that were the case, the divorce rate would approach 80 percent. More likely, women would leave their husbands for being sleazy landlords.

Wait—it gets better. Mary McFadden says in John Fairchild's *Chic Savages* that she's afraid to even let gay men kiss her on the cheek for fear of catching AIDS. Gosh, for the sake of this worrisome ninny, I sure hope she doesn't ever marry someone in a "high-risk group"! And while it's nice that Elton John visited Ryan White (an "innocent victim" according to the guilty media) in his last days, and Michael Jackson called him, wouldn't it be even nicer if, for the cameras, they visited some of their own?

The controversies just keep on coming, sometimes about things that *aren't* as offensive as you'd hoped. Like John Waters's *Cry-Baby*, an only intermittently successful attempt to re-create the spirit of *Viva Las Vegas*, an already perfect film. Luckily, there are lively performances by Kim McGuire as the grotesquely beautiful Hatchet-Face and porn star Traci Lords (the extra i . . .) as a saucy little red riding hoodlum. For extra bonuses, Joey Heatherton speaks in tongues, Iggy Pop's practically butt-nekked, and Patty Hearst says "fuck" for the first time since she was locked in that closet. The film is watered-down Waters, but I guess that's still preferable to watered-down Gatorade.

The film's premiere party at M.K. (which some have been calling M.T.) was so appropriately bizarre we kept waiting for the eggman. And for Joey Heatherton. "Is Joey here?" Waters asked me, the precise information I was about to demand from him ("I had a 24-hour, whatever, virus," Joey explained to me the next day, admitting to having gone to the "beauty saloon" and everything). "Ricki Lake wants to talk to you," M.K.'s Alan Rish insisted, pushing me over to someone who turned out to be Deborah Mitchell of *7 Days.* "She's the new Ann-Margret, " exulted Page Six's Richard Johnson, pointing at "Hatchet-Face" McGuire, though I think he was really aiming for the film's ingenue, Amy Locane (rhymes with a powder that explains some things in previous columns).

Rachel Sweet, who does Locane's singing in the film, lived up to her name (Rachel), though she balked when I dragged up memories of her career as a prepubescent pap star. "Shhh!" she shrieked. "You're dating us both!" *Someone* should date us both. But it was when I mentioned her duet with white person Rex Smith on "Everlasting Love" that the girl completely lost it, saying, "Puhleeeze! Now you're really trying to blackmail me." Sweet said a fan had recently sent that very piece of demonic vinyl to her for an autograph, and she refused with all the willpower of Tracey Love turning down that cabdriver. "Rex is about as hip as my Aunt Ruth," she spit out as an exit line.

McGuire told me the best bars in New Orleans and confessed to having played Ado Annie in four separate productions of *Oklahoma!* ("I cain't say no"). By the evening's boozy end, Rish announced, "John Stamos!" and everyone—well, I—leaped up in wild expectation. "No, it's Vincent Spano," he amended himself. Or maybe it was a fact-checker from *7 Days.*

Grossness finally finds a home in Peter Greenaway's *The Cook, the Thief, His Wife & Her Lover*, which out-Waters Waters with its four lead characters of the type you'd meet on a 970 number. It's set in a freewheeling, absurdist restaurant in which there's a dog-feces wielding vulgarian (the thief), two torrid bathroom sexpots (his wife and her lover), and a corpse in orange glaze (I'm not telling). It's sort of like an off night at Punsch. At the film's party at Morrissey, I asked the distinguished actress Helen Mirren (his wife) if she'd ever really had sex in a bathroom. "Of course I have," she answered, seriously. "Everyone has." In the immortal words of ex-*Family Feud* host Richard Dawson, "Good answer!"

Sandra Bernhard:
The mouth that roared

May 1, 1990

I'm power-lunching at Jerry's with Sandra Bernhard—the mouthy *Mädchen*, the lippy lassie, Martha Raye on expectorants, Isaac Mizrahi's best friend—and she has a few dozen opinions for me. It's an easy game of reflexes: I say the name, Sandra gives the opinion. For example, Jane Child: "I could just rip that nose ring out of her nose. And that hair—please, she is so grotesque. I keep hoping her face chain will get caught, especially on the subway." Milli Vanilli: "My friend Marge Gross calls them Liza Manilli Vanilli. Remember the Grammys, when they said, 'Other artists like us shouldn't be discouraged'? There *are* no other artists like them." Heart: "I'm heartbroken they needed to hire an actress to play themselves picking up guys on the road in that video. Ann Wilson is one of the sexiest women in the world. I don't care if she's a little chubby. *She* should have picked up that guy, with Nancy hanging over the backseat, going, 'Yeah, do it, Ann. Roll, mama.' "

Blue Steel? "It's language meets art meets Kathryn Bigelow's autoerotic female vision. Or better yet, fuck me with a .45. It's that good." Dan Lander, the fat, naked guy on Channel J's *Interludes After Midnight*: "He has a retractable penis. It's getting smaller by the minute." *Sex, Drugs, Rock & Roll*: "Where'd Bogosian come up with *that* original title? Must be a very daring production." Lisa Stansfield: "Grow your hair and give it up, girl. You've been around the world enough times. Your hair should have grown by now." Her *Interview* interviewer, Paul Taylor: "Asshole." *WWD*'s Larry Chua: Ditto. And, lastly, Chastity Bono and her alleged lesbianism: "I'm deeply offended. Cher's response is something like, 'I've had it with your high jinks, young lady. I'm cutting off your credit at Balducci's.' "

That silliness out of the way, we now can talk about just plain Sandra. And Madonna. And Warren. And Sue Mengers ("She told me, 'Take the pussy shots out of the movie. Guber and Peters will be sickened' ").

The movie is *Without You I'm Nothing*—based on her Off-Broadway show—a wry toast to Bernhard that sums up what she does so well it could be an indoctrination film for her cult. Shot in a mere eight days—"on the ninth day she rested"—it's such a whirligig, all that's missing is Sandra's exhortation to "ACT UP. Fuck AIDS" (director/cowriter John Boskovich thought it came off overemphatic onscreen, though I'd say onstage it's her fiercest moment). The movie is rated R, even if the trailer, with the same scenes, got an X. "I guess getting fucked by a black man was too much for the ratings board to take in a one-minute format," muses the new Hollywood Sandra. It will premiere at a May 2 AmFAR benefit in New York, done with a Middle Eastern theme ("the excitement, the glamour, the terrorism. Call 719-0033"). After that, grins Sandra, "it's going to spread like my legs in the heat of passion."

Apropos of that, a *tres* serious woman from the next table comes over to let off steam about—no, not Jane Child—Madonna. She feels betrayed, she says, that Madonna's been saying her *Letterman* lezzie bit with Sandra was only a joke. "I'll tell her," half-smirks Miss Bernhard, and Serious Woman leaves. "It *had* gotten blown out of proportion," Sandra explains to me. "I mean, God, you know, *Madonna is a raging lesbian!* I mean, why don't they take it really literally! At this point it's, like, shut the fuck up. Minority groups are so desperate to be validated. So when they see two women, even if it's totally tongue-in-cheek, they want to believe it's for real so they can go, 'Look, *they're* doing it, we're OK. We're not freaks.' I understand that. The bottom line is they shouldn't need validation from people like Madonna and me to feel good about themselves."

"But we do need you, baby," I plead, all too aware of the need for gay role models and dykons. "I think gays and lesbians feel used. You two had fun and milked it for publicity, and now all we read is, 'We're not, we're not.' I even heard Madonna started dropping you off three blocks away so you wouldn't be seen arriving anywhere together."

"That's not true! But really and truly, how did we use the gay community? Did we go to them and say, 'Look, let's have a private rally. We're going to pull this stunt and convince the American public we're lovers'? We're not making fun of the community. It's strictly between the two of us. In that case you'd better go scream at Guccione Sr. for doing all those lesbian spreads. Nobody's beholden to anybody if they decide to pull a stunt. It doesn't make me any less a friend to the gay community. But I also have a life—excuse me. What is this, the revolution in Russia in 1912? It's very *Doctor Zhivago.*"

I'm getting historically confused, but I do know one thing. Postrevolution—in fact, last year—Sandra had a girl-friend she wanted to hit over the head with a 20-inch-long dildo, just to name one revealing shenanigan she spilled to me for a *Spin* piece. She seems reluctant to talk about such hooliganism this time (publicity pressure?), but at least for that one shining moment she was Little Miss Courage. "I remember that day. I was lying on my couch and it felt so cathartic," Sandra admits. Any trouble she got for putting her sexuality on the line—and I hear she got shitloads—"was well worth it. It blew everyone's mind."

Also "out"—and not just to lunch—the comic Reno is two tables away, inspiring Sandra to murmur, "Reno's back from L.A. The town is abuzz! Jerry's is in an uproar!" I drag her over, and the two, who've never met, exchange frenetic biz talk. Sandra won't give her number. Reno gives hers. Then Reno says, "I've got to get my girlfriend to the gym," and manically leaves. "Enchanting," smirks Sandra.

Alone again, we fall back on more Madonna chitchat, this time about whether she's a friend to the voguing commu-nity. The trend, Sandra agrees, is *ovah,* but not for middle America. "Still," she thinks aloud, "I can't imagine straight guys on Ohio farms voguing and bailing hay. 'Strike a pose with your pitchfork.' " I ask the inevitable Madonna and Warren query (rumors have her dumping Beatty in favor of a Jellybean reunion), and she starts to answer, then scrunches up her two-ton lips. "Oh, I don't want to talk about *them*," she whines. "They get so much fucking promotion. When I have $50 million, I'll talk about them. Let's talk about the movie."

"All right, tell me about *Dick Tracy*," I giggle, and she looks like she's about to lose it and throw her tea at me. Finally, she breaks into a laugh that infects the entire room.

More caffeine, and Sandra decides, "I am a phlegm-o-matic. I walk around hocking." Outside, we discuss *Twin Peaks* and she admits *she* killed Laura. We climax on a discussion of alopecia of the pubes—a rare hair-loss condition—about which my naughty, bawdy lunch date decides, "You have to put a merkin around your gherkin." Bye, Sandra. We need you, baby.

Canada dry:
Kids in the Hall

March 3, 1992

"We're the most sexually confusing troupe in the history of comedy," the Kids in the Hall's Dave Foley told me over a hormone-charged dinner at Coffee Shop. "I mean, with Chevy you knew where you stood." Many "girl drinks" (frosty, fruity things with figurative umbrellas) later, I deduced this much about the HBO quintet: one's gay, one's bi, one's dubious, one's married, and one's a cocktease.

It was quite a midwinter night's sex comedy, this sleazy little dinner. At first I was quite taken with the group's blond and boyish Mark McKinney, but while Mark initially sucked up to me beyond control, he seemed to become a bit apprehensive after I sent him a "hi" note from the other end of the table. The bastard avoided me the rest of the night. My friend, meanwhile, was sure the troupe's doughy Bruce McCulloch was coming on to him, so just for fun he flirted back, only to have the openly gay one, Scott Thompson, jealously threaten, "If you fuck Bruce, I will hunt you down . . . I will kill you." Kevin McDonald, the nerdy one, suddenly seemed the most appealing, his ambiguity less delusional, less mean-spirited, and taunting. "None of Kevin's lovers—male or female—are really sure of his sexuality," Scott confided. "Let's just say no one can place a safe bet on any of us. We're all fruit flies."

And to be sure, Kevin, who'd started out lusting after the waitress, was adopting a more confessional tone, gurgling things between girl drink sips like, "I find the lead singer of Mr. Big very sexy" and "I like Prince!" ("Not me," countered Scott. "I see myself more with lumberjacks.") At one point, he and Scott got into a nasty tiff over who was the sexiest one in *The Wiz*—Michael Jackson or Nipsey Russell—as everyone else fell silent in dismay. And in the corner, the Kids' cheery assistant, Donald Sutherland's daughter Rachel, kept interjecting things about the group like "They're so great! They're so sweet! They're so gentle!" and I could only guess who the real fruit fly was.

Center table, Dave—the faux-cherubic, married one—was trying to divert attention from his own foibles, assuring me that Kevin is kinky and amoral and adding that he was certain I could have Mark in a second if I made a play for him. But I already *had* made a play for him. Besides, Dave now seemed riper for the picking, even though—or maybe *because*—he kept saying how faithful he was to his wife. Funny—after a few drinks, he was intoning things like "Donald Sutherland was so sexy in M*A*S*H!" and I don't think it was just for Rachel's sake.

Our heads spinning, my friend and I went off to Limelight, but we couldn't resist coming back for the kill, at which point Kevin was loudly cataloguing the people he now thought were sexy ("Christian Slater, early Buster Keaton, Michael Jackson in 'Beat It' . . ."). Dave was admitting that he likes sex toys and "some foodstuffs" and wondering, "Have you ever heard of heterosexual fisting? I had to reset my watch afterwards." Scott, on the other hand, as it were, was getting deeply philosophical, crying into his pink vodka martini and murmuring trinkets like, "HBO hates us" and "*In Living Color* stole all our thunder!" And Bruce, smelling my friend's pretend-lust, was racing frantically out the door ("Bruce left," Scott whined, triumphantly).

And then we *all* went to Limelight, which on Fridays is half gay and half straight, aptly enough, and by now some of the party were buzzing on that crazy little thing called Ecstasy. As we waded through the gay ghetto, Dave gawked at the barely clad go-go boys and pinched my nipples from behind, later asking excitedly about the sex room (maybe he didn't *realize* it was gay?). Now I didn't want him either—too easy—but I gamely pointed at my crotch anyway. Alas, Dave could barely stand up, let alone perform (and of course there was that wife problem).

But Kevin was sweet, lying across me as he held my hand and beamed that he hadn't a worry in the world. "I'll respect you after brunch," he cooed, then went into a version of "By the Beautiful Sea" that he suddenly remembered his mother used to sing to him when he was seven. Smelling danger, the Kids' publicist, Nina, subtly pried us apart, while Rachel—knowing nothing could happen between me and Mark at this point—kindly made a space for me to sit next to him. Well blow me down and pick my teeth for gold, why don't you! Kevin was girl-drink-cool to me for the rest of the night; make that two cockteases. And so, while comedy is dangerous, this fable ends safely; we all went home alone.

The coitus was even more interruptus at a kissing contest I helped judge—a shameless stunt (to promote the play *Breaking Legs*) that sadly puckered out before it even started. There were only two contestants, it was announced, and worse, they were a woman and her dog, prompting one onlooker to murmur, "He can't be *that* ugly." But worse again, it was a real dog, and a picky one at that; when the woman tried to kiss her doggie-style, the bitch wouldn't have it. They won anyway, by default.

At least the sex objects didn't shed at Limelight, where brazen boychick Marky Mark hosted the sensual but chaste party for *Interview*'s all-Bruce Weber issue with his own brawny, bad self on the cover. At first no one recognized Marky with his clothes on. Once they did, though, pandemonium erupted, with the rapper shmoozing up the throngs and grinning, "The only thing I can't do is grab my penis. I'll get in trouble." What? Marky not grabbing his penis? What kind of vulgar crap was this? "I do come out in boxer shorts for a number about safe sex," he told me about his newly sanitized stage persona. But as for dropping his pants to reveal those tightly packed BVDs, he said, "Now, I only do it when the audience asks for it." Fortunately, the audience always asks for it.

Marky is a unique '90s sampling of wonder and raunch,

politeness and rebellion. Mostly he's just a nice boy that you want to pounce on. One minute he described his awe over having seen a billboard of himself ("I was buggin' out. I was like, 'Damn!'") and the next, gleefully confirmed my educated guess that he's circumcised. Word. He denied that he's been working out at the gay-laden Chelsea Gym so girls won't attack him (face it, those Chelsea girls would attack him, too). And he even answered non-genitalia-related queries, like whether the New Kids really lip-sync ("They're all talented singers. That's why I couldn't stay in the group. I couldn't sing"). And then he went downstairs, received an honor, and dropped his pants—but this time he had another pair underneath. So two girls attacked him.

By the way, while I signed last week's staff letter to the editor critiquing the anti-Japanese Danceteria ad, I did so because the ad was racist, not because—as the letter also charged—it was in bad taste. Bad taste is something narrow-minded, elitist people—not the alternative press—are supposed to be afraid of. If we start snipping out things because they aren't tasteful and proper, then we've become the oppressors. So let's all drop trow, but nicely.

Summer wishes, Wintour dreams

April 21, 1992

I've visited East Berlin, I've seen the La Brea Tar Pits, and now I've been to fashion week—an alternate universe where all the wrong people scurry about in all the right clothes murmuring witticisms like "Anna Sui is giving total '70s this time" and "Calvin's showing platforms!"; where billions rest on whether a bunch of justified and ancient old bags will either turn up their noses as if smelling caca or announce, in the immortal words of Polly Mellen, "This is not ugly." Still, I loved these seven days of imposed style—they had energy and drama and exposed me to one of the last real scenes in a world with mostly audience left.

The blast-off was at the New York Public Library's 42nd Street branch, where *Vogue* had its 100th anniversary party (and I said it wouldn't last), an event that by necessity brought together every designer alive today. They would become mere remnants if they didn't show up to kiss *Vogue* editor Anna Wintour's hemline, the only truly correct one in the world. On the way in, you stood on a receiving line and waited to greet Wintour as if meeting the Queen Mother. It was her chance to welcome you and yours to encrust her butt with lipstick marks. Too bad that, shaking from having just been accused of crashing by a bouncer, I could barely muster a mild pucker.

Inside, it was a splendiferous who's who of Seventh Avenue chutzpah as well as chutzpah from other avenues. Mickey Rourke and Carré Otis were fighting loudly. *Newsday*'s Frank DeCaro was gushing, "Anna said hello to me the other day and now I feel like I exist!" Cindy Crawford was joking about her MTV's *House of Style* line readings: "It has to be organic. It has to come from within." Ivana Trump was talking up her new novel about—gee, give us a hint, Ivana, who could this be?—a Czech woman who marries a tycoon. Fred Schneider was saying of the departed B-52, "Cindy can't be replaced. Maybe she'll come back." (Come back, little Cindy.) And now DeCaro was exulting, "Mickey Rourke borrowed my pen! Do you want to touch it?" Yes—to grab it and poke his eyes out.

A more civilized idea was to flock to the big room, where Random House sultan Harold Evans praised Wintour's "sense of derring-do," then brought out the patterns pasha by advising, "Please be silent for Anna Wintour, who now steps elegantly out of the pages of *Vogue*." She miraculously did so, and we were so quiet it reminded me of when I was on a plane that was hit by lightning. You couldn't even hear the pages ruffling. "You don't have to be silent for me," Wintour told us nicely, but just in case, we still were.

At the actual shows, we could talk again amid a dizzying

blur of the world's loudest fabrics and opinions. The scene is colorfully intense and circuslike—*Funny Face* meets *Full Metal Jacket*—even if it's only a mere swatch of the pandemonium that's inevitably erupting backstage. Fashion people—editors, buyers, victims, all wearing sunglasses—traipse up and down the runway, aggressively searching out the workers holding up the letter of their assigned section. At the end of the room, a Claymation blob of photographers starts pretend-focusing on itself. And behind the seats stands a battery of real people without even a letter assignation, their realness underlined by the fact that they're there to see the clothes on the models rather than the ones on the audience. The real people seem nice, except that they would clearly murder the fashion people in a second to get their seats. Alas, that still wouldn't make them fashion people.

The stunner holding up the big "B" at the Marc Jacobs for Perry Ellis show was the best statement of all, and he mercifully didn't signal a B-list. There was Jewish Hiawatha Steven Meisel, floating in with a bodyguard reportedly gifted him by Madonna; H. R. H. Wintour, arriving to the chirping sound of "Anna! Anna!"; and Carly Simon and Alec Baldwin, brilliantly standing up and moving to center stage on the runway to have a private talk before about 150 photographers with their tongues out.

New York magazine's Michael Gross passed a note to Meisel, who was now without the benefit of his bodyguard. "Can I call you?" Gross shouted, and, through his *Addams Family*-ish hat and shades camouflage, the photographer emitted a small, magisterial yes. "I'm her mother," said Macy's buyer

Ellin Saltzman to Baldwin, who was catching up with *Vogue*'s Elizabeth Saltzman, who's friends with his brother. They double air-kissed. They fished for conversation. Perhaps something about *Streetcar?* Nahhh. "That's a great jacket," said Ellin, finally. Bingo.

Everyone had on a great jacket, everyone looked so healthy, everyone was so happy to see everyone. Carly gave Alec a tape of her *This Is My Life* soundtrack, which had a price sticker on the back; did the poor thing have to buy her own record? Backstage, Marc was literally sobbing from the pressure. And the show—I mean the *fashion* show? Fast-paced, lively, highlighted by grays and harlequin prints and dripping in—yes—'70s, which is to now what the '50s were to the '70s. It was not ugly, especially when "Dude Looks Like a Lady" played as Naomi Campbell entered in androgynous wear. "I'll never do another show," Marc said as he dried his tears to the tune of a *Women's Wear Daily* rave and began working on the next one.

Other presentations came with such punishing frequency you started waking up screaming that a model was walking in platforms down a fiery runway that led right onto your face. The funky/kiki/kooky one to see was Todd Oldham's "Interiors" theme—not at all based on the Woody Allen movie—which featured a "beaded leopard slink" and a Mona Lisa skirt with what looked like *That Girl* on the back, but was actually a Picasso. It was *very* not ugly, with Ann Magnuson making a particularly hilarious mockery in her frockery. Shockingly enough, the drag model Billy Erb—a dude who looks very much like a lady—had coached all the female models on how to walk. So now it's the women who are imitating the drag queens? Nu?

There were certainly no gender barriers in the funky/kiki/kooky audience; all types were there, plus celebs like ultra fashion- (and cause-) conscious Susan Sarandon, who looked about to break water in the front row. Interestingly enough, it turns out that our pal Susan was all set to address the homophobia issue in her Oscar speech if she'd won the damned thing (as a presenter she felt she should stick to the cue cards). She didn't, of course, so instead we got the confusing spectacle of Jodie talking about how much dignity there is in the closet. But I digress.

For one final blast of finery, the entire fashion industry dug into their own closets and ended up at the Bendel's first year anniversary party for its new store, where they drifted through thousands of streamers, a line of can-can girls, harpists in angels' costumes, a 16-foot-high birthday cake for the store, and Steven Meisel in a hood. "Anna's here," someone insisted, but I couldn't find her and therefore don't exist.

Beauty's where you find it

July 28, 1992

The best place of all to be a fly on the wall continues to be any-where where there's Madonna—like Film Forum, where missy and a bunch of lady friends caught the tough, incisive paparazzi documentary *Blast 'Em*, in which a photographer calls her a fucking bitch. "That's right—I'm a fuckin' bitch!" she gleefully yelled back at the screen, not all that mad. And at her producer Shep Pettibone's birthday party at his duplex, the outspoken superstar proved once and for all that she's in a league of her own when it comes to being in your face with the rude truth. In her more serious moments at the soiree, Madonna went to bat for the AIDS rally that was coming up and plugged Clinton ("the least of three evils," she called him), though she must have been choking on her reservations about cheap Tipper. She also danced freely with the Cuban refried bean/waitress named Ingrid that Sandra Bernhard used to date and whom she and Sandra got into a huge tiff over, as you read here. I guess Madonna won. Ingrid, in fact, had come to town to stay at Madonna's apartment for a weekend, but her little visit had turned into three full-blown weeks. They were wearing matching jeans shorts.

Upcoming Pettibone/Madonna music was playing, one song a "Justify My Love"–type rant called "Erotica" with a similar "Love to Love You Baby" undertow. Another future hit, a lesbianic ode called "Eating Out," is not about nouvelle cuisine, if you catch my drift. But I don't know what you're implying. Anyway, back at the party, a DJ schmoozed up Madonna and then said, "You know so-and-so," by way of introducing her to some bigwig. "I don't even know who I'm talking to," she exclaimed, huffily. Then, teen idol Tommy Page approached Madonna to say that he'd heard her former back-up singer Donna de Lory's version of her song "Just a Dream." "Aren't you excited?" he asked, sincerely. "The only record that matters is my own," Madonna grimaced. "But it's the highest form of flattery when someone records one of your songs," continued Page. "Please! I gave it to her," shrieked Madonna, repeating that for effect as she drifted away.

Ingrid then got in a limo and saw Madonna home, but the gal pal came back to Page's house to party some more, with campily real Truth or Dare director Alek Keshishian, who was also staying at Madonna's and is moving into a guest apartment above hers. He must have won a dare. He and Ingrid had some tasty things to say about Sandra's self-proclaimed beauty, and Alek also read into Clive Davis for scrapping a Taylor Dayne video he directed featuring a guy undressing. But it's none of my business.

That rally Madonna was so hot for—a United for AIDS Action demo in Times Square—turned out to be quite a summer broiler, though I don't recall seeing her or Clinton there. Still, there was an inspiring sea of 10,000 applauding for Jesse Jackson, Gregory Hines, the Addicts Rehabilitation Center Gospel Choir, and Jessica Lange, who was quite eloquent, saying, "Shame to George Bush and Ronald Reagan! Shame to the Republican government that turned a deaf ear to us!" Not as a shameless plug, she then compared our plight to that of her *Streetcar* character, Blanche DuBois, who ghoulishly bemoans "the long parade to the graveyard," and ended with an Arthur Miller quote: "Attention must be paid." Jessica should get a retroactive Tony nomination for her well-articulated and annotated anger; she really said it down. Still, members of ACT UP felt that Jackson hardly addressed AIDS in his lengthy speech, and that the cops corralled them too far from the stage and creepily guarded them with riot gear and winter gloves. "It was a police Disneyland," says ACT UP's Ron Goldberg, "and we were the ride."

The sickest theme-park-like mess overheard, if not overseen, on recent TV was the *All Star Fiesta at Ford's,* a celebration of Latin culture that climaxed with Ricardo Montalban saying *"muchas gracias"* for freeing the slaves to a photo of Abe Lincoln framed under an empty theater seat. That was followed by the only act that could have been any more surreal: Barry Manilow wearing a red AIDS-awareness ribbon as, backed by a nonrehabilitating gospel choir, he sang "America" to the Bushes (in person, not a photo)! There were so many layers of sickness to this that all my white fangs came out. Were blacks freed in order to sing backup for Barry Manilow? Was fey Barry really warbling our nation's praises to the heinous Bushes while wearing a red ribbon? And what the fuck does Barry Manilow have to do with Latin culture anyway?

And—moving on to larger topics—what of those ribbons? As an impetus for awareness, they mean so well that they've necessarily started to provoke some doubt in my darker half. While they probably do open eyes to the AIDS problem, aren't they often cosmetic accessories that take the place of real attempts at change? Don't they tell us "be aware of AIDS" when AIDS is ripping our lives apart every minute of every day? Was I hallucinating or did I recently see someone performing unprotected oral sex while wearing one? Won't we all pretty soon end up dying with ribbons on? And am I just being the grinch or does anyone else also have to repress the urge to loudly sock people wearing them? Much as I can see their value.

Brad Pitt
makes my knees weak

August 25, 1992

The whole world wants to get into Brad Pitt's pants these days, and it's not deterring anyone that they're more than a little soiled. The charmingly laconic actor catalogued all the stains for me in his Mayfair Regent suite, stopping only at a gnarly sepia-toned one that gave him distinct pause. "Looks kind of like butt, doesn't it?" he said, making a closer inspection. "But it's not, it's not. We can do a whole little dot-to-dot thing here. Some red, some purple, some blue, some yellow, some butt. . . ."

In town for the premiere of *Johnny Suede*—Tom DiCillo's alternately winning and lugubrious film about the loves and loserhood of a rocker rebel—Pitt proved himself every bit the quirkmeister you'd expect from someone whose parents had to learn from a magazine article that he never graduated from college. *Everything* he has is stained, and his manner is so evasive but friendly that he can skirt around a million issues with a melting smile that makes him an antihero who's not really against anything, an enigma who quietly forces you to succumb to his ambiguities. You find yourself revealing things to him—like "My mother still does my laundry"—and not being that embarrassed, because anyone who muses openly about butt stains has already disarmed you beyond the realm of shame.

Brad and Juliette Lewis (*Cape Fear*'s troubled nymphette) are Hollywood's new anticouple, a gorgeously grimy twosome who emphatically do it their way and look it. "Maybe it's because we're pigs," he told me, smirking. "I don't think it's a conscious choice. But I believe in Wallabees and boxers, and she's got her own style, too. I'm not going to tell her any differently." They truly are the Pitts, in the best sense.

He speaks of Juliette glowingly, even praising her *Lawnmower Man* 'do at the Oscars, beaming, "She won Worst Hair. I was so proud! That really summed everything up. Just classic." But he balks at the idea that they're gaga in love, though he'll almost settle for pseudo- or semi-gaga. "Oh hell, why not?" he shrugged. "We surprise me." And that's *all* he has to say about "we."

The duo is filming *Kalifornia*—"I think the spelling is temporary. Sounds like a bad Prince song"—in which Brad plays a hillbilly serial killer, and he's just finished Robert Redford's *A River Runs Through It*, for which Redford met with *Cool World*'s director Ralph Bakshi three times to determine whether the actor was worth hiring (the answer was three times yes). As for *Cool World*—in which he plays a cop who makes sure the cartoon characters don't have sex with the humans—Pitt said, "I want to see it. I want to see what went wrong, not like it's a big surprise. I mean I had my fears. Wait," he stopped.

"I don't want to get into this." I crumpled my note paper and dramatically threw it to the floor. "All right, as long as I get to *Suede* later," he said, softening, and I picked the paper up and uncrumpled it. "You see," he continued, "the studio toned the script down because they wanted a PG, and in doing so they left all these holes. And of course new studio heads came in. They're not to blame, but if there was a chance to improve the film, they sure didn't take it. There's politics involved, which is the craziest thing to me. It's anti-art. Ralph's too good of a person, and it makes me mad."

He had nothing more to say on *that* subject, so we got to *Suede*, which makes him happy; it's destined for instant cult status, largely thanks to Brad's hangdog staccato delivery, which matches his dangerously leaning tower of hair strand by strand. About the budget, he grinned, "You got change in your pocket?" Did he have a trailer? "We had a curtain," he laughed. "But it's a good time for it, with all this dogshit that's been out this summer. That film was all DiCillo. Someone should cut open his head and lay it out. I think it would be very entertaining. Him, I picture as a camel trotting through the desert having all these odd thoughts. I mean, what does a camel think about?" His next film, perhaps. "He has this magic, like where everything bounces back and ties into each other. Like, you wore brown pants today so you could spill coffee on them without really knowing that ahead of time." Yes, my pants looked like butt by now, too—how magical—a concept topped only by Brad's desire to add skid marks to his underwear in the film (DiCillo wouldn't let him). Does anyone sense a trend? "*That* kind of magic," added Brad.

I nervously spilled some more coffee and the gentlemanly star ran to the bathroom to nab a towel, assuring me, "You're in good company." As I wiped away, I was now silently writing a country song called "He May Have Stolen Thelma & Louise's Money, but He Only Walked Off with My Heart." As for Brad, he was now on to his recent p.r. blitz, saying, "I didn't ask for it. There are too many magazines, too many talk shows. It's just a 7-11. All this behind-the-scenes garbage. You lose some magic. The E! channel—oh, God! It's frightening." The Discovery Channel's just fine, though, because "I like watching the little animals live their little lives, pop out of their little holes and just forage for food and try to stay alive." Disturbed, I spilled yet more coffee, and this time he just sat back and said in an eerie voice, "There are no mistakes."

The premiere party the next night at Tilt was dotted with both men and women who looked like Johnny Suede losing their martinis all over you. There are no mistakes. Tina Louise—who came back from her three-hour tour to play Johnny's girlfriend Darlette's mother—said of Brad, "He works very organically. Not only is he beautiful, but he's really good." MTV VJ Steve Isaacs was complaining about the ending. A girl was slinking up to Matt Dillon and cooing, "You have my number." And I was snuggling back to Tina Louise to say, "I wish Juliette Lewis was here so I could stick my finger in her mouth." She was dumbstruck at first, then laughed a loud, bodacious laugh.

"Wow, I've got friends here," Brad exclaimed, realizing this might not be the total torture he'd expected. Meanwhile,

DiCillo was working a roomful of them, stopping to tell me, "I think of Brad as a camel, too. Look how slow he is. You know it's gonna take him a while, but he's gonna get there." There was much mutual admiration stuff going down, but DiCillo admitted that there was a lot of eyebrow arching and screaming on the set, too. "It wasn't peaches and cream," he grimaced. "I didn't want any fucking ad libbing. If you ad lib words like *hey, you know?*, and *got me?*, it doesn't work. I said, 'Brad, just say the words!' "

Juliette Lewis—hey, you know—auditioned for the part of Darlette, DiCillo added, and he, like, almost gave it to her. While he admires her boldness ("Actors who play it safe are really disgusting"), he wanted to make sure the character came off at least a little sympathetic. "Imagine having Tina Louise for a mother!" he said. By this point, cute li'l Brad was at the bottom of a stairway to nowhere, avoiding the party in a sunny way that somehow made it the opposite of antisocial.

Slap happy star is anything but Gaboring

June 8, 1993

To assure that you got into Grace Jones's private birthday party upstairs at Le Bar Bat, they stamped your hand at the door with a big old "B." So *that's* the kind of party it was going to be. The cake was shaped like a clitoris, and the highlight came when the insouciant Jones woman—who does birthday parties for a living now—forced a piece from her finger into Marky Mark's mouth. Marky looked surprised—his first taste?

Talk centered on genitalia from the other side when Take That—the Brit New Kids, not the New York band who say they had the name first—swept into town, urging us to take it all, for whatever that's worth. At a Flamingo East dinner for the guys, one of them confided that his mum said he looked "quite big downstairs" in their recent baskety *Interview* spread. "I don't know why she said that. I have a really small penis," he giggled. Take *that?*

I felt like a gigantic wanker while schmoozing recently with the stunning Guess? jeans model–*Playboy* centerfold

Anna Nicole Smith, who's sweet, but distinctly un-neuro-surgeonly. In fact, I wish life was half as simple as Anna. The model citizen told me she'll miss *Cheers*, beaming, "That was a good movie!" Do you consider yourself a feminist? I asked her later. "I don't understand that question," she grimaced, pretty much answering it for all time. Later on, Japanese pop star Nokko left me just as dumbstruck by arriving on our shores to perform in elaborate mermaid costumes, then telling me privately, "I'm a big fan of Gap." Why won't that "B" rub off my hand?

And I went gaga once again when, at Roxy, performer Ty Jacobs—a discovery of DJ Andy Anderson, who might admit it—proved to be a totally original blend of Klaus Nomi meets Skafish via Tiny Tim courtesy of *Sprockets*. Jacobs is a gangly fellow—a pretty little bitch, as it were—who twirls interpretively as he belts out Pat Benatar tunes in an eerie falsetto voice. You don't know whether to laugh or cry, so you just stand there and gape at his singular confidence. Jaye P. Morgan, why'd you gong him?

"Why'd you slap him?" becomes the big query with queen "B" Zsa Zsa Gabor, but one couldn't trouble the Hungarian diva with that old trash when she was in town to promote *Happily Ever After*, the animated film in which she's the voice of a dwarf who says "darling" a lot. Besides, Zsa Zsa wanted to talk about the *Beverly Hillbillies* movie she just did. "I play a Beverly Hills bitch called Zsa Zsa Gabor," she said, grandly, at the Rihga. "We have Daphne [sic] Coleman; a beautiful girl called Erica something, who was a centerfold; and what was the name of the old man?—Buddy Ebsen—is

a guest star. The director was, what was her name? Daphne
. . . Penelope . . . Spheeris." And so on, until just about
everyone was named Daphne.

Both a dream interview and a one-woman filibuster, Zsa
Zsa talks endlessly, and even if she gets the names wrong, she
gets the mood right. Fittingly, she's the queen of the talk
shows and says, "I love Ofrah [sic], Joan, Phil, Mr. Stern."
But she'd rather flee show biz, darling, than be on Jay Leno's
show. "I hate him," she said, without missing a beat. "Son of
a bitch. I could sue him, but the producer's one of my best
friends." His name is probably Daphne.

Not surprisingly, Zsa Zsa's done talk shows all around the
world, in every language that has an expression for *son of a
bitch*. In China, she said, she was with Barbara Carrera and
Miss Universe, "and the press only photographed me. Mother
said, 'They must think you're Chinese.' But the same thing in
Barcelona. I think they like me because I say it as it is. You
only die once." Great, I vigorously prodded—so fork over
the goods, girl. Was Sinatra a good lover? "Never a lover," Zsa
Zsa chided. "He raped me, as you know. He was an idiot."
(In her memoir, she says she "made love to Frank just that
he should leave the house.") What about her hubby George
Sanders's suicide? "I was actually very upset for six months.
I adored George, even though he always cheated on me, the
son of a bitch." George wasn't gay, she added, and yet, "All
English actors are a little bit gay."

And then we tackled Leona Helmsley ("She looks like a
bitch and a half. And don't think Mrs. Trump is an angel
either"), Merv Griffin and her sister Eva ("They travel on a

private plane, not like we peasants"), and John Huston ("He sat there like a dried-out monkey—he was drunk—but he was still the best director in the world").

And how about—at last—her-bitch-and-a-half three-day stay in El Segundo jail a few years back for the slap heard 'round the world? "They treated me like shit," Zsa Zsa snarled, then batted her lashes, and said, "You've heard this language before, Michael sweetheart?" Oh no, not like-a-virgin-eared me! "They wouldn't let me drink Evian water," she went on, regardless, "and I had to pay $85 a night. A motel is cheaper than that horror!

"There was an old lesbian guard there who scared the hell out of me. I told that lesbian woman, 'Why don't you buy some perfume and a new dress?' She showed up the next day in purple velvet, wanting to put me in solitaire [sic]. I said, 'No, I love this cell!' " Methinks Zsa Zsa's watched—or maybe been in—one too many exploitation flicks. "American justice!" she added, for effect. "Well, right after you," her makeup artist interjected, "there was Rodney King." He was *serious*.

As the photographer shot, Zsa Zsa scowled that she shouldn't do so from underneath. ("I read it from Joan Crawford. That looks horrible—I'll have a Mongolian face yet.") The photographer bolted upright, and Zsa Zsa went on, relating how her best friend didn't invite her to a party recently because she's jealous. "Screw her!" she shot out, then she composed herself, and added, "I wish everyone the best. We all have a cross to bear anyway, what the hell. Jealousy's a sickness."

Jealousy-free Zsa Zsa's doing an exercise video "for women over 30-40-50. It'll be better than what's her name, Debbie Reynolds's," she grinned, "and she's a friend." As for *Happily Ever After*, it's a Snow White story that Zsa Zsa said was actually made five years ago (the publicist nervously chimed in that animation takes a long time). "I have a wonderful prince [von Anhalt of Saxony, of course]," she said. "I lucked out the eighth time. How many frogs can you kiss until you find the real prince?"

Which somehow led her to Liz Taylor, with whom she's shared a frog or two, and who offends the heck out of Zsa Zsa because she put her mother in a nursing home. "All that AIDS work," said double Zsa. "Can't you look after your own mother?" At this point, the photographer snapped, and so did our star. "Honey, you're too close," she griped. "You must be further away." But we couldn't get as far away as we wanted—room service had just arrived, and I mistakenly thought we could all live happily ever after for a few minutes. Wrong. The fabulous one eyed the tray from a distance and smirked, "How sweet this hotel is. Only $1000 a day and they sent three more oranges!" Appalling—yet better than El Segundo, darling.

Babs, ageless and evergreen

January 18, 1994

Yes, Barbra was like butter. Like two mounds of whipped butter. Like a giant tub of unsalted butter. In fact, I sat through her concert thinking, "I can't *believe* it's not butter." But before I elaborate, let me delve into the cheesy (can't seem to get away from the dairy section) charms of Las Vegas's other attractions.

The town, as you've heard, has been transformed into a kind of dysfunctional Disneyland for the all-American family that happens to crave flapjacks, blackjack, and Jack Daniels with equal rapacity. The new casinos emphasize tacky but mesmerizing spectacle, luring you with a bevy of gimmicks— from cheap buffets to cheaper lounge acts—that pull you ever closer and more deviously toward the clank-clank-clank of the gambling din.

The attractions are simultaneously jaw-dropping and mind-numbing. Splashiest of all is the Luxor, the hotel shaped like a gigunda pyramid, with the world's largest faux sphinx (not sphincter) as an entrance. The Luxor's big whoop—aside from the kosher-style Egyptian deli—is the Nile River ride, an excursion through the bowels of the place from which you emerge covered with newfound knowledge and processed water ("Ladies, think of the mist as a facial," our tour guide urged us). The day I went, the line for the ride was delayed in order to set aside a VIP barge for a weird man who popped up shielded by a hat, sunglasses, and kerchief (so much for that facial). Despite the crafty camouflage, we brilliantly figured out it was Michael Jackson—a splashy Vegas casino unto himself. Many cheered Jacko's arrival, but I heard one parent balk, "I can't believe they held us up for that asshole!" His entourage included two young girls, interestingly enough—I guess he's an equal opportunity entertainer now.

There's more of that facial mist outside the Mirage, where a volcano erupts every 15 minutes, squirting pseudo-lava that subliminally gurgles, "Gamble! Gamble! Gamble!" The hotel's done as a shrine to those facially misted, ageless lads of legerdemain, Siegfried and Roy, with a giant statue of the duo looming out of the bushes that's surgically correct, voilà. Over at the Excalibur, there are restaurants like Lance-A-Lotta Pasta, a medieval village of pricey carnival games, and a Dark Ages wedding chapel that turns matrimony into yet another tacky spectacle (as it should be). You flee via drawbridge, then mince across the gangplank to Treasure Island, where you're torn between the outdoor sea battle and the Damsels in Distress boutique. Then it's into the mouth of the MGM Grand's lion's head, which freakishly leads you to topiary swans, giant poppies, and a Dorothy mannequin sitting in a rotating Dodge you can win, if you're nasty.

But follow the yellow brick road to the most bizarre attraction of all, even stranger than Caesars Palace's unsettling talking statues. It's the Debbie Reynolds Hollywood Hotel, done as a self-styled white-trash tribute to Debs herself (who's currently appearing in Oliver Stone's Vietnam epic *Heaven and Earth* and at the Debbie Reynolds hotel, of course). Past the large poster announcing "the legendary Debbie Reynolds," there's a souvenir shop that proffers Debbie T-shirts, Debbie workout tapes, items "from Debbie's closet," and Carrie Fisher ties. Not that other stars aren't celebrated; the lobby wall has signed blocks of cement from the likes of Gavin MacLeod, ZaSu Pitts, and Amos and Andy that must have been left over from the Hollywood Walk of Fame. And there's a display window of the "headpiece and personal props" used by Liz Taylor—in *Cleopatra*, not to steal Eddie Fisher away.

But from the cheese bowl back to the butter tub, we filed expectantly into MGM's Grand Garden stadium as Babs worshiper Richard Simmons gleefully shouted, "Are you ready for this?" to just about anyone who'd listen. With Kenny G tapes blaring annoyingly in the background, not really. But soon enough, I was sitting in a $100 seat and peering through my Diana Ross promotional binoculars to spot Barbra emerging tastefully onto the balcony of her beige set—very Fanny Brice meets Evita. "I don't know why I'm frightened" were her first sung words (from one of Andrew Lloyd Webber's *Sunset Boulevard* songs—the one that sounds vaguely ripped off of a *Willy Wonka* tune). "You can't know how I've missed you. . . . I've come home at last," she continued, drenching the song with such personal meaning that every single line got an ovation.

That Babs was understandably nervous only added to the electricity. That she was reading every word—even the spontaneous patter about how thrilled she was—from six monitors contributed to the event's irresistible surrealism. And she obliged with virtually all her hits (except "The Main Event" and "No More Tears"), throwing in for good measure a revised version of "I'm Still Here," with lines like, "I've kept my nose to spite my face." She also performed a duet with a clip of Marlon Brando from *Guys and Dolls* ("Take me now!" she sang to him, re-creating her childhood crush). She dedicated "Nothing's Gonna Harm You"—not "I Am What I Am"—to her son, Jason Gould. And, while the newly empowered Barbra said she couldn't exactly sing vulnerable songs like "It All Depends on You" anymore, she still served up those twin doormat anthems, "The Man That Got Away" and "My Man"—but she groveled splendidly.

In fact, whenever Barbra sang, things were generally buttery. It was when she talked that one often cringed, especially during a long segment with her sitting on various analysts' couches, and other monologues with a few too many platitudes about how we all have to make for a peaceful world. The preachiness made it all the more refreshing when "Coffee Talk"'s Linda Richman—the Mike Myers character—barreled up from the audience to exchange Yiddishisms with her idol (I stole a lot of Linda's

patter for my lead, actually). Linda said she'd canceled important elective surgery—neck lipo—to make the concert, even
though "a woman my age should not look like poultry."
Barbra got all *farklemt* about it and told us to talk amongst
ourselves, even giving us a topic: "*The Prince of Tides* was neither about princes nor tides. Discuss."

Alas, it was platitude time again when Barbra went on to
warble "Happy Days Are Here Again," with newsreel footage
of Clinton's triumphs propagandizing on the video screens.
But her portentousness was cuter when she introduced two
prominent women in the audience. The first was Coretta
Scott King, and when it came time for the second, I pictured
attendees Kim Basinger and Cindy Crawford frantically mat-
ting their lips and preparing to stand up and greet the
applause. Instead, Barbra singled out the prez's mother, in
one of her last public appearances.

"We love you, Barbra," a fan screamed out, at one point.
"You wouldn't be here if you didn't, right?" she countered.
At the end, Babs admitted, "I think I even enjoyed myself,"
and even though she read that off a monitor, I think she
really did. Me too, so nu?

Glenn Close, but no cigar

April 5, 1994

The House of the Spirits, the misbegotten bore of an all-star fiasco, was moved from a Christmastime Oscar-consideration-type release to a spring-cleaning-season lint ball, and we were here to pick at the beautifully photographed carcass. When I arrived at the premiere, that incendiary Latin spitfire Meryl Streep was inadvertently blocking the entrance with her entourage, perhaps wisely. Her costar, that other south-of-the-border bombshell Glenn Close, was nowhere to be seen— so she and Meryl *are* the same person.

We sat down and Miramax cohead Harvey Weinstein quipped, "I'm Anna Paquin's father." No, I'm Anna Paquin's father. *House's* director, Bille August, claimed no relation to the actress at all, instead introducing the cast members present— Meryl, Jeremy Irons, "Maria Conchita whatshername." And then came the film, which mixes commie propaganda with mystic realism, and comes off as a cross between *Like Water for Chocolate* and *Mystery Science Theater 3000,* but without the direly needed robots to make snide comments during the lulls.

The film certainly has *The Piano* beat—Streep's character takes two vows of silence. And it tops *Jimmy Hollywood* in that Antonio Banderas has an even sillier role than Victoria Abril, generally dodging Irons's bullets and overbite on his way to screw Winona Ryder on the beach. As for Close, she does a cross between Maria Ouspenskaya and Boris Karloff, shrouded in black and intoning things like "I curse you, Esteban. Your body and soul will shrink!" Irons deserves the curse; he gives his most unintentionally campy performance ever, using a gruff voice and bizarre American accent to throw endless WASPy/Latin fits through those fake teeth. And Ryder looks like she stepped out of *Heathers*, except when she's bloodied and being fingered by her half brother.

The movie jumps decades, and accents, with some characters aging into ninja turtles, others not changing at all. One actor seems dubbed with two different voices. And another's head was cut off in the original version, then sliced again in the editing room, presumably because the scene disturbed audiences—as if the rest of what's up there is at all soothing to the nerves. At the party afterward at the Burden Mansion, columnists were kept out of a private room in which I can only hope more heads rolled.

Braless vixen
reaches for the knife!

September 3, 1996

I have a new favorite person in the whole wide world. It's the girl everyone says is crashing and burning, even some of her own family members. Funny, I think she's perfectly sane. Sort of. I'm talking about Bijou Phillips, the 16-year-old modeling daughter of John Phillips and Genevieve Waite and half-sister to both Mackenzie and Chynna Phillips. But forget the relations; the troublesome li'l rapscallion has already developed a startling legend all her own. Every day in the press, there's talk of her wild, look-at-me behavior, making Drew Barrymore seem positively nunlike by comparison. She's always dancing on tables, chopping off fingers, and rolling in gutters, before dusting herself off and sashaying like the only pro.

A walking contradiction, Bijou's an adult in a child's body, or maybe vice versa, depending on where you're sitting. Incredibly savvy one minute, she'll then become distracted by minutiae and drift off, suddenly seeming every inch her age. While she's lived more than most 40-year-olds, Bijou's still a glorified toddler, learning how far to go by going too far. But she's always dripping in charisma, whether turning somersaults on a runway or throwing hard candy at the press (that's how I met the girl—she almost blinded me, but I certainly admired the determination).

As her Company models boss Michael Flutie and I wait for the plucky one at Jerry's, Flutie says, "I don't think people make up the stories, but I think everything she does is innocent and naive. The press likes to create a mystique around her craziness, but she's so adorable." Finally, she shows up—"I went out last night" is the only explanation given—but radiates enough spunky charm that you instantly forgive her. You *have* to, since she's not exactly begging for forgiveness anyway. Her actions speak so much for themselves that when Flutie—trying to save her ass on some issue or other—says, "We always cover for you," Bijou responds, "Don't cover for me! My mistakes are my mistakes!" That's not something you hear a lot in the fashion industry.

"I want to be the new Madonna," announces Bijou, who at least isn't preggers or playing Evita. "It seems everything I do is controversial. I could be sitting here and it'll be like, 'Look at her. She's not wearing a bra. Call the police!' " Or at least the fashion police. Rather than roll out the handcuffs just yet, I want to address those alleged mistakes, like that by-now legendary cutting-off-the-finger incident. Bijou gives the exaggerated story a thumbs-down. "I was walking around Spy with a cigar cutter," she explains. "This guy said, 'What do you have in your hand?' I said, 'I don't know. What do you think it is?'—trying to be the real bitch because he was stupid. I said, 'Why don't you put your finger in it?' " He did and—duh—got his finger nicked, and when the guy then asked for Bijou's number, she assumed it was so he could sue her ass. Instead, he called to say, "You cut my finger, and you at least owe me a dinner." He wanted a date! She declined.

Then the press tried to stigmatize the rather charming fact that Bijou kissed another female model on a shoot. When I bring this up, Bijou goes into a pubescent plea for sexual freedom. "Sexuality is the number one thing in life. It's how we get to the earth, it's how we get our pleasure on the earth, it's how we get our pain. Everyone's afraid of it because they don't understand it." Bijou identifies herself as bisexual, and—without any prompting—adds, "I lost my virginity to Evan Dando. Now he's terrified of me. He saw my mother and started to run—but he was running toward my house. He was blushing red. He thinks I'm gonna call the police on him because he slept with an underage girl. If Evan saw me, he'd hide in a closet for two months." That might be a pretty crowded closet.

Suddenly, Bijou notices that I'm grossed out by the fact that my grilled fish seems to be staring back at me, so she impulsively hacks off the head and puts it in a napkin. I'm glad I'm not the guy with the cut finger. She then digs into Dando but calls a few days later to ask me to leave out the negative stuff because they've made up. (Insiders say that when Dando dumped Bijou, she went ballistic and even threw a barbell out a window, but Dando's people have no response to any of this.)

She has other heavy stuff to drop. Bijou—who lives alone in a New York apartment—admits that she's been in AA for two months and says she did alcohol, pot, coke, acid, mushrooms—"everything except heroin. I hardly ever had to pay for any of it—it was handed to me. I reached the point where I knew I was gonna hit the bottom if I didn't do something." The little darling still smokes, though, and says the first time she inhaled, she was so young and impressionable that she jumped on a guy and said, "I want you right now! I'm so fucked up!" Alas, I don't need cigarettes in order to enact such wanton displays. Bijou's parents nobly decided to go along with the habit and even sent her boxes of cigs when she was in camp. "My father didn't want anything in the house diverting us from being together," she says. "He wanted me to tell him everything."

I guess the openness runs in the family. Sis Mackenzie recently told Page Six that she worries for Bijou and has unsuccessfully tried to help rescue her. "Why is she bad-mouthing me?" squawks Bijou. "There's supposed to be a code among siblings. The only reason she got an interview with the *Post*, anyway, is because she told them she had dirt about me. This way, she could get to plug her touring in *Grease*. It's like, I'm sorry your career going down has to be an excuse for an interview trashing me!" She catches her breath and calms down. "But we're very close."

She loves mom, too, though she says she's "schizophrenic" and *also* tries to exploit her for press. "When my CK stuff came out, she called every newspaper to get interviewed. Dad said, 'She's gonna ruin your life! You've got to control her!'" Oh, Bijou worships dad, though she nicely tells me he said I'm "psycho," and mom told her horror stories about me. I'll take it as a compliment.

But I want some horror stories about the fashion biz already, and Bijou nicely complies without slicing off my digits. "There's a bunch of people out there that are losers," she gripes. "It's like, you just cut hair on a shoot, you are not the Queen of Sheba. It's just a bunch of fabric and a bunch of pretty faces and long legs!" In other words, you can drop the attitude, you're just a shopgirl. She singles out photographer Dah Len for particular abuse. "He's the worst. He's, like, having an orgasm—'Oh, baby. You're great'—when he shoots you. He said to me, 'Why are you laughing?' I said, 'Because you're a freak.'"

Next up, the mouthy teen's doing a record, has nabbed a role in the new *Star Wars* venture, and is also in *Stealing Paradise*—one step beyond *Stealing Beauty*, I guess (she likes Liv Tyler a lot, "but I'm not obsessed with her or anything"). But, while she's clearly getting off on making waves, success only seems to have heightened Bijou's unease. "Everyone thinks they can solve my problems," she says, annoyed. "They're the ones that can make me OK. A lot of my friends are my friends because of the challenge of making me a sane person. I'm so tired of, 'When I was 16, I was never as open as you are.' I'm like, 'Don't you have a life?'"

Finally, a Manson
I could like

March 3, 1998

Marilyn Manson's party at Life for his memoir *The Alienist*—I mean *The Long Hard Road out of Hell*—brought out a scary batch of ghoulish creatures, most of them TV reporters. Just sitting there with those glazed eyeballs, wacky Marilyn managed to push a few more buttons and sell a bunch more merch. His glum demeanor was in fascinating contrast to the perkiness of his dressed-in-white escort, actress Rose McGowan, a cutie who greets you with "Hi, sugar! I love your shirt!" I congratulated Rose for holding her own against the sardonic Craig Kilborn on *The Daily Show*, and she said—perkily—"He's an asshole! And that was my first talk show!" As sure as Diana Ross shouldn't have worn those extensions on the Motown special, it won't be her last. In another corner, the more seasoned Janeane Garofalo had her own ideas. "When Marilyn and Rose make out," she said, "can you imagine the gigantic mess of makeup all over the pillow? And the fight for the bathroom afterwards?"

Hoping for some contour tips, I nabbed a quickie chat

with Marilyn and found that he actually seems pretty nice—just a regular guy who claims to be Satan. I asked him how he feels about upsetting Rosie O'Donnell so much. "I think she envies my figure," he said, with a mild snarl. "Also, I turned her down on a sexual proposition." Why wasn't he jumping up and down with joy at this promo party? "This is too crazy," Marilyn said. "It's like culture shock. I've been holed up." In a crypt, probably. I was going to ask if he gets tired of defending himself, but then a news reporter pushed in and asked him to defend himself. Meanwhile, McGowan wondered—perkily—if I'm the one who wrote "Every day's Halloween for Rose McGowan." She seemed irked, which was strange considering she dates an amalgam of the entire Addams family. "No," I said, "I called you *feisty*," which made the li'l pixie happy again. But Neil Strauss, the *Voicer*-turned-*Timeser* who cowrote Marilyn's book, looked permanently stunned. "I definitely got a lot more than I expected [from the experience]," he said. "I probably realized this in Marilyn's hotel one morning at 4 A.M., wearing a blond wig and staring at a bottle of wine, two unidentifiable blue pills, and a nose hair trimmer." Bye, sugar!

And hi, Madonna, that big white pill who's now a sort of mystical presence herself, but one who advocates loving, not killing, your parents—especially now that she is one. The diva's back-to-her-roots Valentine's Day gig at the Roxy was a surprise concert, except you had to buy a $30 ticket in advance to see it. The predominantly gay crowd was so starstruck they needed to be told—by her—to clap their hands and dance, but they didn't require any prompting to scream so loudly that people in trailer-parks must have dropped their cone bras. Her persona? More cabala than canasta, mixing tribal-hippie Goth techno-pop with calisthenics, like Stevie Nicks crossed with Jane Fonda, but purely Madonna. Her voice was in top shape, she never once pulled out the baby for photos, and patter like "For those of you who don't know Sanskrit . . ." certainly proved unique for the dance circuit. And Madonna remained the queen of irony with paradoxes like "I wish you peace and harmony and love. . . . I can't hear shit!"

The first two songs she did ("Frozen" and the Sanskrit tune) sounded on the whiny side, but the third one—"A Ray of Light"—was fabulous, and overall this incarnation should prove more savvy than singing "We Are the World" in a Vegas lounge. "Thanks for coming to my [record] coming-out party," Madonna told the crowd. "If you're not out, you'd better *get* out." The dumb ones who thought she meant for them to leave stayed anyway.

Going in to the CFDA Awards a few weeks ago, one found so many fashion biggies that if a bomb had dropped, the rest of America would have to go naked. It was a gala, if longish, evening and—though I was furious that they deliberately left *Who's Afraid of Virginia Woolf?* out of the video montage celebrating Liz Taylor's "life of glamour"—I loved Liz's dignity, John Bartlett's thanking "my significant tormentor Mark," and the fact that, while screaming fur protestors were apparently swept right in, I was stopped by two cops (who envied my figure) and had to convince them I was on the list! In Sanskrit!

In other awards news, let me address my significant tormentors, the Oscars. I feel that Peter Fonda's a favorite because of lifetime achievement (also because he's very effective in *Ulee's Gold*, which is not about water sports), but is it churlish to point out that after *Easy Rider*, Peter didn't really achieve all that much? But hey. It might also be sacrilege to say this, but the spectacular, massively entertaining *Titanic* has somehow become confused with art, and while Kate Winslet and Leonardo DiCaprio are individually very good in it, they have no real chemistry, even as a duo from opposite backgrounds. But *double* hey. *As Good as It Gets* has a crusty man redeemed by a waitress with a heart of gold, but I way prefer the reverse in *Of Human Bondage*—you know, a perfectly nice guy destroyed by a waitress with no heart at all. And how annoying is it that the nominators went for the gay-victim-played-by-a-straight (Greg Kinnear) rather than the gay-bon-vivant-played-by-a-gay (Rupert Everett in *My Best Friend's Wedding*)?

She's my sister AND my daughter—and my idol!

February 2, 1999

Before the party for the watchable but extremely synthetic *Playing by Heart* ("We're *all* damaged goods!"), I got a PR call warning that Sean Connery would only talk to a few press people there, and I was not one of them. Goshers, was it the wife-beating, the knighthood problem, *The Avengers*, or the fact that they cut him off at the last Tony Awards that they were afraid I'd bring up? Actually, I wouldn't have touched on any of those things—I hadn't even *requested* an interview with Connery—which made this dissing even weirder than my usual ones. And things grew more surreal when the party turned out to be a dismally attended yawner with about 80 tray-carrying waiters per forlorn-looking guest. They should have *paid* me to talk to Connery—and to eat more fucking crab cakes.

Still, it was fun enough to watch the sibilant Scotsman and the two other stars in attendance be dragged around by publicists who kept hiding behind columns, hoping that I wouldn't catch their beady eyes. In a furtive moment, I grabbed Brenda Blethyn—who's not even in the movie—and sat her down for a nerve-rackingly quick Q&A before anyone official noticed. Brenda was nice enough to indulge my impression of her from *Secrets and Lies* ("*What* baby?") and even did it along with me, just for a larf. But she's way more elegant than the harridans she plays and told me that if she ever saw her *Little Voice* character coming, "I would cross the street!" Honey, I'd cross the *country*—especially if she reeked of the "demon drink" that Brenda says is the root of that lady's dizzying dysfunctions.

Completely boozeless, Brenda *was* going to cross the country—she was en route to the Palm Springs Film Festival ("There's lots of spas there, aren't there?"), where she was set to promote *Night Train*, starring herself and John Hurt. "It's quite different from *Little Voice*," she said. "My character is very quiet and she's a reader!" And then, even sooner than you could find the name of a model in *Glamorama*, she was ushered off into the night.

Further evidence that we're all damaged goods came at the screening of *At First Sight*—I'm a viewer—which proves that you don't *have* to be blind to love Mira Sorvino, but it helps. Alas, the audience didn't quite digest the film's romantic message that the sightless see better than the sighted. In fact, when I accidentally bumped into a woman on the way out, she sensitively barked, "What are you, *blind?*"

Not to set my sights on *Playing by Heart* again—I'm damaged goods—but it bizarrely has Ryan Phillippe as an HIV-positive guy who assures his lady love that, by way of intimate romance, they can just hug. It's the most out-there plotline since Phillippe bonded with the old bag in 54 when she paid for his gonorrhea medicine. Hand me some of that demon drink!

I guess movies ain't what they used to be, and that's why AMC revived *Chinatown* last Wednesday at the Guild Theatre, and even got Faye Dunaway to make a live appearance— something she probably wouldn't have done for *Mommie Dearest* or *Puzzle of a Downfall Child*. Fortuitously, Faye is on people's minds again. She's the subject of a little chat in the car trunk between George Clooney and Jennifer Lopez in *Out of Sight*. And the Museum of Television & Radio has been screening a '67 Woody Allen special in which Woody and Liza Minnelli do a bangs-and-all spoof of *Bonnie and Clyde*.

Faye was certainly on *Chinatown* director Roman Polanski's mind in '74, when he said, "I find her tremendously temperamental. Off the stage, I find her impossible. It's hardly worth it, but it's worth it." At the AMC event, alas, I couldn't get Faye to snarl back, as she was exuding her most disappointingly charming behavior. Still, it was worth it. She told me—after publicists actually helped me get to her—that she and Polanski "certainly had our moments, which the world won't seem to forget about, but he's a very good filmmaker." Fixing me with the eyes of Laura Mars, she more topically revealed that her film version of *Master Class* is a go, and she's had a lot of input into the script. When I asked her what took so long, she looked baffled and said that it *hasn't* taken long at all. You don't argue with Faye Dunaway—especially about Maria Callas. And so it was back to *Chinatown*, and how Faye felt "it gave people something to put their dreams on." (It's better than a wire hanger.)

Her cohost for the night, designer Michael Kors, told me that to him, the flick represents "crepe de chine riding jodhpurs, nipples, and veils." "And that's just Jack Nicholson!" we said in unison. Faye was now telling a reporter that she likes "that Calista Flockhart show—I forget what it's called." (It's *Ally Dearest*, I think.) And then Faye gave the crowd an entertainingly rambling speech about the joys of moviemaking, in which she only emitted one unfortunate line: "When I was working with Peter Falk on a gem of a *Columbo* recently. . . ." *That* she remembered? Regardless, Faye Dunaway is the essence of Hollywood diva glamour. I love her so much I feel like she's my sister. My daughter. My sister. My daughter.

Our Canadian brothers came out for a panel discussion at the 92nd Street Y called "Why Are Canadians So Funny?" which efficiently covered every aspect of Canuck humor except for Celine Dion. The evening started with Canadian stand-up comic Sean Cullen telling us, "As Sean Connery would say, 'Enjoy yourselves or I'll kill you.'" Connery never even said *that* much to me. The panel—including Martin Short and Eugene Levy—then ambled out and agreed that Canada is a pretty sad but likable place with a proliferation of doughnut shops where they even sell the stuff you cut out to make the holes! Things got less funny afterward, when reporters craftily shifted the subject to panel moderator Michael J. Fox's Parkinson's disease. But Fox was astoundingly gracious and articulate about it, and when someone's cell phone rang, he even cracked, "That's my doctor!"

My *love* doctor has been recommending return visits to East Village pickup dives like Wonder Bar, Dick's Bar, the Bar, the Cock, and the Boiler Room, which are all hopping with those who are simply wild about penis. But farther west, I'm not so sure. I recently ventured into Florent for an early dinner and found that what was largely a drag queen and clubbie hangout has been taken over by the family crowd— you know, the "Honey, pass the mustard and tell your brother to shut up" bunch. Heeeelp!

I don't know *who* will swim to Float, but it's definitely a new, sleek, medium-sized hangout in the theater district, with lots of lit-up panels and soft blue rectangular shapes. It's all very *Fahrenheit 451* meets *My Geisha* via James Bond (you know, Pierce Brosnan) and could be fiercely festive if it doesn't attract the wrong crowd—you know, the kind that can't pay for their gonorrhea medicine.

Speaking of powder blue spaces, if Toni Braxton was any more lightened on the *Beauty and the Beast* display outside the Palace Theatre, she'd look like Michael Jackson. But another poster—one at the TLA Video store—has been tampered with in a sort of *amusing* way. It's a promo placard for *Halloween: H20*, and they've charmingly inscribed on it, "Michael Myers has broken out of the insane asylum and is going to kill every hermaphrodite on the planet. First on his list— Jamie Lee Curtis!" Good—*her* publicist hates me, too.

La Dolce nightmare!

May 11, 1999

The upcoming Belgian movie *The Red Dwarf*—in which a height-challenged divorce-law worker (Jean-Yves Thual) has a hot fling with a craggy countess (legendary beauty Anita Ekberg), only to dress up in drag as her and go psycho—is not at all surreal. Not compared to the evening I just had with Ekberg and Thual, which was like something out of Fellini's *Intervista* via *Sunset Boulevard*, with huge doses of glamour, insecurity, and barbarism thrown into the poisonous popcorn.

The mood was set when the film's wry writer-director Yvan Le Moine told the premiere crowd, "I hope the person sitting next to you smells OK. Very often films are a punishment, but this one promises to be a torture." People tittered nervously, then a *Christian Science Monitor* critic was bizarrely brought out to introduce the two stars—Thual and Arno Chevrier—and also "Anita Ekberg, who needs no introduction." Wrong! The film goddess looked fit to eat a dwarf. "First of all, where the hell is the light?" she bellowed in the

143

semidarkness. "Maybe we look better this way! And 'the two stars'—he left me out! Then he says, 'She doesn't need an introduction,' so I'll introduce myself. I am Anita Ekberg!" She took in the applause like a giant Swedish sponge. And then, after wildly overpraising her costars, Ekberg returned to barking, "Where is the light? Before we go away, you can at least see what we look like!" They finally flashed the spot on her and, in a sublimely Kenneth Anger-ready moment, you could see that she's a somewhat blowsier version of her former self, but still gorgeously magnetic, with a catlike blond mane, emphatic makeup, and an all-forgiving black shroud. The girl's still standing—and still stellar.

And still a nightmare. Ekberg started to leave, signing autographs and saying, "Quickly, quickly, and then we go where there's air conditioning! It's hot here!" They dragged her into a limo to go to a heat-controlled restaurant a block away, and—though I begged to walk—I was whooshed into the car by a publicist who introduced me to Ekberg as a journalist and old friend. "I thought my work was over tonight!" Ekberg screeched. "And don't say a journalist is a friend. They're not to be trusted! Where's my fan?" Don't look at me, bitch. Arno Chevrier opened a whiskey bottle and Ekberg promptly snarled, "I hate whiskey!" As she made a face not usually seen in nature, I started to think of her as Anita Yecch-berg, but valiantly tried to understand the toll age has taken on her confidence, as well as the conflict she clearly faces between wanting to turn her back on the (decreasing) hoopla and yet desperately needing to be noticed. Besides, I hate whiskey, too.

Alas, things got even more tense when we arrived at Primola. Miss Thing instantly announced, "I want to sit with my back to the wall. Who'll take the coats? I want proper water, if nothing else!" Charmed, I'm sure. Ekberg smilingly turned to her director and said, "I hated you to begin with." I asked the poor guy what he thinks of her, and he said, "She's generous, with extremes—a real personality. I had to convince her to do the movie. She said, 'The only thing is, no dwarf!' I said, 'But the name of the film is *The Red Dwarf!*' You have to love her. She has balls." "Yeah, three," I said, but actually, make that four; she was now roaring to the dwarf, "Why didn't they put the spotlight on us? It's crazy!"

I brilliantly noticed that Ekberg lit up like Rome at night whenever people stroked her ego, so I thought I'd try that approach. I showed her a very flattering cartoon I'd brought of her jumping into the Trevi fountain in *La Dolce Musto*—I mean *La Dolce Vita*—and asked if she'd like to keep it. "No, I'd rather not," she said, as if I'd offered her a dead rat on top of a Dunkin' Donut. "Can I have a napkin?" she suddenly whimpered to a waiter. "Mine has fallen down three times. It's cleaning the floor!"

Averting my eyes from this new play for attention, I realized how hot the dwarf was, especially after someone pointed out that he has big feet and a cute little ass. But now all I could hear was Ekberg yelling, "Why do they keep letting Sophia Loren into the country? She was in jail for a month for tax evasion!" Between courses, other arresting pronouncements came fast and furiously: "Frank Sinatra was not a good lover!"; "If there's one thing I hate, it's people chewing gum. It's like cows out to pasture!"; and "Not being able to smoke in restaurants is against the Constitution!" I never got to argue any of these topics—or even get a word in—but I was certainly never bored.

As I finished up my intimidating-looking crustacean—the one on my plate—two more people joined the table and our diva threw her final fit. "I'm not making any more interviews!" Ekberg insisted. "I thought I saw cameras!" But there weren't any for miles. Oh, well—ciao, bella. I'm now triple-locked in my home, gazing appreciatively at that cartoon of you looking so carefree and adorable. I'll remember her, not la dolce Evita.

Talk is cheap,
but the magazine isn't

August 17, 1999

I've been traveling a lot, but like Holly Golightly, only keep running into myself. At least the *Thomas Crown Affair* premiere in Southampton—a big Bulgari blowout—was a pleasant enough way to avoid too much reflection. The trashily entertaining movie has the guts to put two "older" stars in the romantic hot seat, though the lighting generally whites out their faces and Pierce Brosnan's tight-assed body double is clearly so young he wouldn't even be allowed to *see* the movie. Still, I hope *Crown* clicks; it'll mean the end of those flaccid love stories between denture-wearing geezers and preteen Lolitas. I'm not sure how we can stop them in real life, though.

Before the movie even started, talk had already centered around firm, youngish buttocks. Francesco Scavullo chatted me up about the recent bare-assed Brad Pitt spread in *W*. "He looked like a hustler," he moaned. "When I shot Brad, he said he didn't *want* to look gay. He wouldn't take his shirt off—we put a vest on him." Funny, I look gay in a vest.

We put on our life vests and headed straight to the fancy Club

Colette after-party, where someone was telling Marla Maples, "You should be in a movie like that." "Oh, I don't know," she blushed, holding on to Michael Mailer, who's actually put her in his *own* movie. Like Ivory soap, the girl always manages to float.

And so do I—right back to New York. You get there on the Hampton Jitney, where all the people who've indulged in lock-jawed fake manners in their white smocks and parasols all weekend suddenly turn into the alligator from *Lake Placid*. They push, they shove, they sprawl out over two seats, they scream reservation requests on their cell phones. These are the folks who last year were threatened by the African American invasion and this year by the plethora of "suburbanites" coming in—but they should really be scared of their terrifying selves.

The pert bus attendant announced that everyone should keep his total phone time down to three minutes—hopefully this will go into law soon—prompting the compulsive little blabbermouth behind me to whimper, "I've already exceeded my amount!" As appeasement, the attendant then came around with a choice of pretzels or potato chips, inspiring the princess across from me to brilliantly ask, "Wait—what are my options?" "Pretzels or potato chips," repeated the girl in an exasperated deapdan. The entire bus-load held its collective breath as her choice was . . . drowned out by someone on a cell phone.

At the journey's peak, we were told that the women on board were getting free makeup and an Henri Bendel gift certificate—"though if the men have a wife, they can have one too." That sounded vaguely homo-and single-guy-phobic, so I cornered the waif and sniveled, "But I'm a transvestite," and she nicely relented. I was going to say "a *married* transvestite" but didn't push it since I was wearing a vest. (By the way, the makeup turned out to be a wrinkle stick!)

Back in the city, I looked even younger than Pierce Brosnan but needed to travel all over again—to the *Talk* magazine party on Liberty Island, where media schmoozed media about media regarding media. What's more, to stay in tune with the mag's "Hip List," I had to sport matte hair, scabby knees, earth tones, and a radio. Fortunately, I already *had* scabby knees. On the island, you were greeted by a long line of camera crews, plus Tina Brown, who looked stunning in a green, flowing ensemble. (Oh, that was Lady Liberty.) Past the reception committee, the soiree seemed strangely low-key, considering that everywhere you turned there was somebody massively famous. Maybe the energy was a little down because, though everyone from Madonna to Salman Rushdie was there, it was so dark you couldn't actually see them!

Things picked up when everyone sauntered over to the better-lit picnic table area and scarfed down some potato salad (which, judging from the "Hip List," must have been Vietnamese and/or dotted with thick-cut bacon). I matted my hair some more and forced various notables to respond to Hillary's saucy *Talk* revelation—you know, how Bill was psychologically abused in a bitter childhood struggle between two generations of trailer trash. The answers? Vera Wang: "I'm not at all shocked. Everybody has their past. Why should he be excluded?" Kurt Andersen: "Pathetic. Count me down as a 'pathetic.' " Ann Magnuson: "Excuses, excuses, excuses. That's something I heard said back in the hollers of West Virginia!" Charlie Hunnam, hottie star of the Brit TV sensation *Queer as Folk*: "I have no opinion of Hillary. She's not really a big deal in England." John Waters: "I'm such a fan of Hillary. I've said psychobabble in my life. We all do." Erica Jong: "I think Tina did a phenomenal job. Hats off to that!" Cynthia Rowley: "I feel compassion for people, but only to a certain point. I'd have moved on a long time ago!" And Candace Bushnell: "The thing that killed me was Hillary's remark that a psychologist said the worst position for a man to be in is between two women. For most men, that's the *best* position." But for others . . . well, I was starting to understand the psychological abuse angle.

While I pondered this, earth tones hit the sky in a fireworks display narrated by George Plimpton ("This is dedicated to the advertisers . . .") as Donna Karan scurried for a better view, exulting, "I'm a sucker for fireworks!" But suddenly the sound system crackled with Queen Latifah saying, "All youse very important people, come near the stage." By the time I got there, *Talk*'s publisher Ron "Puffy" Galotti was rapping about the magazine—but then Tina "Misdemeanor" Brown took over, wouldn't youse know, saying, "Ron is sometimes known as Mr. Big, but to me he's Mr. Enormous!" I guess we're talking thick-cut bacon.

In the crowd, Conan O'Brien was rubbing Willem Dafoe's shaved head; Jeremy Northam was telling me that after I quoted him saying "Cate Blanchett's brilliant. I hate her"—chortle, chortle, chortle—the British press twisted it into a *real* feud; and Dr. Ruth—who was *not* the basis for Mini-me—was screeching, "Where are the gift bags? Where are the freebies?" I almost gave her that Bendel gift certificate but basically didn't want to.

Black punks
vs. white trash

November 13, 2001

Punks is a gay B*A*P*S, a drag *Waiting to Exhale*, a black *Broken Hearts Club*, and an L.A. *Priscilla*, but amazingly enough, it manages much uniqueness. The gossamer-thin film—about the love travails of a gaggle of fierce queens—flounders when the catty drag diva becomes Mother Teresa and the loveless hero gets his dream to come, not only true, but on his face. But it's basically sassy fun, the kind of sweet little thing you root for, especially if you're a fan of *Mahogany*, Sister Sledge, or sex with bananas (don't ask).

At the premiere, writer-director Patrik-Ian Polk told me that African American drag queens "have a little extra attitude. I always feel like they mean it more. They grab onto the fabulousness a little harder." And if the stereotypes are true, they have to tuck a little harder, too. But putting together the film's bootylicious ensemble was even more of an uncomfortable challenge. Polk said he cast Rockmond Dunbar as the ambiguous hunk next door "after a string of name actors didn't want to kiss a man." (Interestingly, Dunbar is now a name actor, on TV's *Soul*

Food.) And then Wilson Cruz backed out as the club entrepreneur, so dance-music star Kevin Aviance stepped in, with heels on. "It was shocking," Aviance told me at the premiere. "I couldn't believe I was in Hollywood and performing before a camera!" I can't believe I'm not!

Before the screening, Polk instructed the crowd, "*Punks* is a black movie. Whether you're white, black, or green, I want you to behave as a black audience. Holler, get up and dance, and celebrate!" I did all the above, but in such a distinctly "white" way that my banana is still looking for some whipped cream.

Once home—alone—a scheduled phoner came in from Brett Butler, who isn't a white trash lady, she only played one on TV. The ex-sitcom queen has come back to stand-up comedy and is grabbing onto the fabulousness a little harder. As she told me, "I feel like some girl who's left her favorite rag doll behind. I took two years off and I feel fairly certain it was mutual in the industry. There are a lot of people who say they'll never work with me, and I've never met them!"

What exactly was the career-threatening problem, pray tell? "I worshiped the god of what other people thought of me," Butler revealed, "and I had to find a bigger, meaner one with squinty eyes that didn't laugh at everything I said. Now, I'm not as savage a pundit as I used to be, but I think I'm funnier." I desperately wanted to prove it with a giant guffaw but bit my tongue in my new role as her bigger, meaner deity.

The refurbished Butler—who'll be making funny at the Comedy Garden Forum at Madison Square Garden on November 9 and 10—clearly doesn't miss *Grace Under Fire* any more than I miss *Little House on the Prairie*. "I love that I had the chance to do it," she admitted, "but I deeply regret mistakes or missteps that I made." Still, hotshots are starting to cut the gal a break, especially since she now seems like the most accommodating Butler since *By Jeeves* and is only high on life, thank you very much.

Adding to her pulsing chakras, the self-proclaimed "goyim Episcopal Southern thing" has deeply enjoyed a drop-dead cute boyfriend for some time. "He's younger than me by 10 years," she divulged. "Not enough where it's, like, sad." The modern, domesticated Brett is even friendly with her ex ("because I'm so fucking spiritual") and, in her most shocking move of all, relaxes via needlepoint! On the plane that very day, "people thought, 'Oh my God, she's gotten lobotomized!' But it's not just needlepoint, it's a big orchid that's going to be a pillow!" It'll look great with her favorite rag doll.

Moving back to that Broadway butler I mentioned, *Noises Off* spoofs the kind of nudgy-winky British sex comedy *By Jeeves* really *is*. The revival of the split-second behind-the-scenes romp is silly, daft, and hilarious—an evening of pure, guilty diversion. And yes, the ever cute Faith Prince's bio in the *Playbill* gives her one more Tony award than she really has, but I'm sure that's just another wacky element of the carefully constructed farce.

While you're exploding with laughter, I'll tell you that an upcoming episode of *Absolutely Fabulous* has Ruby Wax as a decrepit woman named Beth DeWoody who attends a workshop for menopausal creatures and announces, "The sands of time are trickling through my hourglass!" I asked the real-life Beth Rudin DeWoody—a well-known New York socialite who's miles away from that kind of character, mind you—how she feels about the appropriation of her name for this bizarre hot flash. "I have no comment because I haven't seen it," said DeWoody, who didn't sound thrilled at all.

Bursting with young testosterone, Michael and Hushi put on a really fun, hypnotic fashion show at the Ukrainian National Home, with model Theo Kogan from the Lunachicks getting the biggest audience response. The girl's making it (in the Burberry and Courvoisier campaigns, for starters), despite André Leon Talley's dismissive comments, not to mention the fact that rock chicks who model are much rarer than model chicks who rock, got that?

But there's been some kooky timing in the magazine world lately. Poor Lisa Marie's on the cover of the new *Gear*, going on about how tight and loving she and Tim Burton really are. Whoopsy-daisy! And a recent *Time Out New York* cover had "Cheap Eats" handwritten in white powder (relax, it was only sugar), a bold choice coming in the middle of the anthrax scare, and one I totally approved of. "Some readers were concerned about that," the mag's editor, Cindy Stivers, told me last week. "It was shot well before any of this started happening. We had the conversation and said, 'Does this look like anthrax? No, it's clearly sugar.' The sensitivity stuff is inevitable, but we're following the mayor's orders to get on with it!" No argument here—I'm downing 16 donuts as we speak, just to be a good citizen.

My appetite whetted, I pranced around on Halloween as a Big Mac and found myself battling even more of that sensitivity stuff. Anxiety-spreading idiots had dampened the celebration by painting it as deeply inappropriate, though a bunch of us brave patriots fought back with fearlessness and fishnets. Still, a visit to the Warhol-themed party at the Gay Center could only last as long as Andy would have wanted—15 minutes.

Speaking of celebrity dress-up, I have some pressing sartorial advice to offer today's biggest stars, like, OK? Alicia Keys, darling, I beg you to take off the headgear. You look like you're hiding from something, and honestly, you shouldn't, because you're not that bad looking—really! And Macy Gray, baby, kindly burn your hats and other doodads immediately. Your raggedy bohemian chic, which was so darned endearing, has morphed into a calculated weirdness that looks like the result of countless bucks and way too much fussing by stylists. Mess it up again! Oh, and Leelee Sobieski, you're fabulash, but please take a little break, pumpkin. You're in everything! Put on a hat!

Celebrities I can stand

August 2, 2005

Not long ago, I scored a gigantic hit with a column telling a myriad of celebrities what they needed to do to get back on track and not be so overall annoying. Well, as much as I'm jonesing to dole out yet more unsolicited advice to sad stars, I'm a little tired of preaching to the perverted—and besides, I'd rather stretch my creative muscles and engage in the flip side of this game. This time I'd like to *congratulate* celebrities— the ones who don't need makeovers, shakedowns, interventions, or even congratulations. After thinking about it for several weeks, I even managed to come up with a few names. And so my bravos go to:

Lindsay Lohan: Yes, perhaps you *are* fully loaded, but there's way too much lip-smacking about that in the press, and what gets lost is that you're effortlessly charming on-screen and have been a slick, capable star ever since you played twins, and even before that as Alexandra "Alli" Fowler #3 on *Another World*. I value you as an actor even as I devour you as a good-copy machine. You're welcome. Now go home.

Glenn Close: I'm thrilled you're getting to re-create your Norma Desmond in the movie version of *Sunset Boulevard* the musical. (I'm still mad about Merman and *Gypsy*.) You belt a love song to a monkey like no one since Michael Jackson. And you've royally earned your niche—playing off-putting yet somehow dignified grizzled old bitches. You terrify me, which is high praise indeed. In fact, no one scares me more except that adorable little Dakota Fanning.

Ewan McGregor: Some critics said your singing in the London production of *Guys and Dolls* reeks of la postnasal drip, but you sounded terrific in *Moulin Rouge*, so try to remember what you did while recording that and kindly do it again when you set down the tracks opposite Glenn for *Sunset Boulevard*. And if not, who cares? You're damned cute and so is your clone.

Madonna: Your save-the-world speech at Live 8 was followed by your icily telling the band, "Come on, go!" Millions found the moment appalling, but hey, it *was* time for them to start already. I love that you amazingly still manage to shock and awe and irritate the bejesus out of people. To those who are taken aback by women of a certain age who let it hang in intimidating ways, I say "Come on, go!"

Demi Moore: You're *also* scoring big time as an older broad—one who's found a steaming plate of hot chicken and won't let go of it. Why should you? He's not just a boy toy or a cheap PR stunt; he's clearly your cosmic twin and quite a dish too. Keep ignoring the cheap jokes and continue to focus on the intensity of your bond and he'll stay on the leash. In fact, keep doing everything you've been doing—just don't ever let him see *Indecent Proposal* or *The Scarlet Letter* or *Striptease* or *G.I. Jane* or. . . .

Here's where the column takes a sharp turn

Fabian Basabe and Paris Hilton: So you both have a problem with African Americans? You pampered, powder-white, "It"-person morons. Get to the back of the gift bag line! Oops, I'm supposed to be doling out kudos. Back to the lovin':

Sandra Bullock: I've always sensed you were way more than just Julia Roberts lite, and you proved me right with your harrowing performance in *Crash* (and by nabbing a man who wasn't attached to someone else). It's never too soon for tired columnists to start beating the Oscar tom-toms, so I'm shouting it out now: If my girl Sandra doesn't get a Supporting Actress nomination, I will not attend the Oscars, even if invited.

Sienna Miller: Cheers for supposedly dumping the lawless Jude Law (though you never should have been wearing a modern engagement ring in a Shakespeare play anyway). Once a cheater, always a schnook, and even if he didn't ever stray again, the lingering doubt would hover over your boudoir like a cumulus cloud of icky cocky doody. Sure, Liz Hurley forgave Hugh Grant and that relationship ended up lasting some guilty time longer, but that doesn't really count because Divine Brown wasn't *half* the skank Daisy Wright is. She's a regular Mary Trampins, a veritable chim-chim-cher-rude slag. Sadie should have known it's better to just strap the kids down and leave them for a while than ever risk having a nanny around. Nannies are the devil's rejects, even worse than babysitters who throw the kids against the wall, if not quite as awful as scummy, cheating menfolk. Just ask Robin Williams, who left his missus for his kid's nanny and who also *played* a nanny in *Mrs. Doubtfire*—one Jude Law would probably even consider shagging. Men are evil, Sienna. Go lesbo and I'll love you even more!

Brangelina: Ignore everything I just said. A little adultery can actually be useful once in a while, as long as it's covert, emotionless, and doesn't interrupt heaping servings of the main course. So couldn't you two have just had a fling on the side? Did you have to throw everything away for a little of the old in-and-out? Have you never heard of surreptitious weekend action in the woods? Yikes, I feel another relapse coming on. Forget all that—you're doing fine, kids. Go ahead and enjoy your disruptive sex making. But just don't cheat on the side!

Smells like team spirit

Gus Van Sant: Congrats, I guess, on having the three balls to make such a nihilistic slice of nihilistic nihilism as *Last Days*, mutter mutter, scratch scratch, mutter snort keel. And kudos to *me* for now preparing to so cleverly hijack the entire thesis of this column (the way Brangelina tried to do in the last graph) and turn it into a straightforward report on the premiere. And so: Before the screening started, I smirkily asked Sonic Youth's Thurston Moore—*Last Days'* music consultant—if the film's torture, as a few critics so rudely claimed. "Completely!" Moore responded. "It's beautiful torture! I love when Michael Pitt is nodding out while a Boyz II Men video is playing—in full." (Yikes—that's Abu Ghraib-level abuse.)

Before I submitted to the film's languid, splotchy trance, I asked Van Sant if it was true that Brad Pitt once approached him to do a Kurt Cobain flick. "Yes," Van Sant said, dryly. "But I thought 'a biopic?' Then after a little while I thought, 'Maybe I'll do a different kind of film. Maybe it should be more obscure.'" And I guess that included using a more obscure Pitt.

Hey, didn't Van Sant ask Courtney Love to play herself in that earlier version? (My spies say she politely declined.) "I heard that too!" the auteur deadpanned, with confirming eyes. Well, let's pin a pretty ribbon of congratulations on my reportorial ass!

Oscar's evil twin:
the annual Felix awards

December 27, 2005

It's time for the eagerly unawaited year-end awards column, which, like everything from *Million Dollar Baby* to *War of the Worlds* to *The March of the Penguins*, will be narrated by the mellifluous tones of Morgan Freeman. Or it would have been had he not been busy narrating the upcoming feature *War of the Million Dollar Baby Penguins*. So let's forgo narration and simply dive into 2005's best and skankiest in fabulous awfulness and rotten-assed bliss. The voiceover-free (and glory-exempt) Felix Awards go to. . . .

Worst feel-good euphemism of the modern age: "He transitioned." Please—he croaked! Dropped dead! Kicked the giant KFC bucket! Went 6,000 feet under! Is pushing up rotted daisies! Turned off the night-light! And he won't be a-comin' back! Learn it, face it, and move on, oh differently mentally abled person.

Biggest disappointments: Jude Law cheated with the nanny, then burnt Sienna welcomed the bastard back; Jacko jurors declared the star not guilty then suddenly started wondering otherwise; the pope transitioned, then they appointed a new one. Kidding! I love the new one—he's great copy.

Clichés ready for retirement: Stick a fork in it—it's done; I didn't get the memo; he drank the Kool-Aid; I can't wrap my mind around that; he's straight—it's his dick that's gay; if you're not living on the edge, you're taking up too much space; she should have her own zip code.

Movies that by all rights should have been better: The Interpreter, Bewitched, and even some things without Nicole Kidman. Stick a fork in her—nah, she's doin' fine.

You know you've seen way too many movies when you realize: The Wedding Crashers was better than The Wedding Planner and The Wedding Date, if not quite up to par with The Wedding Singer. God, Hollywood has range.

Lessons learned from the tidily moralistic An Unfinished Life: J.Lo's character once had a mishap at the wheel and killed her hubby; Camryn Manheim once looked away at the moment she could have saved her daughter from drowning; Robert Redford was once so drunk he failed to protect Morgan Freeman from a grizzly bear's paws (not to mention narration jobs); and you once wasted 10 bucks, 50 cents, and two hours—or, more likely, 40 minutes.

How to ruin a date: Start shrieking, "I can't wait to see Cheaper by the Dozen 2! I've waited so long for that movie! I'm gonna see it right after I catch up with Yours, Mine & Ours!"

How to lose a friend: Screech, "I just decided the war in Iraq is morally wrong! It's totally based on lies and should be stopped! What a travesty!" Please—even Republicans agree with that now. Only Hillary Clinton doesn't.

Enough: Wildlife documentaries (*The March of the Penguins, Deep Blue*) that employ sweeping orchestral music and grandiose narration (sorry, Mr. Freeman) as they show scads of wet critters to be magnificent and profound in absolutely every little thing they do. You don't see any bowel movements or bleeding gums—that wouldn't be all that majestic, would it? No, you're just presented with pure grace and adorableness every step of the way, and I have to say I can see why—those animals are so fucking cute! I completely change my mind. Keep the movies coming!

But back to human biology: Actor Tom Sizemore was caught using a Whizzinator—a fake wee-wee complete with someone else's urine—when he went for a drug test. Sizemore indeed.

Another unwanted lesson in body science: On the big day of testimony against him, master showman Michael Jackson claimed to have back pains and went to the emergency room, showing up late to court in pajama bottoms and slippers. As a result, I was promptly hospitalized with severe stomach cramps and life-threatening projectile vomiting. I almost transitioned. (And that's the last time for the transitioned joke. Promise. It's transitioned. It's croaked! It's dropped dead!)

Something I'll surely never order again: Chicken fingers at Wendy's!

Orange alert: To this day I wake up screaming, thinking I'm still surrounded by those freaking Christo/Jeanne-Claude gates, hung with what looked like giant shower curtains, filling every inch of my beloved Central Park. That much bright orange should never be allowed outside Osceola County.

An exchange I would have loved to see on TV: Martha Stewart: "You're fired!" Firee: "Oh, yeah? Well, you're under house arrest!"

Most shameless whores: The mass media, who'd previously walked on eggshells in addressing Tom Cruise's off-screen life. They were suddenly joined in snark, as they gleefully deconstructed TomKat with cynicism aplenty. Why so bold, pray tell? Because Tom wasn't hooked up to a powerful, big-time publicist anymore—he had signed his own sister to represent him—so they weren't afraid to rock the boat the way they had been during all those oozily polite years of bowing and scraping. And these people have a right to cry, "No integrity!"?

Best gift bag item: A brochure for the Betty Ford Center, which was included in the bag for *Radar* magazine's relaunch party. This was so much more useful than the usual body scrubs and aromatherapy. Alas, Tom Sizemore wasn't there to get one (though he could probably use body scrubs and aromatherapy, too, ba-dum-pum).

Juiciest comment I overheard at a holiday party: The director of one of the big December flicks was gleefully telling a friend, "I don't think anyone's gonna see Spielberg's movie. No one's interested!"

You know my star has fallen big-time when most of the calls I get from TV producers are about: Peter Braunstein, the psycho who went the lam after his alleged Halloween rampage. Yes, he did write for the *Voice* several years ago, but alas, I mean thank God I didn't know him well enough to get booked to talk about him!

Nocturnal omission: A New York daily ran a nightlife-related story that dealt with the sex-laden gay bar the Cock, but they wouldn't say the club's name, I guess because it didn't refer to a barnyard animal. Call me kooky-crazy, but I generally think publications shouldn't write about something if they can't actually divulge what it is. The newspaper I'm referring to, of course, is . . . um, sorry, can't say it.

My latest bunch of unbearably cute drag names to try on like dime-store jewelry: Ariel Photography, Ann Arbor, Sue Donymous, Cindy Cation, Mary Widow, Jennifer Convertibles, Anna Mation, Rosetta Stoned, Rose Tattoo, Pearl Onion, Carrie Okee, Brooke Trout, Sarah Tonin, Ginger Ale, Laurel Canyon, Sybil Union, Tami Flu, and—big finish—Felice Navidad.

Worst restaurant: Parkhill's Waterfront Grill in New Jersey—the place that, as a *New York Post* story revealed, identified patrons by putting descriptions like "Jew couple" or "Dirty Joanne" on their checks. I was sort of tempted to drop by just to see how they'd label me ("Tired queen"? "Greasy wop"? "Unspeakably rude, fat cow"?), but I lost my nerve and just ordered takeout.

Best feel-good musical about Tourette's syndrome: In *My Life*—unless there was another one around, in which case this was the *second* best. When the lead character was also revealed to have a brain tumor and the audience tittered, you *knew* this was a uniquely memorable experience. I also loved how the producer strived to stay anonymous for fear people would hit him up to finance their own shows. I guess he was afraid of that old "If he'll put money in this pile of stink, he'll back anything!" line of thinking. And how right he was; I've been dying to reach him about my seizure-disorder jukebox musical, *Shake, Rattle, and Roll Over*.

Most outrageous showing of pure gall: In a *New York Post* interview with Michael Riedel, Suzanne Somers compared her disgrace at the hands of Broadway critics to the tortures at Abu Ghraib. Funny, I heard some audience members make the same comparison. Kidding once again! I love her!

Least shocking gossip magazine headline: "Marcia Cross engaged at 43!"

Most annoying e-mail: "Kindly update your contact info." If I received the e-mail, then the contact info must be correct, right, douche bag?

Sickest truth: When you call the appropriate number on your cell phone to find out how many minutes you have left, it counts as a minute. It's even more immoral than Iraq.

Oscar flirts with the gays

March 14, 2006

I was cocksure the Academy Awards were going to be even more of a gay Olympics than the *actual* gay Olympics—you know, the male figure skating competition. I blithely assumed they'd be such a glammed-up circuit party they'd have to have a back room instead of a greenroom and a fleet enema in the gift bag. But the show turned out to only be a moderate gropefest for the gays, tempered by the fact that *Brokeback Mountain* had peaked too soon and became abandoned by lily-livered trend pirates afraid to endorse out-of-wedlock buggering outside of their own. I'd probably be more pansy-purple with rage over this if *Crash* wasn't indeed the better movie.

Maybe some people preferred *Brokeback* way back when it was called *Midnight Cowboy. Happy Endings'* director Don Roos certainly did. He just told the *Sydney Star Observer*, "I was so irritated by those stupid, stupid cowboys. . . . It's the perfect film for the Bush years: 'Don't be gay, America!' It's the kind of movie that makes you glad to be straight. Is that the kind of movie we should be rewarding people for? It's an anti-gay film!"

I guess *Brokeback* got it from both ends: The squeamish ran screaming from the lovin' on all fours while the Rooses (and Mustos) couldn't bear the fact that it wasn't fully consummated. (Roos directed *Happy Endings*, remember?) The telecast's shock ending culminated three-plus hours of abuse reminiscent of two classic '05 scenes: the chest waxing in *The 40-Year-Old Virgin* and the fingernail torture in *Syriana*. But as painful as it all was, I was still glued to the set, reveling in the timeless thrill of seeing four people lose in each category. My tawdry thoughts as it all transpired were:

8 P.M.: The very first image shown is of Dorothy in *The Wizard of Oz*, saying, "Toto, I've a feeling we're not in Kansas anymore." Clearly, this ceremony is going to be gayer than a home furnishings store on Super Bowl Sunday.

8:07: Everywhere you look, there are Huffmans and Hoffmans, if not Huffalumps. Alas, things are already so poorly paced it's like the sag awards. A few minutes into the telecast, Catherine Keener is spotted checking her text messages in the audience. Jon Stewart is amiable enough, but he seems self-defeatingly low-key and as declawed as Siegfried and Roy's new pets. Nabbing him as host and not letting him rip into the administration even once is like hiring Sarah Silverman to write greeting cards or Kathy Griffin to hostess a massage parlor. Sick!

8:17: George Clooney praises Hollywood's consciousness, remembering that "the Academy . . . gave Hattie McDaniel an Oscar in 1939 when blacks were still sitting in the backs of theaters." Yeah, but—true story—they made her sit in the back of the Oscar theater!

8:31: The big gay love story won a prize: *Wallace & Gromit*. Let the queer juggernaut begin.

8:46: Is this the same Martin Mcdonagh who writes those impossibly butch, bloody plays of hetero aggression? In accepting for best live action short film, he's coming off all sweet and light and brokebacky. I want to have his babies.

8:51: For no ostensible reason, they're showing the campiest clip of all time—the "wire hangers" scene from *Mommie Dearest*. This shit can't *get* any gayer.

9:00: Whoa, nelly—yes, it can. Morgan Freeman is suddenly quoting from *Sunset Boulevard*. What next? Dame Judi Dench swiveling out with, "But you are, Blanche"?

9:05: The pretaped comedy bits (the montage of gay subtext in westerns, the faux Best Actress commercials) are spot-on, but the live shtick (the overanxious presentations by Ben Stiller and Will Ferrell) is more strained than gay spaghetti. Most annoying of all is the orchestral music blaring the second the winners start speaking. It makes it sound as if the trophy holders are voicing over a Glade commercial. Soon enough, perhaps, they will be.

9:12: Lauren Bacall shakes and stumbles through a prompter read. Finally, some spontaneity.

9:20: It's a good thing the *March of the Penguins* people won or they'd be sitting there all night with those penguin puppets, looking like complete assholes.

9:25: The *Crash* song's production number is very Lilith Fair meets Cirque du So-lame crossed with a Great White concert via a dinner theater production of *Medea*. Make it stop, Jon.

9:31: He can't. He seems defeated. He's not even trying anymore. Are you still there, Jon? We can't afford to lose you to something so silly. Call me!

10:22: I'm so delirious by now that the pimp song sounds just like the *Crash* one. Give me drugs.

10:29: Don Knotts obviously croaked too late to make the cut for the dead-people montage. Note to celebs: Die in early February.

10:55: *Memoirs of a Geisha* is proving that you can have the best costumes, cinematography, and art direction of the year and still have the lousiest movie.

11 P.M.: Oscar loves weight change! George Clooney packed on 30 pounds and won, but Felicity Huffman only shed nine inches. It wasn't enough. Ballsy Reese wins Best Actress. Ryan Phillippe looks suicidal. I give them six weeks.

11:20: Stunner. *Crash* nabs Best Picture. Go to the back of the theater, queens. Race relations trump the gay problem. Oscar is too busy oppressing gays—as a rule, out actors never have a chance—to make homophobia the night's shining concern, even with straights allegedly playing the parts. But hey, wasn't Ryan in *Crash*? Yeah, I'm pretty sure. Reese's marriage is back together again.

And so the straights-love-gays year at the movies ends with a condomless fuck and a stinging slap on the rear. Oscar, I wish I knew how to quit you. By the way, when Rocco Dispirito asked me on his pre-Oscars radio broadcast on CBS, "How do these actors research these roles?" you might have heard a loud bleep, but what I actually said was "They take it up the ass."

Same crime next year
Next year's winner? Probably *Dreamgirls*, which is the kind of gay movie everyone can enjoy. They seem to be doing everything right with that thing, especially the hair and the shoes. But that other kitschy ozone-destroyer, *Hairspray*, has weirdly cast John Travolta, who—after a lifetime of dodging rumors and pushing the wife in front of cameras—now finds he has to don heels and a bra to make a living. It's poetic, I tell you.

More true to form, in the imminent *Thank You for Smoking*—spoiler alert—Katie Holmes plays a sleazebag who gets sexually aroused when the guy she's with pops up on television. I.e., she's a starfucker. Give her a Razzie.

And in the *real* gay Olympics—namely the theater awards—the biggest prize is clearly going to be a toss-up between the exposed chests of Harry Connick Jr. and Chris Carmack. Could you just die, girls?

Helen, shave her

The gays triumph again with IFC's *Fabulous! The Story of Queer Cinema*—my two sound bites are *amazing*—which is a sort of *Celluloid Closet* for the age when there's way more text than subtext. And they even have actual gay people on-screen. Watching the film at the premiere, I was thrilled to see that Jane Lynch—who's stolen everything from *Best in Show* to that Virgin thing—is not only an out lesbian, but she admits to having spent the '80s in a Chicago bar called the Closet, watching the love scene from *Desert Hearts* on constant video rotation!

Another humorous person, Ricky Gervais, was rooting for *Crash* and Philip Seymour Hoffman to win, as he told me at an intimate Oxonian Society reception in his honor at the Princeton Club last week. Recently, *British GQ* named the comic—best known for *The Office*—a more powerful figure than Jude Law and Mick Jagger, if not as much so as Tony Blair. "Take it with a grain of salt," advised Gervais, laughing. Yeah, he's probably *more* powerful than Tony Blair.

After a very quick gossip break—Deborah Gibson is in talks with VH1—let's pull ourselves out of all this fake gay pride and revel in one dark *faygeleh* reality. As I recently hinted, Q television network just went toilet-wise, thereby screwing more people than a prostie without an agent. The channel canceled most of its programming and gave pink slips to about 100 lavender lights, owing them so much back pay it could finance West Hollywood's secession from the union. I know the feeling. I'd been hired by Q (a "premium channel") to do weekly gossip reports and was told they adored me and that this might even lead to bigger things. Yeah, like them lying about the check being in the mail and quickly becoming unreachable, all while the axed throngs file complaints with L.A.'s labor commission! Q clearly stands for quisling (*Webster's*: a traitor, especially one who agrees to govern on behalf of the conquering nation). It's such an unhappy-ending situation Ang Lee will probably do the movie version.

Three hours of pain: Julia Roberts hits Broadway

May 2, 2006

Linda Simpson's *My Comrade* magazine benefit at the Ukrainian National Home was a rivetingly kitschy nutfest, especially if you wandered into the Petit Versailles tent, where two guys dressed as Jesus were blowing the steaming pierogies, as it were, of anyone who unzipped. "I don't get it," I blurted, awestruck yet confused as to what kind of party this was. "They're exhibitionists," responded someone with a "duh" expression on his face.

I ran, crying, off to Splash to present an honor at Cherry Jubilee's Glammy awards for drag excellence, where they were all intellectually immersed in the art of the blowjob, as it turned out. Sweetie, who won best lip-synch artist, touchingly told the crowd, "When I'm sucking cock, I'm also practicing my lip-synching!" Lady Bunny won something but didn't show, so presenter Ariel Sinclair cracked, "She's stuck in a 14-year-old." And Sherry Vine—who cohosted with Shasta Cola—was stuck on the fact that the GLAAD awards seemed to honor gay-friendly straight stars, "but this show is for fags, dykes, trannies, and cross-dressers!" They're exhibitionists! (PS: They're also complete cunts. While I was onstage, someone in the dressing room poured about a pound of sugar into my bag. At least it *tasted* like sugar.)

On Fridays at Mr. Black, the gays start getting aroused merely on entering; it's a Pavlovian response to recognizing the doorgirl, wacky Irene, from all those years at the Cock. And there are other offbeat arousals there. My last time around, a guy approached me to ask if Alexis Arquette should get his dick chopped off. "No way—it's so big," I shrieked, joking. "I know," he replied. "I dated him!" Well, it must have been celebrity fallout night, because another young gentleman later approached me to say he dated [famous person], "and he liked to lick ass. He always had bad breath." Dramatic pause. "Maybe because he liked to lick ass."

But let's stop *kissing* ass and start wondering why *Kinky Boots'* (admittedly minimal) advertising campaign has played down the gender angle as squeamishly as the *Transamerica* DVD cover. It reminds me of the *Brokeback Mountain* spots that almost made it look like the straightest love story ever told. And speaking of straight love stories, I do adore the campaign for *Silent Hill*, mainly because it's allowed so many pervs to change the bus shelter posters into wanky commentaries about Katie Holmes's "silent birth." (By the way, Katie might not have screamed when Suri with the fringe on top was born, but I know I did.)

Another crash-landing epic, *United 93*, is silent about the heroic Mark Bingham being gay, but I'll wait to see it before I decide if that's a willful omission or a lousy mistake.

My life on the Bee list

That flick's more uplifting box office competitor, the spelling movie *Akeelah and the Bee*, is produced by people named Sid and Nancy Ganis, but they're so not punk and suicidal. In fact, at a special screening, the perfectly coherent and well-groomed couple assured us that *Akeelah* is a terrific "family film," as I started getting a tiny bit n-e-r-v-o-u-s and wetting my pants. Well, sure enough, it's formulaic and corny, complete with the *Billy Elliot*–style parent who has to be won over by the kid's talent, but by time they were spelling *pulchritude*, I was a sobbing mess.

And it's pulchritudinous to see Angela Bassett and Laurence Fishburne reunited a million years after *What's Love Got to Do with It?* The Ganises told me that was no coincidence; Fishburne requested Bassett, having loved working with her, and that's supersweet, though I kept expecting him to bash her face in.

At my table, omnipresent celebrity lawyer Mickey Sherman refrained from punching me out when I asked for his secrets to TV-commentator glory. "The key," he said, "is being able to start and finish a thought in 14 seconds, before being interrupted by a screaming female prosecutor. Look straight at the camera, don't drool, and know that the moment you're sitting there, your mic is hot. Once, during OJ, I was on a show with Mike Walker from the *Enquirer*, and we argued. They cut to a commercial and I said, 'Is he a fucking asshole or what?' Walker [who was being beamed in from elsewhere] heard it and said, 'I don't appreciate that.'" How do you spell 'tense moment'?

That kind of conflict is always welcome in reality shows and even more so in speculation about them. Like: Now that Ivana Trump's doing *Ivana Young Man*, should Melania Trump launch the inevitable answer show, *Ivana Old Man*?

A cut above (though she had a cut below), Amanda Lepore is striving to launch her own reality series, and at one of those crazed Tuesday nights at Happy Valley, I asked her if it will be similar to Anna Nicole Smith's. "No," she cooed. "I'm already thin."

It's Weill all right

On Broadway, reality has filtered in, but in a deeply artifical way that adds excess poundage to the proceedings. At first, I was excited by the *Threepenny Opera* revival because it seemed almost like a drag awards show at Splash. But like this column, the production anxiously tries on anything for size: bisexuality, coke, subtitles, modern dress, sing-alongs, house lights going on in the middle of a song, a gay marriage joke, New Yawk accents, belching, and everything but getting stuck in a 14-year-old. It's the *Spamalot* approach to Weill, and it's also the *Pajama Game* approach in that loud weirdies (normally my favorite type of people, but not all at once) make up most of the cast. And things are even more spelled out than usual. Lucy, for example, is played by a man in drag, and if you don't get *that*, he lifts up his skirt and flashes his pierogi. Ana Gasteyer puts the ill in shrill—though she's talented, she sledgehammers every syllable—but Nellie McKay is sweetly affecting, Jim Dale is an old pro with the right vaudeville moves, and Alan Cumming works his haunting heinie off. By the end, the piece's power can't help but surface through the gimmicks.

Another anticapitalist tract getting a pricey revival, *Awake and Sing* reads like a Jewish *Raisin in the Sun*, and the new production treats it as such, with a loving if not always transcendent result. Some of the actors shine, while others seem to have stepped right out of Turner Classic Movies—but at least the opening-night audience was awake and singing its praises. "I'm enjoying it so much!" gushed *Light in the Piazza*'s Victoria Clark, who's apparently never had a dark moment. (By the way, while *Threepenny* breaks through the fourth wall to slam you over the head, the *Awake* set has no walls by the end. This trend has to stop, or Wal-Mart will go out of business.)

A wet set is the basis for *Three Days of Rain*, which the kids on the message boards call *Three Hours of Pain*, one noting that Julia Roberts can't even get the Southern accent right—"and she's from Georgia!" But of course they—and the critics—are indulging in a bit of that insider snobbery that automatically derides slumming movie stars. My Julia does fairly well in Act I, and she probably comes off remote and glacial because her *character* is remote and glacial, OK? But in Act II, where she gets to do more capital-A Acting, she sadly fails to convince, leaving you with the overwhelming sense that she's a great movie star. At intermission, I heard people talking about the really important things: "She's huge! She's even taller than Cate Blanchett!" "She's actually not that tall," Tatum O'Neal assured me in another row. "She just looks tall. She's so pretty!"

Hugh Panaro is awfully sweet looking as the lead in *Aida*,

I mean I *Bite Her*, I mean *Lestatic*, I mean *Lestat*—the Elton John musical that's way gayer than the Tom Cruise version and is generally not as rotten as some had hoped. It has some style and soaring melodies, though admittedly too many of them are showstoppers that stop the show for the wrong reason, and the lyrics tend to be overly explanatory ("The thirst—I feel it coming on") or downright absurd ("See me, wolf killer!"). It's brave that they show Lestat escaping a disaster in New Orleans. But a friend summed up the main problem with Lestat: "It spans 300 years, but it still seems slow!"

Teri Hatcher is sweet and other disturbing possibilities

May 23, 2006

The best line heard at Duvet recently: "What did I promise you again—a blowjob or a palm reading?" The most memorable utterance heard at Beige: "Is Happy Valley still good? I haven't been there since a creature with tits and a penis sucked a whiskey bottle into her ass." The most choice comment at Happy Valley, as a drunken girl was being dragged out by security: "It must be because she's wearing a tube top." The juiciest nugget played by the Cuckoo Club DJ, John John Field: a set-to-music version of those crazed phone messages left by Faye Dunaway for a TV biography show producer, fuming that she doesn't want to be interviewed about Terry O'Neill ("a big, big liar"), Andrew Lloyd Webber ("a terrible person and everyone knows it"), or *Mommie Dearest* ("a stupid cult movie"), but instead wants positive things emphasized, like her artsy, barely seen movies with Depp and Brando ("I was brilliant in it," she admits of one such chestnut—and she was "wonderful" in the other). "I'm really fed up," Faye whimpers at the climax, threatening a lawsuit. (Fantastic, Faye. Sheer hate has never been so dance-able, so keep spewing, baby.)

The *second* best communication, according to sources, had Jared Paul Stern asking the *Post*'s managing editor last week about when he can come back and start working on the next Page Six magazine. (The answer: "The 12th of Never"?) The most heartwarming press release from porn guy/self-promoter Michael Lucas had him rekindling with ex-hustler Rupert Everett at the Cuckoo Club. (Hmm. I wonder who paid whom?) The oddest line emitted outside the Cock by someone trying to avoid the whopping three-dollar cover charge: "Don't you know who I am?" The most flattering experience ever at Rawhide: Two weeks ago, the doorman wouldn't let me in because I didn't have ID showing I'm of legal age! The most astute interpretation of the new *X-Men* movie, which deals with an attempt to normalize the mutants: It's a giant metaphor for the ex-gay movement! And the most gay-straight-whatever scene of the week: Club queen Susanne Bartch invited her zany tits-and-a-penis crowd to see a performance by Cedar Lake, the dance company run by the controversial yet cultured Wal-Mart heiress. I haven't seen such a mixture of drag queens, dancers, and department store execs in one room since I went to see Martha Stewart promote her blue-light special at Kmart.

The best celebrity run-in happened outside Cain, which is like a Carnival cruise filled with Applebee's customers. There, perpetual charmer Esai Morales—whom I'd love to give a palm reading to—told me he got fed up with being signed to a big agency, where you get lost in the shuffle.

"This lady here is changing my life," said Morales (*NYPD Blue*, *La Bamba*), pointing to a blonde sporting a frozen smile. "I'm her only client," he added, exultantly. The woman started glaring at him, as if to say, "Put a lid on it, dude," and he promptly did so and moved on. See—you can't *get* that kind of attention with a big agency.

A more wanton broad became the star attraction over at XL's *Faggoty Feud* game when the MC, Trai La Trash, dragged up the only biological woman in the place and grilled her about her sexual preferences. When the busty gal declared that licking guys' butts is her all-time favorite activity, the place erupted into five minutes of hooting and cheering. It takes so little to make the gays happy.

Heading uptown to respectability, I kissed Teri Hatcher's impeccable ass at Gilles Mendel's party at Bergdorf Goodman for Hatcher's happiness manifesto *Burnt Toast*. First, I had to shimmy past the crush of labeled ladies who were forming human crop circles around the *Desperate Housewives* star just to get a peek. "She's so sweet!" cooed an employee who was going to try to introduce me. "How disappointing," I deadpanned. "No, it's refreshing!" she oozed. Whatever the case, she couldn't get Hatcher's attention, so I chatted up the star's stylist, who unsurprisingly gushed, "She's very confident and wears clothes well. She's a stylist's dream." "And she's so sweet!" repeated the employee, who then slipped away and left me totally adrift. (I guess the sweetness wasn't contagious.)

Fortunately the stylist made the introduction, and Hatcher turned out to be . . . well, so sweet. "Has anyone mistakenly thought Burnt Toast was a cookbook?" I wondered, cutely. "Only Liz Smith," Hatcher said, laughing. Whatever the book is, does it mean Hatcher's horning in on my territory? "I should only be so lucky," she said, correctly. "But I've always written. I wrote an episode of Lois & Clark. I wanted to be able to give women tips for how to live their lives, and I'm grateful Desperate Housewives has given me the exposure to do it. If I didn't have that, no one would take me seriously." And speaking of that colossus of camp programming: Has anything on the show shocked the absolute bejesus out of her? "I was surprised that Gabrielle [Eva Longoria's character] got away with sleeping with an underage boy," Hatcher admitted. "That's a sensitive issue in our culture. We seem to attack a lot of men for going after teenage girls. I was surprised the writers let that slide. I'm not suggesting she should have gone to jail, but the storyline dropped and it's a serious issue." Great answer—and even though I then dove lustily on a piece of chicken, I can assure you it was just an hors d'oeuvre.

Another Man's Poseidon

On the big screen, very young disaster queen Emmy Rossum ran from chunks of hail in The Day After Tomorrow and from bad music in Phantom of the Opera, and now she's got water in her lungs in Poseidon, the remake about an ocean liner turned topsy-turvy by a "rogue wave" or maybe just an upsidedown camera. Just like the original version, this one introduces a bunch of starlets, B actors, and Oscar winners (well, one Oscar winner—Richard Dreyfuss), then makes them battle the waves while tying up their messy personal problems. It's like a Carnival cruise filled with Applebee's customers. There's about 10 minutes of backstory, and then the water becomes the star, destroying some good sense in its path, though it's interesting to see Dreyfuss play a gay architect with a diamond ear stud who's been dumped by his lover and has decided to end his life with $5,000 bottles of champagne. Sad? Pathetic? Maybe, but at least unlike so many screen gays he *had* a lover.

(By the way, *United 93* probably would have been a hit if they'd only gone for the kitschy, all-star, Irwin Allen approach, with a romantic subplot and a lounge singer. Nah, maybe not.)

Staying in the wet zone, every critic clobbered Julia Roberts's dual-role performance in *Three Days of Rain*, many rhapsodizing about how much better the admittedly fab Patricia Clarkson was or must have been in '97. But I did some research and it turns out Peter Marks's *Times* review back then said Clarkson was effective in Act I, "but less convincing" in the second half. So there. (P.S.: I wouldn't be surprised if Julia signs on to the movie version; stage actors whore out for Hollywood all the time.)

In other Broadway news, someone on "All That Chat" heard that Judy Kaye might follow Patti Lupone in *Sweeney Todd*. A gorgeous choice—but can Kaye play a tuba? Meanwhile, a certain new leading man with his own lovely instrument has reportedly been sleeping his way through Broadway—well, *half* of Broadway, namely the male half. "Gay guys are so hot!" as Katie Holmes exclaimed in *Go*.

You Can Call Me Al

I'm hotter than Faye Dunaway's breath these days—if I can
steer the conversation back to myself—but while I get recognized all the time, unfortunately it's not always for being
Mikeypoo. (Don't you know who I am?) Thanks to my neb-
ulously nebbishy face, panting folks have been convinced
I'm either Al Franken, Eugene Levy, Michael Richards, Tony
Kushner, Elvis Costello, or the guy from NY1. A woman was
near tears last year as she told me what *Caroline, or Change*
meant to her, and the more I assured her I didn't write it, the
more she was convinced I was either a painfully shy genius
or a shameless liar. Others have absolutely adored me in
projects ranging from *Seinfeld* to *American Pie*, despite my
shrieking protestations that I've never even seen those
things, let alone been in them. By the time a scary guy was
chasing me down the street and squealing, "Mr. Franken!" I
just went along with it so as not to disappoint one more
person (and to not get killed). "Yes!" I said, still running,
"that's me!" But when the freak *kept* chasing me, begging for
an autograph, I demurred, not thrilled at the prospect of
forging Franken's name. "You asshole!" he shouted. "I tried
calling in on your radio show and I couldn't get through—
and now you won't even give me a fucking autograph? You
suck shit!" Sorry, Al, you now have one less fan—but he was
rather psychotic anyway. Now everyone leave me alone. I'm
really fed up.

The Legend of
Miss Baltimore Crabs?

April 14, 2006

The kooks are cocky and cooing at the Cuckoo Club, Sundays at the Maritime's Hiro Ballroom. The other night there, a lovely young man with no shirt and the hint of an ass crack sticking out said he was a major porn star named Josh and he was thrilled to meet a "famous actor" like me. We bonded and posed for photos—I adore hobnobbing with other cognoscenti—and then he introduced me to his "husband," gushing that the guy had just purchased him a really expensive car. Honey, we all need a deeply appreciative spouse like that. I reached out my withered hand to greet the hubby/daddy, but the lovin' ended when he threw me a fishy look and whinnied, "You've written so many mean things about me!" "That's how I show love," I tried unsuccessfully before grabbing my clutch and crawling under a table.

Well, based on my research, the guy turned out to be Adam Shankman, who directed *Cheaper by the Dozen 2* and who's helming the new movie of *Hairspray*! (He also, interestingly enough, played the washerwoman in a TV version of *The Wind* in the *Willows*. Yes, imdb.com fills in all holes.) Anyway, I was left in the lurch as the porn star lovingly straddled Shankman on a banquette, and they made a big spectacle of deep tonguing each other, only occasionally interrupted by Vegas star Joey Arias gamely grabbing at them both. (You can't stop the beat.) And then they were off—no doubt in a really expensive car. That's not a mean write-up, it's just the truth—and by the way, it's the first time I've ever mentioned Shankman!

Farther downtown, Bank—the Saturday-night bash at Element—has become so popular there isn't even room to straddle your porn star boyfriend. The last time I went, the dance floor was more packed than Clay Aiken's hookups' anuses. The balcony was as tight as the Queen Mother's vagina. And even the downstairs lounge rooms were more crowded than Ricky Martin's throat (when he's eating a supersized Cuban sandwich, I mean). After a while, you couldn't even get near the bar to buy a soda, let alone grab a free one, and for this little washerwoman, that spelled panic attack. But in the distance, you could sort of hear the live entertainment—a woman with a frizzy wig who belted out Spanish versions of dance hits by Kylie Minogue and Katrina and the Waves. Ay, caramba.

By the way, I don't just haunt penis-filled nightclubs—I also go to Broadway shows about incest and pedophilia. But my heart sank when I realized that *Festen* was adapted from that Danish movie *The Celebration*, which mixed TV-movie potboiler dramatics—child abuse! interracial love! a note from the deceased!—into an overheated stew posing as avant-garde drama. Fortunately, the play is hypnotically directed and works better than the film, sustaining a nicely creepy mood, especially in the silences and eerie, faraway kiddie laughs. Critics have eviscerated Ali Macgraw's performance, but I thought her awkwardness worked perfectly for the part of the ever smiling, monstrous enabler. Then again, I liked Sofia Coppola in *The Godfather III*.

Turn the Page?

Kiddie sexual abuse is hinted at in *The Notorious Bettie Page*, which has great period detail, a lovely performance by Gretchen Mol, and lots of naughty posing, though it adds up to more of an extended photo shoot than a psychologically compelling drama. They've failed to come up with much of a story around the '50s pinup's controversial rise. Basically, Page comes off as a nice, mishandled girl who's asked to model. She does so. She's asked to take if off. She says sure. She's asked to do bondage. She says great. Oy! Yes, there's the crackdown trial, plus her religious awakening, but otherwise, it's her life that seems to have been bound and gagged here.

At the premiere party at, appropriately, B.E.D., I asked director/co-writer Mary Harron if today's conservative assault on porn is the biggest one yet. "Nothing could be worse than the '50s crackdown," she said, "because porn was scarier and not as familiar then. But porn is the biggest moneymaking industry, so for people to get moralistic when everyone's on the Internet is all show." For her next show, Harron wants to do a punk movie about CBGB, though she said, "It's always a battle to get a film made." More immediately, she was planning to return the gorgeous Dolce &

Gabbana dress she borrowed for the premiere, "and then I turn back into a Brooklyn housewife!"

Let me turn back into a raging queen with a blood-soaked ax to grind, if not a pricey car to escape in. As you know, the troubled Q Television Network recently gave queers a bad name by laying people off and owing shitloads of gay money all around (including to me). Well, they've had a corporate overhaul, but a knowledgeable source tells me, "The new president has no TV experience. They're just making the same mistakes over again. It's probably just going to fizzle away. They've done such damage to the brand, I can't imagine anyone would ever take them seriously again." That's so true, but while the sad sacks are trying to rise out of the scum bucket, let's please take the following inside jizz *very* seriously: I hear one of the network's on-air personalities is having a lesbian affair with one of its "straight," married-with-kids senior executives! They should film *that*.

In other sexual entertainment news, I was just interviewed for a documentary about the notorious Paris Hilton that promises to be her *Truth or Dare*, maybe even with the same Chihuahua. It's backed by Warner Bros. and authorized by Paris (who's fully cooperating), but it looks to be balanced, and she even curses in it! That one will never be bound and gagged.

Stern und Drang

Last week, I ungagged myself to give commentary on a TV news show—no, not about how Britney and her baby are now *both* brain dead. It was about—what else?—the Jared

Paul Stern scandal, which I said will have to prompt a purge "for there to be a light at the end of the tunnel and everyone to be able to dish more ethically." "Did you just hear him say 'dish more ethically'?" the anchor remarked, smirking, before her costars erupted into giggles. (And then they went on to a really urgent story about TomKat's "silent birth.")

Hey, freaks, why is the prospect of ethical dishing such a joke? Has gossip become such a cesspool of conflicts that the Stern hoo-ha is just the tip of the insidious iceberg? Don't answer that! Believe me, I know the industry I'm part of is partly a subtly tangled mess of paybacks and backstabbing. But I don't think it's that laughable to say that this particular situation can be used to help flush out the bad stuff and emerge with (free-food-filled) heads held high. We columnists can do so in the following ways:

(1) Never think a publicist is your friend. They're actually the enemy. We strive for truth, they usually aim to subvert it. (2) Still, let's call for the other side of the story. Even if flacks are generally paid to lie, let's try to include their BS in the item just for equality's sake. (3) Fuck favors. When I hear someone say "I need you to do me a favor," I turn into Naomi Campbell. (Of course, if I want to call a plug about myself into a column, I'm still allowed to do so, in my most tremulous, pleading tones.) (4) Don't dis blogs as inaccurate when your own column (or tabloid) happens to be more fictional than a Bush war excuse or an Oprah book of the month. (5) Please realize that anonymous or unnamed sources generally have an agenda. I knew that when I quoted that person about QTN,

but I put it in anyway because I have an agenda, too. (And the source isn't anonymous to me.) (6) Go ahead, go on junkets and free tastings if you're hungry and they're approved by your paper. Just trash them in print afterward. That's what I do, belch. (7) Quit with the endless plugs for that Italian guy's restaurant and that horrorhouse publicist. You may have inked a deal with the devil stating you will gush about them through eternity, but readers signed on to no such agreement. (8) The rival dailies that have reveled in this story so gleefully should probably step back for a little self-reflection. In the *Daily News'* case, their biggest scoop ever only happened because of the *Post!* And in the *Times*, all the articles on Stern's fuckup are second only in length to their corrections page. Wow, that was cathartic. Cigarette?

The devil wears diapers

June 13, 2006

The first big fright at the premiere of *The Omen* came when I noticed that the seat behind me had a sign saying "Liza Minnelli Guest." I thought it meant she was still married to that creepy guy! Thankfully, I calmed down after realizing the key word was spelled differently. Moments later, Liza showed up with her Gest, I mean guest—a radio-host twink named Jason Drew—and revved into her best Liza mode, acting as effusive and agreeable as if she were on *Larry King Live*. Someone in my row asked Liza if she planned to be afraid. "I have a protector!" Liza responded, chirpily. "He's my best friend!" She meant her guest. "We'll be under the chair in five minutes," the guest whimpered, not all that protectively. "But it's not like *The Exorcist*," assured Liza, adding many consonants. "*The Exshorshist* was shhhhcary!"

Another jolt happened when Griffin Dunne came running up to Liza and said his daughter recently sang "Maybe This Time" in school, but she coughed on the last note. "I did that, too!" comforted Liza. "Tell her I think it's kosher!" (Her sudden

Yiddishism may have been because the premiere was in a former synagogue—long story—which at one point prompted Liza to cutely exclaim, "I'm in a shynagogue?") By the time Liza was calling Mia Farrow over and vowing undying love, all I could think of was that Jackie Susann wanted them both to star in the tawdrily fabulous movie of *Valley of the Dolls*! Imagine Liza playing Neely, the part based on her mother—a singer-actress who loses roles because she's a druggy mess—while Mama herself played opposite her as Helen Lawson until losing the role because she was a druggy mess? Alas, it was neither kosher nor meant to be.

But back to this camp classic—a sleek bunch of hooey about a kiddie Antichrist, which really stretches credulity since *The Da Vinci Code* says there wasn't even a Christ, let alone an anti. As the darling demon seed causes suicides, beheadings, and doggy discomfort, no one does anything about it, even with Pete Postlethwaite's tremulous, overacting priest screaming over the thunder, "He must die!" Daddy Liev Schreiber finally jumps to action, and as he does so, you see a totally not-gratuitous product placement of a KFC sign! Now *that's* scary.

At the din-din after the movie (which wasn't fast food), Cynthia Rowley wisecracked, "I'm gonna go home and shave the kids' heads."

I was terrified all over again when a screening notice for *Strangers With Candy* asked reviewers who plan to abbreviate the movie's name if they could please just call it *Strangers*, not *Candy*. That's because the same company has a Heath Ledger film coming out called *Candy* and would rather not have any kooky confusion around it. I'm just going to call it *With*. Or maybe "alternately hilarious and flat." Or maybe "four-alarm migraine," since I waited forever at the film's NewFest party for AMY SEDARIS to show up and she didn't. No, I worship the woman, and I'm sure she was just busy taking off her prosthetic teeth.

At the same fest, everyone showed for *Another Gay Movie*, Todd Stephens's very funny gay spoof of teen sex romps, which I insist on calling *American Quiche* (or maybe just *Gay*). It's refreshingly crass, from the carrot fucking to the spoof of the prom scene in *Carrie* with cum instead of pigs' blood. Porn star Matthew Rush cameos as an OD'ing drug bunny, and survivor Richard Hatch shows up to get naked and stick his face in the underweared butt of a guy who's had three enemas and who calls his friend to gloat, "I'm about to get anal from a million-dollar bear!" After the movie, Stephens said Hatch was his "dream of a cheesy reality TV celebrity. I thought, 'What would it be like to finally see his penis?' I asked him if he'd show it. He said, 'Fuck yeah. I'd love to.'" And fortunately it was sizable enough to not get voted off the island.

I wittily asked Stephens if the million-dollar bear paid tax on his income from the movie. "The $250? Yes," he said, laughing. "Actually, he wanted to wear a cap that said 'Fuck the IRS,' but I thought that whole thing would blow over by the time the movie came out." But now that Hatch is jail-bound, it's *he* who will either get fucked or blown over.

Survivors of A.D.D. lined up for the Golden Trailer awards—given to movie trailers, not mobile homes—which started with host Jim Gaffigan saying, "I've never heard of me either," and got even giddier as it went along, a *Beer League* star accepting Trashiest Trailer just because the real winners (for some skanky epic called *Three*) had done a Sedaris and not shown up. "I'm too big for this," deadpanned presenter Rich Vos. "I've got to go to the Ringtone awards."

A slice with extra sausage

And I had to get to a shynagogue, I mean to Fire Island, even though Fleet Week had just ended and boy was my butt sore. Alas, the slushie machines weren't even filled yet, and there was hardly a single tick-infested deer (or gay) in sight, let alone licking your face. I guess the queens were busy waxing their pubes and alphabetizing their Madonna remixes. Still, it wasn't hard to locate the usual overhanging cloud of relentless sexual innuendo just by glancing at the community bulletin boards. A pizza-eating contest at the Ice Palace came with the slogan "How fast can you swallow?" (Not very, it turned out; the competition dragged—and you had to buy the slice to enter!) And one of the big theater events being promoted had the guy who sang "Boom Boom Boom (Let's Go Back to My Room)" costarring in some three-enema romp called *Two Boys in a Bed on a Cold Winter's Night*. Actually, after a Broadway season of overdressed British drama, that sounds exactly like my cup of jizz. I'll swallow it quickly.

Back on the mainland, the nights seem hotter now that Bailey Bartsch Barton—the son of party queen Susanne Bartsch and gym titan David Barton—just got his first love letter. From a girl. And he's not repulsed. "I guess he's straight," Bartsch told me over the din at Happy Valley. Oh, dear Antichrist! What went wrong? (Kidding. Straights are people, too. Except in the White House—though I must say Dubya does stand for change: changing history to blame Iraq for 9-11 and changing the Constitution to stop gay marriage!)

While we're talking sexuality talk, Egan Elledge was one of the biggies at the late, unlamented QTV, which screwed tons of people (like me) out of oodles of money. Well, insult has just been added to gay injury. Ex–Q personality Jack E. Jett says Elledge recently contacted him to try to get his name off the imdb.com credits for Q's old *Queer Edge* show! (Elledge refused comment when I asked him about this.) Elledge told Jett he feels that some people in the biz aren't cool with gay credits, and I guess he wants to do whatever it takes to fudge things (or un-fudge things) and secure his next job. "Our number one concern is to help Egan get a gig," says Jett, wryly. Meanwhile, ex–Page Sixer Jared Paul Stern is staying on the offensive, as it were. He tells me by e-mail, "Ron Burkle and the *Daily News* are both completely full of crap and they'll find they've made some very costly mistakes in launching this ridiculous smear campaign. Burkle will have to crawl back down his diamond-paved hole and stick to being Bill Clinton's fluffer. If there's any justice at all, he'll end up with his old pal Anthony Pellicano in jail. And even the mouth-breathing morons who buy the *Daily News* will find out just what a sack of shit it really is." Rather than ask if he prefers the *Post*, which fired him, I deleted the e-mail, shaking. That was shhhhcary!

A heck of a Heckie

But let's end with some cockle warming and—for those who found my *Valley of the Dolls* section too au courant—a little education: Eileen Heckart was a brilliant stage-movie-TV actor who filled her acerbic roles with layers of humanity, most notably in life and as the mother of three sons, including theater guy Luke Yankee. Well, Yankee's memoir of Mama, *Just Outside the Spotlight*, is a multihankie Heckie-thon that's one of the most compassionate and illuminating showbiz books ever written. There are gossip flashes—Lucille Ball and Mary Pickford as nasty drunks—along with dizzying opening nights and offbeat confrontations, but mostly you come away with the portrait of a towering talent, with an allergy to BS, giving a master class in life—complete with some very challenging assignments—to her awestruck son (who probably has a birthmark of the Ticketmaster number on his head). It's a privilege to be privy to it. End of shinsherity.

Mel Gibson
hates the gays, Too!

August 7, 2006

Mel Gibson looked terrific in his mug shot—not just because plugs are much easier to control than actual hair, but because, though he had just been drunkenly screaming epithets at uniformed law keepers, he cagily remembered to gently smile for the camera. What a star! The resulting photo is reminiscent of that last image of Norman Bates in *Psycho*, where he's eerily grinning in the police station, with the corpse's teeth superimposed on him, as you hear his alter ego think, "I wouldn't hurt a Jew," I mean "fly."

But while the photo wasn't that messy, Mel's initial claim that he isn't anti-Semitic, he was just drunk, definitely was. I had no idea that an open bar is all it takes to turn Mother Teresa into a hair-plugged Hitler. My aunt the nun had better stay off the sacramental wine or she might end up grabbing a rifle and mowing down children in the nearest ghetto. We'd *all* better lay off the booze or, at perfectly sophisticated dinners, we'll suddenly find ourselves singing "Tomorrow Belongs to Me" with right arms extended. That could be embarrassing.

Mel's excuse prompted a friend of mine to snicker, "Well, he must have been plastered when he made *The Passion of the Christ!*" And he must be shooting down doubles because, let's remember, his filmography also reads like a laundry list of big-budget slaps in the *gay* face. There was his icky spoof of a flaming hairdresser in *Bird on a Wire*; his draining all the gayness out of the tender *The Man Without a Face*; the controversial Prince Edward II character, whose lover was thrown from the castle, in *Braveheart*; and of course the mincingly buffoonish Jesus baiter Herod Antipas in *Passion*. (He wasn't portrayed like that in the Gospels—in fact, he was a rabid womanizer—which tends to deflate Mel's Jews-killed-Christ defense: "But that's what it said in the Bible!")

What's more—as is now legend—when a 1992 interviewer asked what Mel thinks of gay men, the star pointed to his rear end and elegantly replied, "They take it up the ass. This is only for taking a shit." (No, in Mel's case, that would be the *facial* orifice.) In the same delightful quiz session, Gibson revealed that he had worked with gays at acting school, and "they were good people, kind. I like them. But their thing is not my thing." In fact, he remembered freaking that people might think he was one of them—but magnanimously enough, "I became an actor despite that." And the world breathed a huge sigh of relief! "But it would be hard to take me for someone like that," Mel added, perhaps sardonically. "Do I sound like a homosexual? Do I talk like them? Do I move like them? What happens is when you're an actor, they stick that label on you." No, they stick the label *homophobe*, you friggin' anti-Semite. (Update: Poetically enough,

199

in the upcoming movie *Under and Alone*, Mel gets to play a character named Billy Queen. At least he isn't Billy Queenowitz.)

Mercifully, Mel will be undergoing sensitivity training—which reminds me that in 1997, he did some gay penance by working with GLAAD and allowing queer filmmakers on the set of *Conspiracy Theory* for a seminar. They must have been thrilled to get to know his paranoid-nutjob car-driving personality—in the movie, that is.

Feta Accompli

At a press dinner at Geoffrey Zakarian's Country restaurant in the Carlton Hotel, a guest claimed that *GQ* is dropping Mel as their man of the year, and Zakarian quipped, "They should make it Manishewitz of the year." Some of us then expressed empathy for Mel's publicist, Alan Nierob—who's reportedly the son of Holocaust survivors—though there's a feeling Mel has calculatedly used Nierob's Jewishness to soften his own blows. And Nierob, turning this into a "fighting for his life" issue for Mel—along with a "source close to the Oscar winner" telling a reporter that Mel was suicidal because he was "helpless to alcohol"—verges uncomfortably on more blame-game spin. It makes Mel the victim—much like Jim McGreevey's "Throughout my life, I have grappled with my own identity" speech—recasting an unsavory wrongdoer as a deeply ethical person who's poignantly struggling and finding himself utterly "helpless" (though admittedly Mel has sought help in the past—for his boozing, anyway).

With each apology, though, Mel's gotten a little closer to a full disclosure. "It's like playing Operation," Zakarian cracked.

But let me get back to that dinner, where I was absolutely helpless to Diet Coke—with a wickedly corrupting lemon wedge! As we enjoyed Zakarian's "arpeggio of feta cheese," the restaurateur moaned that golfers used to dress much snazzier, before Lee Trevino changed everything into "an elastic orgasm of crap." I was suddenly tempted to point to my gay butt and exclaim, "That's what this is for!"

Counting Quos

Culture is coming out of everyone else's. Nightlife legend Fred Rothbell-Mista has launched a plucky quarterly pullout magazine called *No Status Quo*, featuring—among many other things—an interview with rock icon Richard Hell, who gets queasy when asked if he's bisexual or still does drugs. Either way, he'd be a perfect *No Status Quo* reader. Exults Rothbell-Mista, "I want left-wingers, right-wingers, drug addicts, everything. There's no target audience because that's what ruins magazines. We have no target anything!" That way your demographic can't possibly desert you.

In music, the downtown kids seem to have one thing on the brain—or in the mouth. To wit, Rainblo's song "East Village Cocksuckers" is a hard-driving ode to metaphorical pipe smokers. Cazwell's "All Over My Face" is a rap-happy dance tune about, you guessed it, the squirting powers of the devil's penis. And Kenny Kenny's "Stiletto Kickback" is a danceable romp about fetishy footwear, though he tells me, "It's not overtly 'stick it in my pussy.' It's very me, very androgynous. I'm effeminate, but I have a deep voice." (He does? Then I guess he'll never get in a Mel Gibson Bible movie.)

At Happy Valley, I swatted off an admirer three weeks in a row, only to learn he's the guy who was just bumped from *Project Runway* for being a total cheat. Now I desperately want him back.

But back to the bigotry. In a broadway.com piece, the incorrigible John Simon rails against "show queens" who he says have bad taste and laugh too hard and stand and cheer too easily (though he graciously concedes that they support the theater and occasionally like something he feels "worthy"). Can't wait for his article on "show blacks" who encourage Oprah musicals or "show Jews" who start wars at the concession stand.

A member of Lord knows how many minority groups, the *Times* critic turned NPR reporter Elvis Mitchell was recently nominated for "hottest gay journalist in New York" by a blog named Left Behinds. "You know what they say about the length of a man's dreads?" was their teaser for Mitchell (who lost to current *Times* man Patrick Healy). "But is he even gay?" some voters wondered. I don't know; he never sucked my dick.

In the movies, it's the year of the sad, pathetic gay who's dumped by the boyfriend and ends up feeling so suicidal he wouldn't mind being thrown from a castle—by himself. *Poseidon, The Night Listener,* and *Little Miss Sunshine* all have just such characters—but at least some of them eventually rally in a way even little miss Christie Brinkley could learn from.

Of course being "that way" myself means I'm capricious, malicious, wear eye makeup, and can now return to some other irrelevant comments about mouthy Mel: Don't you love how the celebrity showdown on the subject has basically amounted to Rob Schneider vs. Jackie Mason? (And you thought they were the same person.) Why on earth are Jodie Foster and John Travolta so vehemently defending a homophobe? When Mel threatened the officer with, "I'll fuck you," was the old truth serum arousing his real feelings once again? Does his lethal weapon have hair plugs, too? And don't you think that female sergeant will get over her hurt feelings in time to start hawking her "sugar tits" to *Playboy*? Sorry, I didn't mean to say any of those things. I just drank another Diet Coke with lemon.

YOU SAY POP CULTURE HORROR, I SAY FEATURE STORY

Nudge, nudge,
Tinky Winky

February 23, 1999

Here's a first: I'm totally aligned with the Reverend Jerry Falwell! I thoroughly agree with the guy that Tinky Winky is a Pansy Wansy—we only seem to differ on what to *make* of this information. While Jerry's convinced that the Teletubby's supposed gayness is a menace to society, I feel it teaches kids the welcome lesson that it takes all types to make up the world, from purple, flouncy moppets to blue-in-the-face windbags.

Incredibly enough, I may be indirectly responsible for Falwell's remarks that Tinky is a cuddly receptacle for Satan. Early in '98, I told *Entertainment Weekly*, only half tongue-in-cheek, that Tinky's seemingly homosexual ebullience provides a great message to the impressionable—"not only that it's okay to be gay, but the importance of being well-accessorized." The comment went relatively unnoticed, but in their year-end issue, *TV Guide* gave it a bizarre "Jeer" that even raised GLAAD's ire, and this was apparently one of the media moments that spurred Falwell into his all-too-predictable blatherings. Never mind that press discussions about this subject started way back in '97 when the show debuted in the UK. And forget that Falwell actually thought what *TV Guide* had printed was an interview with the *Teletubbies'* creators, in which they unveiled their elaborate plot to perpetrate a gay kiddie character. (That's how Falwell's office explained his motivations to a toy store's publicist, as the flack later informed me.) Logic and real information go right out the window when you're dealing with this level of invective. Whether he's missed the bus or is just plain at the wrong station, Jerry simply has to vent.

And typically, he did so without much backup, readily admitting that he's never even seen *Teletubbies*. (Funny, it's designed for his intellectual peer group—and it's the only show on PBS that is.) "I believe that role-modeling the gay lifestyle is damaging to the moral lives of children," Jerry told the press, clearly nervous that, years from now, all those 'Tubbies watchers will robotically choose anal penetration as a result of their babyhood viewing practices. Alas, Jerry's off on some of the details. In his esteemed *National Liberty Journal*, he wrote that Tinky's purple skin tone is the color of gay pride, "and his antenna is shaped like a triangle—the gay pride symbol." Pardon my rainbow, but I seem to remember that lavender is more of an out shade, and a pink triangle is actually the symbol—though I may be betraying my own Martha Stewart-loving sisterhood here. It doesn't really matter anyway, since there are enough other queer signifiers to justify Falwell's gay panic. Tinky carries a patent-leather handbag, prances around in a tutu, and does pretty much all the same things that I do. He's so gay, in fact, that he verges on a stereotype—he's as flaming as Richard Simmons, Bert, Ernie, and one of those kids on *Barney* combined. (Come on, *you* know which one.)

But Falwell should probably relax (just as a whole other bunch of idiots recently had to when they realized that one of the Teletubby dolls was actually *not* saying "faggot"). Beyond those superficial traits, Tinky couldn't possibly get any action, since he has no orifices in the right places. The corporate types behind Tinky and his pals are probably sincere when they emphasize the character's conspicuous lack of sexual organs or drive. It's absurd, though, that they haven't at least copped to his effeminacy—are they even *less* astute than Falwell? In the course of last week's media mayhem, a damage-controlling rep for the *'Tubbies'* American licenser made a point of announcing that Tinky's alleged purse is actually a magic bag. (A fascinating distinction—I guess Boy George can pull a rabbit out of his Prada.) Another spokesperson repeatedly used words like *sweet, innocent,* and *harmless* in defending the program's lack of gay content—the implication being, of course, that a gay character would be full of danger and blasphemy. A much higher-road approach would have been to say: "Yes, Tinky seems gay to some people, and that's fine. Femmes should be loved, too—if they weren't, we'd have to ban *Hollywood Squares*—and if a dwarf in a fuzzy suit who doesn't even speak intelligibly is all it takes to 'warp' a child, there must be real trouble in trailer land."

But despite all the spin control, I can't be all that mad at the *Teletubbies* team. Unlike Falwell, I've actually watched the show and happen to enjoy the characters' diversity, their warmth, and the way they giggle under that big baby sun (though I could stand to hear "Again!" a few times less often). I even carry a Teletubbies handbag, though it's not a patent-leather one, and it's definitely not magical. What's more, I'm fairly confident that the Sexgate-era masses—who for the most part have rejected the ambush against Clinton's consensual sex acts—are way too sophisticated to heed Falwell's maligning message. These kneepad-sporting swingers have had their earplugs in ever since Jerry urged sponsors to abandon *Ellen*, and more recently, they shoved in some extra swabs when he said the Antichrist is a male Jew who currently lives among us. (Who—Buddy Hackett?) By now, when we hear this putrid hot-air balloon spewing about some imaginary evil, most of us have learned to respond: Again? Again?

Those Lips, Those Eyes: Michael Jackson's weird evasions

December 2, 2003

Rude comments about the state of Michael Jackson's face don't exactly raise the level of discourse, but come on, when that mug shot hit the news, you had to stop and shriek a little. Had Jacko spent the entire flight to Santa Barbara playing around with his M.A.C. products? (Or maybe the eyeliner and lip color are permanently tattooed—yeah, in fact, I'm pretty sure I read that somewhere.) Did he—desperate to avoid a Nick Nolte—end up uncannily echoing the pleading eyes and near grimacing mouth of that other alleged child abuser, Joan Crawford? And how 'bout that nose, huh?

But wait a Neverland minute! We need to separate the blusher from the bullshit. I'm terrified that we may be turning into a tabloid version of Brandon Teena's lynchers, making merciless fun of any celebrity's gender nonconformity or fashion extremism. I of all people shouldn't be casting stones, having spent my entire adult life celebrating drag queens, freaks, and kooks (though most of them are openly gay and the worst thing any of them has ever done to

211

a kid is scream, "Sit down!" at a birthday party). Are we all just afraid to accept a female-bloused Cat in the Hat who simply provides a playland of wonderment and life lessons to needy little ones? Maybe we need to decide if Jackson's giving drag queens a bad name or people are giving him a bad name because he's a drag queen.

But—end of compassionate sidebar—back to the lip jokes, all right? It's way more fun to ick-ify Jacko, and besides, it's not too hard to argue that his cosmetics (and cosmetic surgery) are less self-expression than cover-up. Our collective "eew" can be justified—after all, this guy hasn't been straight with us! Any remaining fans I knew lost faith when Jacko bought off his last accuser in '94 because he didn't want to bother with a trial. ("Extortion!" he cried, then promptly paid up.) Since then, even when coming off completely out of it, Jacko's often reeked of sheer calculation, from getting various women to farm out babies for him to dangle, to bizarrely thanking Britney Spears for the Artist of the Millennium award on the VMAs when all she'd offered was a piece of birthday cake. Jacko marches so loudly to his own arrested-development drum that no one was surprised when he turned up as an ick-tegral part of Liza and David's wedding party last year. (These people all shill for each other's dysfunctions. They're—this feels so good—*freeeaks!*) Worst of all, he loves children—but mainly if they're drop-dead gorgeous, and in some cases even ready to drop dead.

Yes, Jackson's aggressively weird, and inspiringly enough, this has united a nation in political disarray! His excesses bond us against a collective enemy—he's much more popular to attack than Iraq—while fueling our desperate desire for the charges to be true. No, we're not rooting for anyone to have been molested, but we want Jackson to be the repository of all our fears so we can agree on something, send him away, and bring on the sunshine. We couldn't get Rosie or Martha to melt—and we can't even find bin Laden or Hussein—but if Jacko would just agree to be a pedophile, we could have our kook and eat him, too.

The trouble is that no one else has exactly been behaving with any restraint or dignity either. For all his insistence that he's not making this into a vendetta, D.A. Tom Sneddon Jr. has been grinning like a rat with a ham hock. Sneddon's smug press conference last Wednesday inappropriately started with a jokey tone and a plug for Santa Barbara commerce and went on to spew a little too much bluster, which was undercut by Sneddon begging anyone else who'd been molested by Jacko to please come forward and help the case.

Even less credibly, the level of around-the-clock "experts" wrapping their unlicensed pop psychology around the subject quickly became thinner than those pained ruby lips. Alternating squeals of "He had no childhood!" and "How can these families leave their children with him?" (this from the same pundits trying to make a living off his name) proved as obvious as a Chanel top with Peter Pan hair. One cable channel proudly featured a Jackson family friend who'd brought his two girls to Neverland and said they absolutely loved it. Yeah, well, they're *girls*. Another one had the usual array of chattering heads, under which absurdly flashed the fun fact, "Michael Jackson once dated Brooke Shields." (So he *does* like girls? This *was* getting shocking.)

And the Jacko camp was sending out its minions, convicted sexual assaulter Rick James damagingly coming to the singer's defense and brother Jermaine making his usual rounds, coming off a little like he'd be at home on Christopher Street himself. In his brief Barbara Walters interview, jaunty Jermaine cried racism, invoked the power of his family (which *my* crazy ass thought was the most dysfunctional one in pop history), and even suggested that the cops may have planted evidence. With OJ, we had to at least wait for the evidence before people were accused of planting it. The persecution of superstar sociopaths is happening faster and faster these days!

Things reached an even more feverish pitch when I got a press release from a child sex-abuse expert who feels Jacko should submit to "a penile plethysmograph"—a device that measures your sexual arousal patterns to various pervy scenarios. All righty, who wants to be the one to hook up the plethysmograph?

Eventually, some cleansing truths will flush out all the murk, but until Bonnie Fuller outs the cancer kid (which at least one Brit tab has already done, in addition to breaking the love-letter scoop that gave us twisted hope), we're only left with more trash-minded questions. Like, if the kid ends up detailing Michael's penis on the stand, couldn't the defense argue that he might have just read all that in the book about Michael's *other* molestation charges? (Not that I've read the epic work nine times. It's circumcised, with very little pubic hair, and pink and brown patches on the testicles.) And when the *Daily News* outlined the secret passageway to Jacko's kiddie stay-over room, were we sick to relish lines like, "In the back of Michael's closet, there's a hidden door"?

And psst, how 'bout that freakin' schnoz?

Alien vs. predator:
The sickening
McGreevey scandal

August 24, 2004

I'm a gay American—applause, applause—so I've been especially mesmerized by McGreevey-gate, the most sweeping allegory about the dangers of the closet since David Gest was allegedly brutalized by flying pieces of Halston furniture. By his own admission, New Jersey governor Jim McGreevey has been a poster child for duplicity, finally forced by a legal wake-up call to come clean while wearing a patterned red tie that would have outed him anyway.

The gay revelation was a momentous event that, sadly, could have only happened out of shame, not pride. Even more so than showbiz closets, political ones are generally so airtight that it takes flat-out blackmail (or at least a possible sexual harassment suit) to fling them open and a smoking butt to keep them that way. The days when a married pol announces "Yep, I'm gay" just because he feels like it are as far away as Michael Jackson begging the FBI to chaperone his next date.

Still, even if only because he had to, the wandering-eyed

Jerseyite spoke out and did so with enough rising-against-oppression authority to make you feel, yep, he must be gay. In his August 12 speech saying he'll step down into Garden State ignominy, McGreevey seemed as dignified as his administration was unpopular and as well-intentioned as his reign was called corrupt, failing to register as any kind of stereotypical gay psycho killer or colorist. At least that's how it all seemed at first. When the pixie dust cleared, it became more obvious that the Drumthwacket-eer had played the lavender card and blinded us to the fact that he'd apparently put gayroll on the payroll and used taxpayer money to fund dubious jobs for what was basically a glorified trick, whether real or imagined. "Sexually confused" is what the press first came away with, all misty-eyed, but by the next day they were thinking "jaw-droppingly sleazy," and that hasn't helped the gay cause any more than McGreevey's last scandal helped fundraisers-don't-hire-prosties-to-entrap-their-brother-in-law awareness.

In his statement, McGreevey insistently portrayed himself as a survivor of hormonal bewilderment, not a gleefully flaming queen who's been cruising for a bruising for years between dutiful ribbon-cutting appearances with the wife. He looked heart-tuggingly contrite as he declared, "It was wrong. It was foolish. It was inexcusable." What, his marriage? No, he meant cheating on his marriage, though he neglected to add that it was with a not unattractive, overage rent boy/underqualified employee whose only apparent terror advising was in advising himself to be a terror when scorned. Adding fuel to the flaming-queen flames, the guy,

Golan Cipel, then swore he was the victim of predatory advances and horny vindictiveness, and by the way he isn't gay, no matter how close he lives to Don't Tell Mama! (Not that it matters if people call him gay, blah blah blah.) By the time that item leaked, there was more confusion and blame flying around than in the *Queer as Folk* episode where Justin discovered that Brian didn't go to Ibiza.

I'm not buying into theories that the guy (who's straight, by the way) must be some kind of soigné Mossad spy, but I am still amazed by Golan's heights of nerve. His accusations, seemingly right out of Gore Vidal's dirty-politics drama *The Best Man*, couldn't come at a better time for Republicans, who, led by gaydar-activating Christie Todd Whitman herself, are demanding that McGreevey step down immediately, presumably so one of their own illustrious, sexually unconfused ranks can get voted into the job.

And speaking of confusion, the biggest shocker of all is that McGreevey's gay-gay-gay revelation has somehow spelled unemployment for him but so far not anything resembling marital termination. In fact, right after the admission, the scandalized politico and his missus went away for some quality time together. Where-to the Fire Island "Meat Rack"? What's it gonna take to break up this arrangement? The whole point of a fake marriage, people, is to keep it going only until people find out it's fake. And you certainly wrap it up when the wife finds out it's fake!

But—someone's gotta say this—Dina's no dummy and he's no genius of discretion. She had to have known! Everyone else, from reporters to Web posters, had buzzed about the supposed liaison for years, so how could she not have gotten the memo? Despite the anonymous source running around claiming that Arianna, I mean Dina, was homo-clueless, I bet the McGreeveys have a de-lovely, we-know-what-it's-about situation and enjoy sharing a home base, even more so when power is tasted. Did you see wifey's face at the press conference? This was no Mrs. Kobe Bryant-type squirmer. The woman almost looked proud! She practically seemed at peace with his having gotten a piece! Maybe this is the marriage of the future-one completely open in its duplicity.

Lord knows McGreevey's first wife, Kari Schutz, seems to know the score. Last week, the *New York Times* asked Schutz if she knew before their divorce that McGreevey was gay, and she tellingly replied, "I'll leave it at that." But funny, the next day, when the *New York Post* and the *Daily News* trotted out the very same question, she shrieked, "I didn't know!" Clearly, Schutz had been visited by the same checkbook-wielding angel who contacted Kevin Federline's suddenly ecstatic dumped girlfriend.

McGreevey can take comfort in the fact that he's no more alone in his double life than Scott Peterson is the only guy with a murdered pregnant wife. Public figures are constantly driven into surreptitious love by the way society's underlying disapproval of gays fuels their own self-doubts. In fact, the same day "I am a gay American" became the hottest catchphrase since "Shove it!," the California Supreme Court routinely invalidated 4,000 or so marriages. The hilarious result is that Rosie O'Donnell is now living in sin, but McGreevey's marriage to his beard stands by law! (That's good news for him, since he's possibly sticking with it.) Adding yet more ironic texture, McGreevey himself helped fuel this very climate by arguing against gay marriage (though he did sign Jersey's Domestic Partnership Act). I guess hypocrisy is not the exclusive domain of the Giuliani-Gingrich-Limbaugh-Ryan-etc., party after all.

And sex scandals, as we know by now, are not the exclusive domain of any group. When it comes to the proverbial casting couch, the effect is always corrosive, whether the couch is from Seaman's or Ikea. Deliciously enough, on the very page after its McGreevey story last Friday, the *Post* reported that Bronx state senator Efrain Gonzalez had given a longtime gal pal a cushy job. (Obviously Golan Cipel wasn't available—probably busy launching the inevitable handbag line.) Well, unless Gonzalez gives a weepy "I am a straight American" speech and steps down in shame very soon, I'm moving to Canada.

With all these lurid layers wrapped around the McGreevey story like a Dolce & Gabbana suit, the gay pundits are having a foofy field day. Reaction has been impassioned and mixed, from out Massachusetts congressman Barney Frank (who survived his own escort scandal in '89) welcoming the closet flinging to Chelsea bar patrons pontificating over sour apple martinis, "I never realized McGreevey was so cute!" (Or that Cipel was so straight.)

Choire Sicha, the gawker.com blogger-turned-overseer, told me he loved the spectacle of Anderson Cooper and Shepard Smith having to roll around in the story on camera. But what does the whole squalid soap opera represent? "You can read it really traditionally," said Sicha. "This is why J. Edgar Hoover used to say the CIA wouldn't let gays in. They could use it to blackmail you!" Especially if you're fully gowned like Hoover. But just as traditional was McGreevey's claim to have had an affair with one man. "Like, oh right," smirked Sicha. "A man this week."

Conversely, author-Barneys creative director Simon Doonan feels McGreevey was too forthcoming. "With his wife standing there," Doonan told me, "he could have at least said, 'I'm bisexual.' It really elbowed her out of the picture big time, which made him seem a bit less than charitable. Gay people are usually a little sweeter than that."

Charitable gay person Michelangelo Signorile—the godfather of outing and a talk show host on Sirius Satellite Radio's OutQ—has his own problems with all the McGrievances in the air. "What I hate," he told me, "is that in every one of these stories, there's always an evil queen doing something horrible." Or two evil queens? "Well, there are several possible scenarios here," he offered. "One could be that Cipel is telling the truth and he just wanted to work and McGreevey started harassing him. I've written about harassment—it's so typical of closet cases.

"Or it could be the complete opposite, where Cipel's been extorting McGreevey from the get-go. How do we know his jobs were not based on maybe one sexual romp in Israel and the next morning this nut says, 'I have pictures of this. I want a job'? The reality is probably somewhere in the middle."

Either way, the upshot is that the carefully chosen words

"I am a gay American" have been resonating beyond all the pulp-fiction details of the story. "A lot of people will find sympathy with that," says Signorile. "People are beginning to distinguish between the fact that he's gay and these other issues. In that sense, it's a good thing."

And you certainly have to find sympathy with the fact that, as of last Friday, channels were still showing the suddenly riotous commercial for New Jersey tourism that has McGreevey and his family cavorting on a beach (no, not in Fire Island) as the shark-mouthed gov urges, "Come out and see what's new in Jersey." Thanks, honey, but I came out and I'm staying right here.

Pope springs eternal
—but why?

April 7, 2005

I'm surely going straight to hell if I say anything critical of the late pope John Paul II, but according to him, I was heading there in a handbasket anyway, so what the fuck. The truth is I am a bit fed-up with the wall-to-wall lionization of this man, who admittedly brought inspiration and faith to millions, but who also propagated some ancient, reactionary viewpoints that—just my humble fag opinion here—fanned the flames of widespread oppression, all in the name of God's will. Not since Ronald Reagan's death last year—when the prez became painted as a forceful, flawless leader, with nary a reference to his callous, longtime refusal to acknowledge AIDS deaths— has there been such a wacky whitewash of someone's controversial canon. This time around, all the cable channel phonies—few of whom have been known to live lives of quiet piety, especially the gays—took on a nauseatingly hushed, reverent tone as they indulged themselves in nonstop slobbering over the icon they exclusively portrayed as noble, divine, and even well-accessorized.

As evidenced by the overwhelming response to his passing, the guy surely tapped into the hopes and dreams of loving throngs around the world, all fighting for hotel rooms in Rome. But as I've clicked the channels for days on end, I haven't heard a single person question the "man of the people"'s rabid anti-abortion stance, his aggressive anti-condom platform, or his intense demonization of gay marriage as "a new ideology of evil, perhaps insidious and hidden, which attempts to pit human rights against the family and against man." Of course maybe someone's death might not seem like the right time to say, "He furthered sexual guilt, disease spreading, and hate crimes," but actually, when there's exhaustive, weeks-long coverage of a man's life, what better time could there be? (At least a pundit on an ABC special did note that the pope may have disliked democracy as much as he hated Communism.)

The reality is that, as the world—and even the church—started inching forward and becoming more accepting, John Paul II tried to hold things together with a moral vise that often proved intolerant and unrealistic. As women gained more control over their bodies and gays developed some rights of their own, he was frantic to push down the progress by promoting absolute respect for human life, except for individualists and "deviants." This was no shock—religion has traditionally specialized in messages of love that double as tools of persecution, and fanatics have always picked sections of the Bible at random to oppress unpopular people, while ignoring other parts that might put a damper on their own fun.

Just recently, Christian, Jewish, and Muslim leaders all got together to denounce the upcoming Jerusalem WorldPride march and to agree on one thing—gays suck. The protest was an eye-popping reminder that so many of the different gods people pray to seem to have the very same queers-are-the-devil message. Even these groups' usual distaste for each other was effectively buried as they united in fear of the common gay enemy.

As a shameless queen myself, I was brought up on strict Catholicism but strayed after brilliantly sensing I wasn't that welcome in my own religion. Not only did the ruler-wielding nuns seem scarier than the flames of hell, but the church clearly wanted me to stay and be terrorized only if I'd admit I was a sinner and grovel for forgiveness. Given a choice between "immoral" nightclubs where people shrieked, "Girlfriend! You look fabulous!" and a place of worship where everyone snarled, "Heal your soul!" I chose the clubs and haven't looked back since.

John Paul couldn't have been too upset about losing one more messy miscreant. A 2003 document issued by the Vatican reminded the world that "homosexual acts go against the natural moral law." (So what, I always wondered, should someone growing up with gay feelings do? Get electroshock treatments? Become a priest? Or simply be honest about them and live as a papal disgrace?) The report compassionately took pains to add that "allowing children to be adopted by persons living in such unions would actually mean doing violence to these children." This from the church that silently condoned abuse of children for centuries.

The beloved pope was also dead set against the use of condoms to curb disease and unwanted pregnancy. After all, that would be acknowledging that humans actually have sex. Instead, the pontiff stood for the loftier goals of abstinence and/or marital monogamy, the kind of family values that, when preached too fervently, often result in scandal headlines. To further this no-nooky agenda, the church has long promoted the idea that condoms can cause disease more than they prevent it! Yes, listen to the Vatican and you'll believe that scumbags are inherently unsafe (gee, so is pushing abstinence or monogamy) and they actually encourage promiscuity (though the more scientific-minded tend to recognize that condoms don't cause sex any more than a coat brings on the cold).

To the pope so mourned on cable, any kind of contraception was an absolute no-no because it blocks children, as if the world is somehow lacking in people. (And if condoms don't work anyway, then what's the problem?) You'll recall that his recent book went so far as to equate abortion with the Holocaust because both are supposedly a result of usurping the law of God. So an indigent woman who considers aborting an unaffordable baby (which, let's say, exists because Mama wasn't able to use condoms, and has AIDS for the same reason) was suddenly Satan *and* Hitler combined.

And then there was the pedophilia-in-the-church scandal, which blew up in 2002 after decades of hush money payoffs and the transferring of accused child molesters to different parishes the way you'd move a rotting vegetable from the fridge to the freezer. The priesthood has long been a place for ashamed gays to hide (along with the truly devoted). In the old days, you usually couldn't make your Catholic family proud by coming out, but you certainly could do so by stuffing your sexuality, marrying God, and becoming a man of the cloth. The church loved the deception, too—so much so that it turned a blind eye to the twisted intergenerational acts these self-loathing closet cases perpetrated while abusing their power. When it all finally exploded, the media erupted in GLAAD-protested reports that gleefully equated gay with evil, triumphantly playing right into the church's long-held theory that homos are bad people.

I'm certainly not rejoicing that the pope has passed on— I'm not a big fan of human suffering and death, even if it brings one closer to God. Still, it's hard to forget that John Paul's love of society's fringe characters always had a big but attached. You know, we care for PWAs, but they're in this predicament because they're sinners. We denounce gay bashing, but—according to official doctrine—"the proper reaction to crimes committed against homosexual persons should not be to claim that the homosexual condition is not disordered." Oh, yeah? Well, I think a lot of your moral decrees were disordered, O holy Father. I certainly loved you for the sanctity and uplift I kept hoping I could turn to you for. But. . . .

Death of the Dumb Blond: Why peroxide rot is, like, officially over

November 15, 2005

The biggest pop-cultural message of the aughties so far is that smart people bizarrely worship dumb blonds. With the communications explosion bringing savvy to every household, you can't necessarily feel smarter than the person next to you, but you *can* enjoy intellectual superiority to a bevy of bimbos and himbos with dark roots instead of gray matter—ding-dongs with a burning taste for fame but no idea whatsoever how to live off-camera (which works out fine because thanks to reality TV, they never *are* off-camera). Watching these entertaining dull tools act out in relation to their low self-esteem has become a sadistic feel-good experience that has us cheering on the golden-chunked desperation while gleefully handing out more Clairol.

This is nothing new. In the darker recesses of our culture's consciousness, dumb and blond have always equaled messy, malleable, sexy, and guilt-free. Dumb blonds of both sexes will pleasure you in the backseat and never look up. They'll let the video of the encounter slip out and feel certain it'll help your career, too. They might not even wince when you return their lost wallet, all emptied out. (It was Daddy's dough anyway.) No wonder this phenomenon is tawdrily timeless.

But the recent craving for DBs has been so extra-voracious that even some natural blonds have managed to become popular. Millions become aroused watching platinum petunias fall out of limos and onto booze-stained red carpets, while others delight in sitting back and clucking, "There but for the grace of God go . . . aye, aye, aye!" Either way, the dummies win, writhing on to even greater ditzy glory and better salons.

Why now? Partly because women have come so far that the inevitable backlash has men anxious to see them take a giant step in reverse (even if they're making millions in doing so). Meanwhile, women can feel less envious of successful beauties when these idols are barely able to stand up without puking through their nose jobs. As the ladies get a firmer stronghold on showbiz, the biz responds with, "Fine—as long as we can go back to representing you as hapless and hopeless," and the jaundiced audience approves and enables.

But now the dimwits are dumbing themselves out of the picture, jumping the shark without even knowing what that means. The backlash has suffered a backlash. A surfeit of pesky peroxide addicts who had face-lifts at age 12 and turned their abortions into handbags has made things so oppressively dumb-tastic that Charlize Theron has to wear boils and a modified babushka to elevate herself from the tragically superficial morass into respectability (though ever a trouper, she bravely still sports luscious blond locks).

I swear on my obsolete Uggs that dumb blonds are, like, officially over. It's just not cute anymore to watch people who, thanks to raging insecurity issues, insist on being both stick-thin (because they want to look "good") and camera-hoggingly self-humiliating. The spectacle of boobs popping out, drug dribble leaking out, and vaginas *wearing* out, all in the name of career advancement, was extremely amusing for a while, but everyone's too smart to stand by and applaud this sideshow any longer, especially if they can't get close enough to grab some.

The last time I saw Paris
Come on, someone please lock Paris Hilton up ASAP—get her to a nunnery! Admittedly I'm a fan; the heir-head's blank-slate quality allows millions to project whatever feelings they want onto her, which has allowed her to soar in every medium imaginable. (Even her book—written without her ever having read one—has gone into multiple printings.) Paris is actually quite slick on talk shows, rising above bad situations with surprising aplomb. But her messy behavior, stemming from an inbred sense of entitlement, has long been tiresome. Paris peaked when she had the nation searching for her missing chihuahua, only to realize she'd left it with Grandma. (But where she left Grandma, no one knows.) When she and blond co-star Nicole Richie screwed up *The Simple Life* shootings with a tiny, little hitch— they weren't talking to one another—you wanted to yell, "Wake up, dingbats! It's all pretend anyway—just speak!" But now I feel that for my sanity's sake, neither should ever

speak again. (By the way, their feud is second in dumb-blond hall of shameness only to Courtney Love heckling Pamela Anderson at the latter's roast, which may have been a battle of wits with an unarmed opponent.)

Gossipeuse Liz Smith tells me she thinks Paris is a cipher, but still a wildly popular one. "I think the power of the old Hilton name has a lot to do with it," she said, "and that is interesting to me because I began working for society columnist Cholly Knickerbocker back in the day when Hilton still meant something. Times change, but the snob appeal of a lost social climate endures."

Page Six pooh-bah Richard Johnson agrees that Paris still has it, saying of the blond brigade, "I don't think they're so dumb—here we are talking about them—and they aren't truly blond either. You've got to give them credit. Paris looked great for Halloween in a white garter belt. I guess she was a hooker, or a stripper." She must have left her neuro-surgeon costume at Granny's house.

But this cycle has to end before the blond hair falls out and reveals pinheads. In fact, it's definitely all-aboard time for the blond reality-show survivors, who should start busing it to one of those New Jersey autograph conventions, along with the fake blind man from the diabetes commer-cial and the guy who played Chewbacca.

Clawing her way out of the wreckage, Britney Spears was brave enough to let her trailery antics subvert her singing career (says Liz, "Britney can stage a comeback—if she is not required to speak"), while fellow pop princess Jessica

Simpson, says Richard Johnson, "is starting to tick people off because she's a liar, pretending to be happily married to Nick, and getting paid by OK! as some kind of career move." Telling too much has steeped the blonds in irreversible shit and so has blatant BS'ing, and as a result, the only sensible blond way to go—I *repeat*—is racing toward the Garden State with stripped-down boobs and a clenched mouth.

Of course the high-water mark in low living was set by Brit's and Jess's predecess-pool Anna Nicole Smith, who staged a comeback by giddily falling apart in public while gamely eyeing the gold. (Quips Liz, "Anna Nicole is a simple girl who accepts the old anatomy-is-destiny proverb. As long as about $500 million is attached to it.") She's dumb as a fox—a nouveau Marilyn Monroe, but more death-resistant—and tons of fun, though she's in for an awakening if she thinks mattress humping and corpse shtupping are soul-fulfilling talents with a future. (Wacky sidebar: I once asked Anna Nicole for her views on feminism and she widened her eyes and replied, "What is that? I never knew what that was.")

Whether these gals are really dumb or just faking it like their last orgasm, they've managed to rise to the top while finding an angel standing there with a giant baseball bat, ready to slam them over their rinsed heads. Even a smart blond like Martha Stewart slipped off the brain wagon when she felt she was above the law and—even worse—when she started overexposing herself with dueling TV shows. (No, I won't leave out all the other smart blonds just to prove my thesis. There's Amy Poehler, Ellen DeGeneres, Meryl Streep, and also . . . um, er, um . . . never mind.)

Bombs make for bombshells

Movie blonds are especially popular during wartime, balmy bombshells inevitably lifting spirits and raising flags. The more the casualties escalate, the better the career chances are for golden-tressed sirens with parted hair and lips. Back in the '40s, Veronica Lake was a sultry icon with sophisticated bangs and a tart mouth; Lana Turner was so shrewd she survived her boyfriend's death by her own, I mean her daughter's, hand; and Marlene Dietrich was a smart woman *and* a brilliant man.

But so many of today's blond dummies are only that—windup wildcats with no *there* there. They've given us relief from the Iraq situation, but only in the way a malapropian clown takes you away from the meat of a Shakespeare play. (Dumb-blond response: What's a Shakespeare play? I never knew what that was.) For example, Cameron Diaz is a winning actor, but *In Her Shoes* was a box office momentum killer, and offscreen she spends too much time fighting the press about her past or her blond boyfriend Justin Timberlake's present. Once, I asked her if she'd wear cum in her hair to a certain awards ceremony (admittedly a dumb question). "We'll see," she replied, even more weirdly.

Hollywood's pampered princesses rarely fail to annoy, but even the squeaky-*cute* kids end up jumping into the fame vortex, checking their minds at the gift bag counter, and falling apart while saying "Cheese!" The blood-red carpet is littered with the memories of Lindsay Lohan's wicked ways, the Olsen twins' bony, homeless chic, and all the other flaws that plague the prematurely processed and eagerly overexposed. And let's not forget Tara "I'm an Actress" Reid, who fought the press about her party image, then signed on to host an international party and travelogue show. "People are fed up with Tara," concedes Richard Johnson, "but that's probably only because she put on weight, became a lush, and lost her hotness." It's a tough world that allows you to be a skinny drunk, but not a puffy wannabe recoverer. No wonder the blonds are self-destructing for our nightly delectation.

At least some guys are keeping the gals company at the (un-)happy hour, particularly Brad Pitt, who humiliated his main course by moving in with an overbaked tomato, and Harlow-haired Eminem, whose cheesy family battles and bitter fights with both Moby and a hand puppet proved him to be the kind of wimp-ass extraordinaire he would normally beat up.

But the backlash culminated when Camilla Parker Bowles (the "other woman" in frump's clothing) dove onto America last week to curry favor with winged hair, and one realized that ill-advised blondness knows no nationality or social rank. Camilla's acceptance-craving visit provoked a multitude of yawns, cementing the fact that blond is officially as over as a Times Square hooker heading to an outlaw party.

The next step? A rising up of the cultured blonds (Patricia Clarkson) and an embracing of the sane ones (Nicollette Sheridan, Jenna Jameson), but mostly, an appreciation for people who aren't afraid to lay off the bottle.

TWITTER AND BE GAY

Act up! Fight back!
Book a hotel!

October 25, 1988

The long D.C. AIDS weekend boiled down to a choice between crying or screaming, looking back or looking ahead. These tacks weren't mutually exclusive—you could conceivably grieve over the quilt and then be inspired to demand that the government stop that symbol of mass tragedy from growing—but for the most part the two moods seemed as separate as the quilt's panels, which are all joined together, but very distinct.

The quilt reflects love and grief, expressed in a painstaking and personal way. Its value is awesome—we must never let this crisis make us so callous that we don't continually stop and remember the individuals, one by one. But there should be a warning sticker on it: "Don't feel that by crying over this, you've really done something for AIDS." A lot of mourners seem to think that catharting over the quilt is the best they can do. That's also partly true of some media, which avoid-like-the-plague detailed analyses of AIDS issues (there wasn't nearly enough New York paper press on the

237

FDA saga), but cover the quilt at length. "How sad," they tsk-tsk, attracted by the maudlin quality they can wring out of it, and by the big-name celebs sometimes involved in the viewings. (One of these celebs, Susan Sarandon, recently went to an ACT UP meeting, but no major star has yet participated in one of their actions.)

The quilt—a tragic national celeb in itself, with its own tours, even its own "Making of the Quilt" play—can't be allowed to become too much of a religion about which we can only quietly sob. It can't be misinterpreted as a wet blanket, a sop to soak in our sorrow and let us blithely go on. Grief isn't the only answer. D.C. quilt viewers were reminded of this by ACT UP fliers urging them to "turn the power of the quilt into *action*" against the government that's helped make it possible.

Some activists' anger has been directed at NAMES's Cleve Jones, the quilt's organizer, for often saying that, though he hopes the project has political impact, it was not intended as a partisan political statement. Sorry, guy, but whether it was intended that way or not, it is, *has* to be, because AIDS is by necessity a political issue. So is being gay, black, an IV-drug user, or a prostitute. Our leaders' lack of urgency in dealing with the disease is a political, not medical, issue, and every death by AIDS has been encouraged by their homophobia, racism, and fill-in-the-hatred.

Since Reagan has only shed clouds on the crisis—ignoring it for years, then assembling advisers whose recommendations he still disregards—the only practical response is furor. Bush says he gets so depressed when he sees people "wringing their hands" about AIDS and other problems that it makes him "want to switch over and see *Jake and The Fatman*"—typical of our do-nothing government's inability to deal. Maybe if the Fatman got AIDS, then George would give a shit.

Jones probably can't openly make too many outrageous political statements for fear of antagonizing potential backers or visitors. "It's semantics," he told me. "We're organized as a nonprofit community arts organization, but we seek to be a catalyst for action." Still, the pressure to overtly politicize seems to be shaking all that up a bit. Saturday in D.C., Jones was quoted as saying that history will record "that our nation's failure was based on ignorance, prejudice, greed, and fear not within the heartland of America, but within the Oval Office and the halls of Congress." He also put in a coded plug for the angry demos that were about to happen. After that, even the most quilt-dubious ACT UP member refused to say a word against it.

Other battles bubbled under, and above, the surface that long weekend, typified by the driver who recklessly tried to ride through—or over—ACT NOW's Department of Health and Human Services rally. (Amazingly, the cops chose to chastise the ralliers who beat back the car, instead of the driver.) Even among the activist groups, there were differences in approach. The ACT NOW rally, for example, featured a courtroom dramedy—replete with drag characters, a rabble-rousing speech by Vito Russo, and lots of shtick—in which Reagan was unconditionally proclaimed guilty of murder. This show-biz angle had at least one ACT UP member running around saying, "Why are they doing a fun show in front of an empty building? They don't see this as an emergency. This is so '70s-gay. And why are they doing a nuclear song? They're aligning themselves with too many other causes." ACT UP, of course, got to storm the FDA the next day with its own show.

Divisions or not, come the pre-FDA demo meetings, the mood was as high as backstage before a high school sing. "I'm not into crystals. I'm not spiritual. But you're totally beautiful," gushed facilitator Maria Maggenti, addressing ACT UP NY. "Everyone here loves everyone. We should love each other because it's great!" They hugged and kissed; very few stopped to cry.

Tuesday, ACT UP/ACT NOW all came together, and nothing else mattered. Some 1200 people screamed outside the Rockville, Maryland, FDA site ("It's a lie, it's a sham, it won't work"), held signs ("Time Isn't The Only Thing The FDA Is Killing"; "FDA—Fucking Disaster Area"), and enacted events of civil disobedience, each stunt as rehearsed and accessorized as any Royal Shakespeare production. On the sidelines, a media person called out to reporters, "We have someone who's dying to do an interview with you . . . living to do an interview with you." Some yards away, a Reagan effigy was strung up on a flagpole. When the wind blew its pants off, dozens seized the chance to yell, "Reagan's been caught with his pants down" and "Look, he has no balls."

The unsmiling cops, wearing gloves that didn't match their shoes, tried hard not to arrest too many people (they got 176, but more were willing, to make this a better story), inspiring the event's tag line, "Who do you have to fuck to get arrested around here?" A 67-year-old Texas widow named Sylvia Ayres, meanwhile, *was* arrested in some crazy mix-up and became a media star, demanding that "these beautiful kids" get their drugs.

Delta Queens, Tell Me Why, and other united-in-outrage affinity groups marched and chanted all day, blocking traffic, demanding the testing and release of specific AIDS drugs, and preventing FDA workers from coming in to perform "business as usual." Many wily workers had gotten into the building anyway by showing up before 7 A.M., but after that, the only ones on the list were ACT UP members who broke in and put up "Silence = Death" signs. For hours at a time, the workers stood motionless by their windows, watching and hearing the message—"We die, you do nothing."

Dear Pat Buckley:
Kindly eat caca

November 14, 1989

A message to Pat Buckley:

I don't scoff at the money you've helped raise in the fight against AIDS. I applaud efforts to gather funds for a cause that desperately needs them. But for every dollar you raise, your husband sets the fight against the disease back a long, long time. A monetary statistic can't erase the damage done by a man who stews in hate against people who are already suffering— a man who wants to brand them as lepers who've conspired in their own demise. A man who recently wondered in his syndicated column why he didn't read more editorials saying, "Why in the name of God did this dope addict or this sex-driven gay take such chances as he now suffers the consequences of?" That damage has no price tag attached to it. I know a lot of PWAs who will probably never enjoy the benefits of the money you've helped elicit, but feel the brunt of your husband's hatred every time they're shunted, blamed, or persecuted by the neglect his biases contribute to.

Pat, just by calling yourself Mrs. William F. Buckley, you're fueling his fire. Some would say your actions automatically distance you from him, but everyone knows there are all kinds of reasons for doing charity work. I hope your reason is wanting to battle the darker, less rational ideas on the subject, like those espoused by your husband, not just the bad press they've engendered. If so, I'd like to hear it from your own lips.

I'd also like to know whether you understand that money is not the real issue of AIDS. The real issue is the discrimination against people with the disease, which must be overcome or there won't *be* money, medicine, and support. The real problems are prejudice, contempt, and the compulsion to judge those who deserve compassion, not bigotry. You can locate and research all these things within your own household, Pat. Remember, charity begins at home.

You had a chance to assert your distance from your husband's views when *Newsday*'s Jim Revson called to get your feelings on a critique of those views (and the media's perpetuation of the Buckley name) by *OutWeek*'s Michelangelo Signorile. Your comment? "I will not address this." Earlier, your response to a friend about this columnist's admittedly excessive but strongly felt attacks was a sadly inarticulate, "Ignore it."

Ignore it, Pat? Ignore your husband's proposed tattooing of PWAs? Ignore his repeated insinuations that PWAs bring the disease on themselves and, in fact, may well deserve it?

This is 1989. A woman can have views that conflict with her husband's and even (gasp) express them. Do you shrug off your (presumed) disagreement with him the way you'd shrug off an argument over what color paper towels you buy or what movie you see?

Barbara Bush openly disagrees with George on gun control. But still, you stand by Bill in stupefying silence. You're even slated to go with him to a masquerade ball on World AIDS Day—that'll be some party.

Even more telling are Revson's actions after he gave you the chance to speak out against AIDS-related hatred and you chose not to take it: he buckled in to the Buckleys, fed the hand that bites, and ended up lauding you anyway. You have quite a hold on the media. Why don't you use it to do some greater good (as ACT UP tried to do by hanging banners on the Buckley agenda across from your "Skating for Life" benefit)?

I feel for you, Pat. You say you care about PWAs, yet you're married to a man who must find that view anathema. But you're allowing your husband's outrages to become even more real. Until you speak out, every time you're mentioned in a column for having a luncheon or losing your luggage, you're adding luster to *his* name. You've done some positive work and are mobilizing wealthy friends to start caring—with their wallets at least. But if you stood up to the deeper issues you could make a *real* difference. Keep raising money, Pat, but how about talking to your worse half (and the press) and raising some consciousness, too?

The AIDS era:
life during wartime

July 31, 1990

These are the times we live in. Times of depression, denial, frustration, and compulsive nail-biting. In between the good deeds you didn't know you were capable of, you're split by three emotions that never let you rest easy: mourning, worry, and rage. You're mad at it, at them, at yourself, and ultimately at the world. You want to turn time back or forward—wriggle your nose and be transported to another century, another planet where there's no such thing as AIDS, never was, and never will be, not even in the most diabolical imagination. Mortality—which you never really thought would catch up with you or your friends—confronts you every day, as you wake up and realize that AIDS is still out there, still looming, still destroying with its silent, invisible assaults.

Your biggest problem used to be a routine rent increase or the closing of the nearest dry cleaners, but now it's a marathon race from something a millionth your size that could be waiting to attack your motor skills, your memory, your sight, your breathing, and every other function you never used to give a second, or even first, thought to. You start wondering if something you did 10 years ago that you didn't really want to do anyway might end up killing you. Just in case, you vow to live every day to the fullest, as the cliché goes, but that's impossible with the rough sketch of a 24-hour-a-day guillotine dangling over your head. You can only live life to the fullest when you're not trying to, when you don't have to.

You start to have self-conscious fun, anxious amusement. Every second is laced with an undercurrent of uneasiness you want to deny, but it keeps grabbing you by the neck, pushing you against the wall, and reminding you it's still there, still menacing. There are moments when you actually forget that the disease exists and you go back to the relatively angst-free complacence of late-'70s–early-'80s hedonism. Then you come across the word in a newspaper, on TV, or on the phone, and it starts choking you again, even tighter. It always seems to come back twice as defiant, twice as imperturbable.

You get mad at cab drivers, then realize you're not mad at them, you're mad at AIDS. You shower in the dark so you won't see anything—or won't imagine anything. You hate yourself for being so stupid. You start getting religious. You almost engage in a "probably safe" activity and then spend six months wondering just how *almost* and how *probably* safe it was. You never used to think of sex as a transaction. You contemplate marrying the person.

You remember when it was called "gay cancer" and might have been caused by poppers. You remember when they said 10 percent of those with the virus came down with the disease.

You remember thinking you were in the clear if you hadn't had sex in three years. You remember when Rock Hudson was the first famous person to die of AIDS. Since then there have been Liberace, Michael Bennett, Wayland Flowers, Sylvester, Way Bandy, Charles Ludlam, Perry Ellis, Willi Smith, Peter Hujar, Antonio, Amanda Blake, Robert Mapplethorpe, Seth Allen, Cookie Mueller, Ian Charleson, Keith Haring, Halston, Ryan White, and even some whose families claim were killed by brain tumors or rare bone diseases. And there are people who still say it isn't an important enough problem. They avoid the word—on death certificates, in conversations, in the media—but the word won't go away. You're bored with it, mad at it, terrified of it—but it *won't go away.*

You run into someone you haven't seen in a year and think, "He's aging terribly," then you realize: he has it. You fight the impulse to prematurely mourn sick friends—to treat them as if they're dead. You become so callous from grief overload you don't even flinch as you learn someone else has come down with the disease, or tested positive. The absurdity of the situation has numbed your emotional reflexes into a deep chill. You can sit down with a pen and paper and in 10 minutes come up with 100 names of people you knew who are gone. It used to be 25 names, then 50. Soon it'll be 200. You force yourself to remember that those were people—full-fledged individuals with far-reaching lives—not just notches on a morbid belt. You're almost glad to hear that someone's died in a car accident or from a heart attack. "Natural causes" has become the most welcome phrase in the lexicon. Gradually, AIDS bulldozes closer, as it takes distant role models, then friends of friends, then friends. People talk about how it's a more treatable disease now, and days later someone else dies. You want to shoot it—throttle the virus with your bare hands until it knows what pain is and goes away. You want to yell at it, talk sense to it, blow it up, make it run far from this place.

You never used to know about anything remotely medical, but now you're conversant in endless details about drugs, treatments, machines, and procedures. Words like *seroconversion*, T-cells, and *immunodeficiency* have become staples of everyday conversation. You could be a doctor. You *should* have been a doctor. You debate taking the test. If you have it, is it better to know and do something about it or not to know at all? Knowledge is power, of course, but at this moment it's not nearly as powerful as HIV.

You watch some of your gay male friends shack up with girlfriends and talk about how deep down they always knew they were straight. You watch the rest become not only open, but vocal, defiant, and filled with a fury that's sometimes misguided, but always hurtles sincerely from the knots in their stomachs. You're angry, too, because the disease has tapped into so much hatred and prejudice it's become a tool to further bludgeon the suffering. Your God wants compassion, not persecution. Your God wouldn't use disease as a punishing tool.

With awe, you watch people shirk off the negativity because there's no time for it and fight the disease with hope and courage. You applaud those who combat fear and panic with rationality. You follow those who loudly inform the government that it's betrayed us and that it must correct its mistakes before anyone else has to die. You treasure those who live with AIDS—not just survive with it, but live with it. You admire those who give time and money to AIDS charities that try to make a difference. You laud those who volunteer, who seek answers, who aren't afraid of the truth because they're searching for a greater truth, who fight for their right to information, dignity, and good health. You ACT UP. You fight back. You fight AIDS.

Rosie's b.s. isn't cutie patootie

March 18, 1997

First off, let me say, blah blah blah, that Rosie O'Donnell's daytime talk show is generally hilarious and watchable, and Rosie's a bubbly, fun personality worth tuning in to. But the girl's self-denying attempts to be embraced by the American heartland are becoming a bit excessive, and someone's gotta pipe up already.

There was her on-air pooh-poohing of Marilyn Manson, a demonizing so intense I could have sworn I was watching Rush Limbaugh's show. There was the time she tried to "in" Richard Simmons, freaking when guest Kathy Kinney dared to be unashamedly honest. And there are those supposedly mirthful attempts to convince us that Tom Cruise is her boyfriend, a travesty she even pulled as a guest star on *Suddenly Susan!*

But the sickest thing of all is the way the media's letting Rosie get away with this shtick in a self-appointed goodwill mission that's actually quite twisted and hypocritical. Out of a misguided love for their new hero, a conspiracy of silence has taken over the journalistic world, with everyone blindly parroting the Cruise stuff and covering up everything else.

It's one thing for the Queen of Nice to think being gay is an unmentionable horror, but does every single media outlet in America have to agree with her? It's been downright comical to see magazine after magazine (except for the tabloids) tripping over each other, writing long-winded treatises about Rosie without a single reference to her romantic life. And these are the same mags that will report practically anything personal about anyone remotely famous in the name of fair play and good copy. Talk about homo-*phobia!*

The *Entertainment Weekly* cover story was especially amusing, tiptoeing around the subject as if trying to describe a country-and-western singer without using the word *hair*. The piece began, "Go ahead. Ask Rosie O'Donnell anything," and then asked her everything except THAT. It unapologetically addressed Rosie's "larger size," her mother's death, her absentee dad, and her past alcoholism (Rosie says she adopted her son Parker rather than give birth because she didn't want to pass on the alkie gene). But meticulously, it avoided anything to do with love, something I assure you no other know-it-all showbiz cover story would dare to do in the age of David Duchovny and Pamela Lee.

The profile quoted Rosie as saying that her only extracurricular activities these days are spending time with Parker, watching TV, and playing Scrabble with friends. "That's it," she added, almost threateningly. "You want some colorful details for your story? Go play with Parker, because he has a much more active life." That boundary-drawing made it even stranger when the piece contended that Rosie "bubbles over with a casual frankness rare in her new business." (Ken Tucker, who wrote the piece, casually refused to speak on the record to me about his choice of focus.)

We did learn from the article that the openly lesbian comic Kate Clinton—who worked as a writer on the show—often came up with biting, political jokes that Rosie admired but rejected (Clinton split the show because, as she told me, the workload was too demanding). What's left on *Rosie*—and in her media coverage—is mostly high-spirited enthusiasm, often done with veils. Once, the host slipped and blurted something about a close friend named Michelle—presumably the same Michelle the tabs named as Rosie's then live-in lover—but immediately she seemed to catch herself and switch the subject. She got a little warmer joking around with Ellen DeGeneres and saying, "Maybe I'm Lebanese." But usually she'll say stuff, without any irony, like how unsettling it is that people know Parker's name and address him as such when they're out together. As if this is some great mystery of the universe! Just maybe it's because Rosie talks about Parker by name practically every day on her show. In fact, she mentions him almost as much as Kathie Lee plugs her little emblems of apple pie-ism. This even though Rosie obviously believes in celebs' "right to privacy."

The rebirth of irony didn't start there, though. At a party last year, Rosie brought her brother over to tell me something he was just dying to unload. It turned out that the guy absolutely loved what I wrote about Lily Tomlin's closet status and how absurd it was in relation to her involvement with the movie of *The Celluloid Closet*. And that's the truth.

Oh, there are more indignities I've been forced to suffer lately in the name of journalism. When I went to interview Howard Stern the other day, Stuttering John thanked me for being one of the few people who'll answer his bad-taste questions at those black-tie galas, where his microphone generally sends socialites scurrying for the exits. "Who'd be afraid to talk to Musto?" chimed in Stern, laying on the movie-star charm with a trowel. Funny, I thought he'd twice canceled interviews I tried to set up.

I guess I just tend to inspire fear. I recently learned that Oprah Winfrey was supposedly going to play the shrink Ellen comes out to on April 30, and, having missed my own deadline with the info, called my beloved columnist pal to bestow it on her. She was away, so one of her assistants fielded the call and acted a bit imperious, saying, "How do we know this?" and "But it's been published before" (I told him it was already in an online newsletter—hardly common knowledge yet, though I later heard there was a reference in *Variety*). Well, they passed on it, and three days later, it made huge, gigantic newspaper headlines. Fine enough. But then the next week, the same exacting column stole an item from my column—that Toni Collette doesn't care for Jennifer Jason Leigh's acting—and not only didn't attribute it, but embellished it into a completely wrong tidbit about how they both worked on the film *Cosi* and hated each other. To which I say: "How do we know this?" and "But it's been published before!"

And then came the premiere of *Gentlemen Don't Eat Poets*, a/k/a *Angels and Pigs*, which I'd call in to someone if I thought there was any chance they'd believe me. The film is an uneasy satire brimming with murder, mayhem, and much humping of the hostess. Surly servant Sting alone does it with everyone in the household except the dead piglet, though the rest of us got to commune with it at the preparty. There was so much pork being served, in fact, that *Poets*'s director, John-Paul Davidson, apologized, saying, "I forgot this was a predominantly Jewish city." But he had only good things to say about the rump of his producer-star Trudie Styler (Mrs. Sting). "It's not often that you can ask your producer to do a retake with bare buttocks," he beamed.

Gentlemen ate pig and everything else at the opening of 107, "the party with an altitude" at the Windows on the World's Greatest Bar on Earth. Going along with the trend of ironic club names—Plush isn't, Chaos has none, The Room has two rooms, and Boy! has some girls—107 is actually on the 106th floor (there's no 13th, though that obviously hasn't cemented any good luck for the World Trade Center). It's still pretty high up, but there was no view that night due to the impenetrable fog. That gave me all the more time to concentrate on the blood spurting out of my ears from the elevator ride.

Finally, self-exiled publicist Bruce Lynn may not have a view of Erie, Pennsylvania, for long; he's already broken up with his drag queen boyfriend and may want to get out of the sticks sometime soon. I've got a great new guy for you, Bruce—Tom Cruise!

Not so GLAAD tidings

April 7, 1998

While GLAAD does a lot of good work, I've always been unnerved by the way the gay watchdog group seems to grovel before the mainstream and thank them for throwing us crumbs. The most recent example: *As Good as It Gets* was nominated for a GLAAD Media Award! Excuse me? This slick, Oscar-winning vessel from Hollywood hell might not be worthy of a full-scale street riot, but a GLAAD award? For the 800th time: Yes, Greg Kinnear's gay character is sweet and ultimately appreciated, but for most of the time he's a professional victim with a dour face and (phony-looking) scars. Having been bitterly shunned years ago by his father—the same nutjob who thought Greg was sleeping with mom!— this adorable doormat is now abandoned by practically all his friends when robbed and beaten by gay hustlers. For such a success, he's a complete loser.

Furthermore, Greg has to rely on two straights (one being the homophobic-but-learning Jack Nicholson character) to get him back on his feet, and in the process he helps *them* ignite into a sexual, loving, and highly improbable relationship. Of course, Kinnear-infection never manages to grasp at any romance of his own—he's gay, remember?—though there is a subtle flirtation between him and Helen Hunt! He, in fact, is only queer because he says so and has frosted hair and a foofy dog. And though the filmmakers clearly see him as a lovable survivor, one mainly remembers the fact that he's no closer to an actual human being than a department store mannequin with a limp wrist and a "Beat Me" tattoo. Thanks, Hollywood!

And now, though I won't even dredge up again what GLAAD's Chastity Bono said about *Ellen*, I do want to whine about how every dummy on earth seems to be blaming the show's anticipated cancellation on the public's distaste for lesbianism. I guess the demise couldn't possibly be because maybe *Ellen* wasn't promoted enough, had already run its course, or was considered distasteful by the network (its ratings aren't any worse than those of some series that are being left on)—it has to be because the masses simply can't take lesbianism! But the folks who promote this theory are the same ones who, when Ellen and her character burst out of the closet, screeched, "This is just a desperate act to boost her ratings!" How can it be both ways, you misbegotten monsters?

In *Primary Colors*, Kathy Bates gets fairly good ratings as a heated-up lesbian who's the conscience of the movie (the character's mental breakdowns can perhaps be chalked up to her eternal disillusionment). But—do not read this if you haven't seen the film—the idea that John Travolta's campaign opponent, played by Larry Hagman, is flawed because he was once involved with a guy and, of course, drugs (after all, he didn't know what he was doing) primarily colors one's ultimate reaction red, white, and blew (chunks).

Watching the Oscars without (that many) pharmaceuticals, I knew exactly what I was doing—wincing. Especially quease-making were Neve's nerves, the bear's refusal to maul the crowd, Fay Wray's confusion (though I loved her having no idea who Matt and Ben were), James Cameron's I'm-so-fabulous-but-let's-have-some-silence-for-the-dead stunt, the flying dancer, and the fact that too many of Billy Crystal's jokes relied on ancient reference points, from Marcel Marceau to "Here come da judge." Plus, Kim Basinger now acts as if all the artistry of *L.A Confidential* was simply designed to help her win an Oscar. (By the way, I hear that in the press room after the show, a reporter with an accent nervily asked Kim, "Do the best things in life for women come after 39?" and because she didn't understand, he had to repeat it loudly two more times!) And though the old lady in *Titanic* was mostly nominated for proving that good things for women happen after 79—and for being a legend we never heard of—it seemed like kicking your grandma in the groin not to give her the prize after all that buildup. For shame!

Meanwhile, mama Madonna appeared to be straining for dignity with her stick-up-the-ass presentation, at least until her involuntary eyebrow raise at the name Celine Dion and her "What a surprise" at another *Titanic* victory (though in person lately she's seemed so warm and friendly—the up side of the karmic and career reawakening that's had her subtly renouncing her past and even advocating sexual discretion). But I loved the "family portrait" of former winners (especially since Harold Russell sold one of his two Oscars), adored Cher's outfit (a big fuck you to all the folks struggling to look so tasteful as their breasts popped out of their Badgley-Mishegosses), and marveled at Cameron Diaz saying, "Ever since *The Jazz Singer* amazed audiences by have characters speak. . . ." Perhaps they should have stayed silent.

As for *Movie*—I can't have speak the name anymore—I now realize how truly genius the casting of the lovely, but less than supermodely Kate Winslet was. Her nabbing Leonardo DiCaprio onscreen makes the audience feel that perhaps *they* have a chance with him, too. This device has always informed straight porno films, which generally feature ordinary-looking actors nailing all the hot babes without the tiniest struggle. Kate is the highbrow Ron Jeremy.

The highbrow Kate Winslet—but over 39—Blythe Danner is everywhere lately, playing women who fly into a tizzy over ordinary-looking men. In *No Looking Back*, she looks back a lot while holing herself up in the house for six months because Hubby left her behind (and the rest of her, too). And onstage in *The Deep Blue Sea*, she tries to gas herself when her adulterous affair with an ex-RAF dude crashlands. Cheer up, Blythe. You're a fine actor—and so are your daughter and her last several boyfriends!

Younger offspring will probably love *Teletubbies*, a Brit preschooler comedy debuting this week on PBS in between all the arias and fundraisers. The invite for the show's launch party at Roseland asked us to dress as 'Tubbies Tinky Winky,

Dipsy, Laa-Laa, and Po (no, there's not a gay one called No Nookie, though the purple one *did* used to carry a handbag). Well, I came as a composite character named Dipsy Ho and learned that the *real* buggers are absolute dolls (and backpacks and CD-ROMs) who believe that "Magic happens when the windmill turns," whatever the fuck *that* means. These blank-faced-but-terminally-up-beat kewpies play with vacuum cleaners, eat custard, and giggle—all with much repetitiveness and adorableness—and no matter what they're doing, they're such a smash that people in England have run in front of speeding trucks just to get near the merch. Not me; when the windmill turned, I went home.

Oh, in case there hasn't been enough sheer hatred in this column, let me end by gratuitously confessing that I detest the fashion crowd. I dislike them for being drawn to a life spent looking at models in dumb dresses and then complaining about how boring it is. I abhor them for whining that the Chelsea Piers, where the shows were last held, were too far out of the way. My heart bleeds! Imagine someone in Bosnia being irritated that the fashion shows are too inconveniently located. And yet I'm one of these horrid people. Thank God the shows are closer this year!

Gay pride and prejudice

June 26, 2001

It's Gay Pride Month, tra la, but President Bush refused to proclaim it as such because he "does not believe in politicizing people's sexual orientation." That's funny—Dubya certainly used his to get into the White House, arguing that his solid relationship with wifey made him a supremely noble candidate worthy of your butterfly ballot.

But what the fuck—Gay Pride without Bush's endorsement is like Earth Day without an oil spill. And whatever the official word is on our right to be openly proud, being gay in 2001 New York still has its undeniable joys and intrigues, along with the usual headaches, all of which I've personally experienced just from watching Showtime.

It's a life filled with contradictions, beginning with the fact that our adulterous mayor is on a phobic spree that includes closing down anything sex-related that isn't a $100-a-pop Broadway show. Of course there are ironies within the gay community, too—like Andrew Sullivan's high-tech sex outing, whereby the conservative critic of gay promiscuity was revealed to promote himself on barebacking Web sites as a wanton studmuffin who likes to turn tricks with his bum. This saucy scandal showed that we're *all* torn between our intellects and our dicks, though only some are able to yell at gay men for being too stereotypically hedonistic while also screeching, "Give it to me, you hot, tempestuous pig!" In the midst of the uproar over Sullivan's travels, one onlooker commented that the most fun to be had was calling up the guy's personal Web site and seeing the phrase "downloading Andrew Sullivan."

Naturally, showbiz is what I milk for juice, and it pays off, providing a glitzy reflection of society's absurd responses to queer life. For each step forward lately, there's a giant one back, with every Barbara Walters daring to "go there" paving the way for a Ricky Martin shaking his bon-bon at inaugural festivities (did he really need the exposure?) or a Madonna righteously defending Eminem's verbal carving of gays as refreshingly un-p.c.

And the absurdities keep on coming—like the fact that *we're* still not allowed to marry, but the law fully permitted Barry Diller to tie the knot with Diane von Furstenberg, their wedding seemingly attended by more gays than last year's Pride parade. On the bright side, our parents probably don't have much sex either. At least these two like each other!

But the biggest, kookiest gay story of the year involved divorcé Tom Cruise suing a gabby porn star, stating that the gossip the guy was spreading was erroneous and could devastate Tom's career. And why? Because, Tom's lawyers explained, our star needs to be convincing as a hetero action hero and doesn't want to lose the sizable chunk of his following that's antigay! Funny, I don't remember Tom Hanks threatening, "Don't tell anyone I like women—I'm starring as a homosexual in *Philadelphia* and I need people to believe me." Cruise has *also* never been mad about being called straight, even though such reports could conceivably diminish ticket revenue coming from gay audiences and hetero bashers. Yes, Cruise has a right to sue for what he deems are untruths, but he shouldn't have fed into that old bull that gay talk—in an obscure French magazine yet—is deeply detrimental and vicious (though of course he added that there's nothing wrong with being gay, blah blah blah).

Tom *used* to focus on suing anyone who said his marriage to Nicole Kidman was a sham, but now that their union's as shattered as Tom's Oscar hopes, he's had to vehemently chase down other targets. On DataLounge—my favorite Web site, filled with bitchy, opinionated postings—someone put up a mock article titled "Tom Cruise Sues Long Island Man for Masturbating to His Image." But the real saga was even more fascinating. Nicole was suddenly announced as having been pregnant—this via the man she was on the verge of breaking up with! (Sadly, she miscarried.) And after the split, the tabloids quickly had Cruise dating another woman, Patricia Arquette—a false story later exposed as a case of mistaken identity.

If Tom somehow *is* worried about losing his gay fan base, he should relax; Rosie O'Donnell still gushes about him on her talk show! But who can keep track of *her* love life? Soon after she said, "I love you, Kelli!" at the Daytime Emmies,

Rosie explained that Kelli's just a very close friend and later raved on her show about a hot-looking man she'd spotted at a movie theater. Maybe he'll take her mind off Tom—if not Kelli.

On nighttime TV—well, cable—we've had a phalanx of gay characters humping and bumping, but all the progress instantly dissolves whenever *Queer as Folk* actors run to the press to blather about how they washed their mouths out with Listerine after kissing scenes. If these people ever played murderers, I'm sure they wouldn't bother to hold press conferences saying, "By the way, I was deeply repulsed, never having killed anyone in real life." But playing gay? *Eeew.*

Thank goddess that Gale Harold—who stars as *Folk's* hot-to-trot Brian—showed great enlightenment recently when a TV interviewer asked if he was afraid he might lose jobs as a result of playing a gay character. "I wouldn't want to work for homophobes anyway," he said as thousands cheered. Yay—someone saying the right thing! I love you, Kelli—I mean Gale!

Such clarity of thought is extremely rare these days, especially since in the media, we're still pretty much the last frontier of legitimized prejudice. (Even last week's American Fashion Awards ceremony dabbled in fag jokes.) As is now legend, John Simon complained on *The Charlie Rose Show* that, while fellow critic Ben Brantley likes "the homosexual play," *he* doesn't, adding that some dramas carry hidden gay messages that he finds especially repellent. Couldn't your gay skin just crawl? It's so true, Mr. Simon, they're totally taking over—homophobes, that is.

The gay-panic defense turned up again when the *Post* ran a lighthearted gossip item about a scribe who's "quite the jokester." At a restaurant, this happy douche bag made a big scene banging his spoon on the table and shouting that he deserved a discount "because I'm the only one here who isn't a fag." This was all presented as if it were the height of levity and wit, which would never have been the case if the punch line had led to the N- or K-word.

Adding anguish to injury—if we can get to the *real* horror—AIDS turned 20 this year, an unthinkable landmark accompanied by reports that infection rates have soared (though Andrew Sullivan denied them at length and partied on). Despite medical advances, the plague is still a guillotine-like reminder that not only are we second-class citizens, but we may be doomed anyway. Recently, I told *Poz* magazine that, as the epidemic has dragged on and on, so have my grief, fury, anxiety, bouts with denial, and annoyance that gay life's become a terrifying sci-fi movie. Today I'm stunned to still be forced to care about this hideous cosmic joke. Happy birthday, AIDS, you fucking freak.

And happy Gay Pride Day, all! I hope I haven't depressed you.

Gay pride '02: We're oppressed but hilarious!

July 2, 2002

Being gay in 2002 means we might not necessarily be able to marry, adopt, or join the armed forces, but honey, we *are* in every sitcom! We're a regular riot, girlfriend, our flouncy gestures and bons mots providing a cathartic giggle for the entire TV-watching populace. We've got a place at the table, all right, even if it's only a fictional table that's dismantled at 10 P.M.—and by the way it's usually not even remotely adjacent to the bedroom unless the show is on cable.

Am I sounding an itsy bit bitter? Well, as Gay Pride Day approaches and the nipple clamps tighten, I'm going to throw off all negativity as if it were a Century 21 shawl and appreciate what progress we *have* made, even in the land of neutery second bananas and laugh tracks. Take *Saturday Night Live*—take it all. For decades, the show wallowed in homophobia and stereotypes—and I'm sure it still will—but now that queerdom is the new navy blue, it's been pushing a way more gay-friendly agenda to the sound of cash registers ka-*ching*-ing. Back in March, guest host Jon Stewart made yay-gay remarks that straight comics once would have run from, holding their crotches and screaming. And just a week later, Sir Ian Mc-Kellen did a bracing comic monologue, saying he felt much more welcome on the show than at that morning's Saint Patrick's Day Parade—"they don't seem to mind the priests, though, do they?" Sir Ian climaxed his appearance by planting a big, old, juicy smooch on Jimmy Fallon while in full drag. (Too bad so many cynics pounced on the esteemed Brit for having such a hot young boyfriend in real life that he stopped being photographed with the guy. This happens all the time with gay celeb relationships—the threatened media and public race to declare them horribly corrupt.)

Anyway, the week Sir Ian did SNL was the most gay-licious one ever, especially since it was the same week that Liza Minnelli married David Gest! Also flaming up the airwaves were no less than two Matthew Shepard TV movies (if you're gay, it helps to murder or be murdered to get a film project green-lighted), plus the sight of daytime darling Rosie O'Donnell finally coming out, eventually calling me and Michelangelo Signorile "morons" and "gay Nazis" for trying to push her there. I could handle that, but I had more of a problem with Rosie's refusal to admit that she'd been cagey all those years, and for careerist reasons. Instead, she insisted she'd never misled her audience and claimed her Tom Cruise shtick was not meant romantically. (Please—even a promo for her final show, while acknowledging how gay it was going to be, trumpeted an appearance by her "dream man," Tom.) But Rosie could be an extremely positive force, and she's getting more sensitive by the minute, even dropping her argument that Ellen DeGeneres was "offensive" in the way she came out. (How—unapologetically? Though sadly, Ellen herself has felt the need to recant, telling *Next* magazine, "I think [Rosie] just studied what I did and learned what *not* to do." Tellingly, in her latest comedy appearance, Ellen didn't do a single gay joke.)

In another case of "better late than never," *Frasier*'s David Hyde Pierce went to the Emmys with his partner—how semi sort of bold of him—but the tabloids are still filled with your ambiguous performers who, the second rumors pop up, make sure to get caught licking whipped cream off female strippers at some paparazzi-laden hooch bar. Methinks the ladies doth protest too much.

The coolest public figure around has been Mike Piazza, who didn't avoid questions about his sexuality when the issue cropped up due to some very slippery reportage. With a refreshing sense of calm, the comely Mets catcher simply said he was straight, but it wouldn't matter in the least if he weren't. The directness and affability of his response made all the other people screaming that Piazza's name had been "dragged through the mud" look a bit foolish.

Alas, we're striking out in movies, kids. As prevalent as we are on the small screen, that's exactly how invisible we are again on the large one (except for the smash *Spider-Man*, which couldn't resist a piece of homophobic shtick). For any kind of representation or safety, you have to stick to the theater, where the line between blue-haired matinee lady and onstage male talent blurs by the minute. On Broadway, the big attraction once again will be queer pioneer Harvey Fierstein prancing about in drag (in the musical *Hairspray*). In the last three decades, Harvey was right about everything—from the way the world was noticing us as a result of the devastation of AIDS to the importance of gays' adopting—and if he now wants to sing and dance in a housedress, I say let him.

Of course gay adoption still has its critics—stay with me, folks—one of whom is *New York Post* columnist Victoria Gotti, who vehemently feels children deserve parents of both sexes. Alas, *her* kids can't enjoy that exalted situation, since their father's in jail, and he and the columnist are divorced anyway! (As Liz Smith wrote about the woman, "She has been struggling to liberate herself from an unhappy and old-fashioned lifestyle.")

But the whopper issue, naturally, has been Sacramentgate—you know, the dangerous lives of altar boys—a crisis that became an excuse for the church to bash gays one more time with a sledgehammer made out of crushed rosary beads. As the situation turned into a modern-day revival of *The Crucible*—but with most of the screaming accusers telling the truth—officials in gowns reacted by targeting homosexuality (and the media) as evil, forgetting that their own intolerance, denial, and insistence on the closet may have fanned the flames of hell. At one point, the Vatican went so far as to suggest that gays shouldn't be allowed into the clergy anymore—as if *that* wouldn't lead to an empty cathedral. Excuse me, but while there are many self-loathing offenders here, gay doesn't equal boy-snatcher any more than church always equals accepting. One thing's clear, though: When it comes to policies and priorities, the church needs an even more massive overhaul than the FBI.

Things got even more absurd when, at the height of the insanity, the Vatican put out an edict criticizing stars like Cher for wearing jewel-studded crucifixes. Shouldn't they be thrilled that celebs are making the holy image massively visible? Publicist Liz Rosenberg shot back brilliantly with "Why don't you tell the pope to clean up his own house?" I guess John Paul II wants to pick and choose exactly who can wear the cross and with what outfit. Not surprisingly, he hasn't exactly gotten behind the campaign to canonize Father Mychal Judge, the 9-11 hero who was gay and apparently not ashamed of it. I suspect even I'll be named Saint Mychal before he is.

But the real martyrs continue to be people with AIDS, and though the accepted line these days is that the illness is more manageable, you should go tell my friend how manageable it is—the one who keeps having to be rushed to the hospital with all sorts of infections and disabilities. Go tell all the people with sunken cheeks, their facial wasting acting as a banner that screams, "I've got it." When it comes to AIDS, it's still 1981 in too many ways.

Oh, we may not live an unhappy and old-fashioned lifestyle, but we still have a long way to go, people—and the best example of that is the fact that I've barely mentioned lesbians, bisexuals, transsexuals, and the intersex community. "Hello, kettle! It's pot!" (Laugh track, please.)

Happy Gay Day.

Zip it up: Assessing the new AIDS scare

March 1, 2005

It's déjà vu all over again with the panic over this new, drug-resistant strain of quickly percolating AIDS that was detected in a New York man a few weeks ago (followed by another possible case in San Diego). The same AIDS pundits from the late '80s and '90s are being called upon to address all the familiar responsibility and prevention issues, and there's even a patient zero for the new millennium, though it's not been determined whether he's really a point man for a terrifying new strain or someone whose personal genetics made him susceptible to a hideous anomaly.

Even if the latter's the case, at least the media are covering this mess! I'd rather they be a little alarmist than totally speechless. In the early '80s, as I emptied half my Rolodex in horror, the press was shockingly silent about the creeping terror of "the gay cancer." It was an unspeakably dirty subject, especially since gays and druggies were potentially scary fringe characters, so ignorance begat terror, which begat a near reportorial blackout (whereas some presumed straight vets who died of Legionnaires' disease a few years earlier nabbed international coverage—not that I was jealous, mind you).

But having learned from that unbelievable fuckup, today's more seasoned media have just lifted their heads out of the sand again to stop the proverbial band from playing encores. Out gays have moved so far into the mainstream culture that the observers have had to notice this new possible threat to some of their favorite reality show stars and designers. Unfortunately, with the frothing support of gay leaders, they may be going *beyond* the realm of a little alarmist. Some commentators seem to be scapegoating the victims more than reaching out to them, with a frenzied approach reminiscent of last year's "blacks on the down low" mania.

In a *New York Times* article by Andrew Jacobs that detailed community leaders' reactions to the new strain (and that did present both sides of the controversy), historian Charles Kaiser blared, "Gay men do not have the right to spread a debilitating and often fatal disease." Well, er, I guess—but why only gay men? Yes, I know the new patient zero, like the old one, is gay, and I'm quite aware that the article centered on the surge in crystal-meth-assisted gay infections. But AIDS transmission isn't the exclusive domain of anyone (nor is crystal meth—straights have done it, and not just on *Beverly Hills, 90210*). In fact, when I criticized a God's Love We Deliver commercial a few years ago for taking pains to reveal that the client shown had children, a rep bitterly responded that gay people could have children, and besides, "the number of new AIDS cases in the heterosexual population is currently rising at a faster rate than in the homosexual population." That was before the crystal boom, but still, did gays go from being not quite visible in compassion-urging ads only to wind up as the exclusive face of the new recklessness?

And if gays *are* the devil, why not factor in the responsibility of the other person engaged in the sex act, not just the spreader (or "murderer," as the most extreme moralists would no doubt call him)? Even way back in '89, when Marc Christian won big bucks after claiming his late lover Rock Hudson had sex with him without disclosing his HIV status, I remember thinking, "And you had never heard of AIDS risks? And you had nothing to do with the sex acts?"

Willful ignorance—like President Reagan's all through the '80s—has always been the AIDS epidemic's best friend. No wonder power figures are anxious to attack the return of it head-on rather than putzing around in haunted confusion like last time. According to the same *Times* article, various gay and AIDS-prevention leaders "want to track down those who knowingly engage in risky behavior and try to stop them before they can infect others." They might even want to go so far as to penetrate certain Web sites and confront revelers at sex parties. That sounds admirable—if impractical—but where do you draw the line when it comes to preventing health risks? Do you throw rocks at a restaurant that serves burgers? Tackle a guy who gives his girlfriend a cigarette? Oh, I forgot, only gays are the culprits here. So should all gay bars be shuttered because people might hook up there and go home to have unsafe sex? Or can we just shake up and educate the denial-prone without sounding like our own oppressors?

These desperate measures are clearly motivated by concern, but they risk putting gay leaders in bed with conservatives (where I hope they'll use condoms; a lot of conservatives have secret double lives). Interestingly, some of the same gays who were horrified in '86 when William F. Buckley Jr. suggested that poz people should be tattooed are now advocating keeping track of them and their tricks. At least they can't be accused of complacency.

And this all comes just in time to fuel the real virulence going on—Bush's anti-gay-marriage stance, a cornerstone of his recent rah-rah freedom-and-democracy State of the Union address. "Look at the self-destructive gays chasing death all over again!" the right-wingers can cluck along with us. "They're not worthy of our sacred institution." Of course, as one pundit suggested, being denied rights like the ability to wed is exactly what fuels the kind of angst that drugs and quick sex are often used to self-medicate. But I doubt Bush would change his mind on the issue just so gays could be less promiscuous.

So what's the real cure? Well, forget about thinking you can close down every venue where people might have unsafe sex—where there's a will, there's a gay (or a straight or a bi). Instead, we have to get to the heart of the crisis and figure out why a part of the queer community supports crystal usage and lethal sex rampages. Free answer: Because they wrongly feel AIDS is over or manageable. Or that nothing is more important than unprotected anal sex. Or because some of them already have AIDS and want to lose themselves in a spiral that seemingly distances them from the specter of death while it ironically adds to it.

So here's the deal: Education on the subject needs to be more direct and harrowing—show 'em what a messy crystal addict really looks like, not a hunky guy who's "crystal free." Hold up a mirror. Keep investigating and publicizing this horrid new strain, which may be a diabolical reminder that everything happens more quickly these days. Pick up the ball on *all* AIDS reporting; most media, like the public, had gotten beyond bored with it. Bring back condoms. Try doing drug interventions with friends. (The community might not have the right, but you do.) And drum up some experts and activists who still have a whopping sex drive. Crusty old Nancy Reagan types screaming, "Just say no!" don't always ring younger gay chimes.

A whole other safer-sex revolution is in order, just like in the '80s. But urging people to "zip it up" will only work as long as the finger-pointers do the same.

Did I blow my chances with Anderson Cooper?

March 17, 2005

In addition to some touching support, I've gotten a steaming heap of flack for my current *Out* magazine article in which I examine why CNN's fabulous Anderson Cooper hasn't come out or been at least asked about his sexuality in the lengthy but guarded profiles written about him. A lot of the people attacking me haven't even read the piece, which references my *Voice* writings and which is not a screed at all—it's just a questioning look at why Cooper's open-secret life hasn't gotten ink, a practice he obviously goes along with.

Still, I'm getting all the same old arguments from the early '90s and have to drag up all those hoary, old defenses in response. You know: "How do you know he's gay?" Gee, well, I'm a reporter.

"His off-camera life is private and I don't care about it." Good, then I presume you'll scream the same sentiments at anyone who dares to write about Brad and Jen, Ben and Jen, Katie Couric's fling, Diane Sawyer's marriage, Lindsay Lohan's gropefests, and so on and so on. And don't let me catch you reading any of those items, by the way. You're not interested, remember?

"But some of those people have been spotted doing stuff in public." Well, Anderson's been seen at gay spots.

"No one's forced to come out." I never said anyone was (though they certainly should). In fact, I gently examine the reasons why he won't.

"But he IS out." Sort of, but not on the record. And if he IS out, why are you so upset about the article?

"But he never said he was straight." Yeah, that's in the article. And I never said he was straight either. I said he was gay.

"Outing is disgusting." But you didn't think so with David Gest, Al Reynolds, Fabien Basabe, or even the false rumors about Marcia Cross coming out or all the Jacko jokes (which started way before his public travails). Not one person complained to me about any of those reports. So producers, party boys, "freaks," and women are OK to report about, just not newsmen (and former Mole hosts)?

"I thought it was disgusting with them, too. Outing is just gross." But what's gross about saying someone's gay? It's OK to be gay, remember? Project much, dear?

"But my cousin was outed and. . . ." Wait, your cousin is not a public figure. There are different rules for celebrities.

"We should only out our enemies and hypocrites." So I should only reveal when HORRIBLE people are gay? That would really advance the gay cause, wouldn't it? In my book, outing isn't only trotted out as a revenge tactic—it's a statement of equalizing and truth.

"You're just outing someone to get your activist credentials." Please—I was doing this before it was cool. I outed Methuselah.

"You're just jealous of Anderson." No, I'm actually very proud of Anderson and in fact the article is wildly apprecia-tive of his talent and charm. It's just saying he's smart, suc-cessful, and happens to be gay, too.

"You're out of line!" But I write about celebrities' per-sonal lives for a living. To leave out anything gay because it might seem distasteful to someone would be extremely hyp-ocritical. And the media certainly didn't omit mention of Anderson's brother's tragic suicide. Nor do they avoid cov-ering all kinds of celebrities' adulterous affairs, out-of-wedlock babies, narcotics problems, bad movies, or gross misbehavior.

"But after your writeup, someone on Don Imus's radio show made homophobic remarks about Anderson." So I should never say anyone's gay because someone else might make a dumb comment about it? In that case—you heard it here first—Jamie Foxx is white.

"This will ruin his career." One 800-word article in a gay magazine? And a pretty gushy one at that? Besides, I'm not making him gay, I'm just saying he is.

"If he came out himself, it could hurt his career." But the article addresses that. The article, in fact, covers practically all the bases. You should read it.

"You didn't ask him for comment." I asked CNN for a comment from Anderson and/or themselves. They apparently didn't even forward it to him, they just responded by sending me a blanket no comment. Besides, in the past, Anderson's turned down the chance to be labeled "gay." And when *New York Daily News* columnist Ben Widdicombe asked him if he had any comment about the *Out* piece, he said "No."

"This is sick!" Oh, really? And you're on that Web site all day where the fake Marcia Cross thing started and where they relentlessly out celebrities, including a lot of people who aren't even gay? I'd say you're conflicted. Oh, and probably gay, too!

BLIND BOMBSHELLS

Shameless nameless items

June 2, 1992

So you want I should tell some more blind gossip items to gnash your teeth over? So you want to tsk-tsk again about who did what creepily subversive thing they'll never admit to? So you want I should start? So what am I waiting for?

What rock star's wife has no ostensible talent except the uncanny ability to pee when she comes? What black heart-throb is none too faithful to his unsuspecting wife? What little star's internal organs are growing faster than his body? What same star's *external* organ has no need to grow any larger, thank you? What male scion of a wealthy, powerful family has a penchant for big, bodacious "Mandingo warriors"?

What metropolitan actress and married rocker are having a torrid May–December affair? What musical star changed her name, her face, and her public sexuality shortly before making it? What two bosom buddies brightened up an L.A. house party with a vicious catfight over one of their girl-friends? What pseudo-virginal teen star is preggers by her Mexican boyfriend? What vehemently antidrug sports figure was recently found cutting lines of coke with his credit card in a hotel?

What comedy star threw a fit after a surprise guest appeared in his TV skit, even though—or maybe because—that appearance was the highlight of the show? What veteran rocker and his wife met at a gathering of an s&m society, and, rumor has it, it was love at first nailing-of-the-dick-to-a-board? What member of that fictitious rock group lost out on a TV pilot because she's not committed to staying thin? What then sexy movie star, between husbands, made a pass at a female DJ a few years ago to the chagrin of guys who'd been unsuccessfully hitting on her? What offbeat songstress blew her bandmate in a nightclub display window in the mid '80s?

What sweet ol' star is, truth be told, a holy terror to work with? What fading model can strike quite a pose with a crack pipe? What talk-show regular who won that magazine's contest flaunts his "girlfriend," but is one himself? What singer was all set to sue that tabloid for outing him until his lawyers realized that no one gave a shit? Who participated in improvisational rehearsals for her upcoming movie, then when the cameras started rolling stole the other characters' best lines? What two top female models have been known to make out in public, purely as a goof, I'm so sure? What other three models, who have nothing to say anyway, are no longer speaking to each other? What controversial actress had to have her hair formula sent over to the set of the film she was working on so her exposed pubes could be dyed to match her golden tresses? What retired politician used to be set up on dates with men, who'd reject him, forcing him to dig into his wallet and romance the same old hustlers again?

What late star's husband went home with a female impersonator dressed as his dead wife? What two famous brothers can be occasionally spotted sharing spoons in bathroom stalls? What sometime local news regular's favorite sexual activity involves the wearing of gloves—not for anything intrusive, just plain old-fashioned boxing? What trendy artist is "a real bore" in bed, according to one disgruntled conquest? What other trendy artist keeps that young boy in clover even though the boy isn't putting out anymore? What concerned celebrity used limos and hotel rooms for her family and flew in friends to attend her charity's event, all at the charity's expense?

What model's party at that swanky restaurant was not paid for until the management threw repeated fits, upon which a check mysteriously arrived from a foreign country? What alternative-rock band lead singer's recently had several dermabrasions and hair transplants in a vain attempt to beat the clock and punish nature? What long-haired rocker didn't like the way he looked in a video, so he promptly had a dimple added to his chin, a nose adjustment, an eyelift, and an attempted transplant of fat from his butt to his lips that failed when they couldn't find an ounce of fat (they used collagen instead)? What comic's dentures popped out once while she warbled "My Funny Valentine"? What children's icon was caught out of costume—and character—shopping for dildos on the West Side? What '92 marriage is a shady attempt to benefit both stars' images, if not their love lives? What former Olympics hero now apparently has breasts?

What moonlighting photographer is trying to get a photo book published but isn't telling agents that the pix were actually taken by his late roommate? What part-time writer brags endlessly about his safe-sex exploits but privately craves partners who will "take the cum"? What chickie with dickie was caught getting boomed with her panties down behind a curtain at Limelight? What socialite called a hotel concierge to ask for recommendations regarding Broadway shows but specified, "No black musicals, please. They're talented sometimes, but a whole stage of them is hard to handle"?

What music biggie regaled a prospective male trick with his braggadocio, insisting that he's well hung and is just 38, ha ha ha, only to have the guy race for the exit, upon which the biggie screamed, "I can have any hustler I want in New York!" and the trick replied, "Well I'm not a hustler and you can't have me!"? What new sitcom lead has beefcake pix up in his apartment, where he oftentimes traipses about wearing lovely gowns? What drag queen got his girlfriend preggers, and everyone expects the child's first word to be "Mama?"? What current Broadway lead whom no one thinks is gay is gay? What baby girl on that TV show is actually played by twin boys?

What club impresario has handcuffs and a whip near his bed but is actually very gentle during sex, according to survivors? Who vehemently disapproves of sexually explicit (read: gay) art but happens to be a lesbian? What older designer is so verging on senility he stumbles into work saying, "What did I do yesterday?" What Brit singer was a bug-eyed, sobbing mess on drugs and booze when she visited New York clubland recently? Ditto what once-hot bratty actor?

What scribe and her girlfriend recently went shopping for a Connecticut country house to share and bickered over things like closet space? What sitcom star and his wife are leading separate lives in separate bedrooms, no questions asked? What artsy multimedia married man is dating that classy older actress? What young TV star got his start as a cocktail waiter at a hustler bar called Numbers, snagging big tips for hefty services? What dead artist was not asexual at all, grabbing boys' dicks and begging, "Please come home with me," settling for a forced utterance of "those three little words"?

Who, what, when, where, why?

June 22, 1993

If I used names in the following gossip items, I'd be promptly run out of town by a posse of angry sleazeballs. But by keeping the information "blind," I'm most welcome here, surrounded by wildly approving people quizzing me, offering bribes, and telling me how irresistibly witty and provocative I am. So I'm not using names.

Here goes: What wandering art critic regularly tries to get a struggling East Village artist to fellate him in exchange for a good review? What explosive Oscar-winning actor recently pulled out his penis and shook it suggestively at that virginal former child star, who shrieked, "What are you doing?" and turned away in revulsion? What late ballet dancer had his Italian friend send him a black hustler, whom he denuded for appraisal, only to call the friend and scream, "How dare you send me someone with such a small dick!"? What kooky rock group's third wheel is obsessively into servicing big truck-driver trash, the sloppier the better? What coked-up movie actress—once a steamy looker—tries to pick up guys at parties, and when reminded that her husband's there, snorts attractively and says, "So?"? What same actress has been holding things up by falling down drunk and slurring her lines on the set of her latest (intentionally) campy flick? What faded Warhol star won't do AIDS benefits because she feels they detract from cancer and other diseases? What Scroogelike rapper was gifted with an $8000 watch from his brother for Christmas but gave him zip in return, also winning cheapskate hall of fame status by selling a pair of sneakers he'd gotten for free to one of his backup crew? What '80s Oscar-winner regularly tongues her teeth with Vaseline so her unnaturally heavy upper lip won't get stuck to them when she talks?

What enduring black superstar frugally forages for wigs on 14th Street? What boozy British journalist says, "I want you to meet someone," as he guides girls' hands under the table and straight to his loglike member? What famed but blasé goddess of song has been munching with that local chanteuse/former junkie of foreign descent? What comic got his comeuppance from two drag queens he slept with— one sashayed off with his credit cards and the other read him for not having done anything for his people? What writer has been publicly dredging up much dirt on that supermodel, possibly to stir up interest in the book he's secretly ghosting on her? What sidekick's macho hubby (who's rumored to be a closet case) asked for a different waiter in that touristy New York restaurant because the one he and wifey had was just "too homosexual"?

What editor from that defunct magazine, while buying glow tape for a club event, bought an extra roll so she could tie her husband up with it? What female pop diva ripped off her producer/writer of most of the publishing rights to that smash song, which served him right because he'd already ripped practically the entire song off his engineer? What other top female singer's wafer-thin voice often has to be programmed into a science-fiction machine that raises it a third and thickens it? What exotic beauty was reported to be dining with her then paramour (the same one who showed his privates to the ex-child star) one festive holiday last year, but was actually running around a club dining on a lady friend? What male club hag now admits to having done both that Oscar-winning blond actor and that '70s macho series star in the late '80s, with no small assist from a truckload's worth of a certain white powder?

What male movie megastar's 22-year-old brother is gay and lives with his lover on the other side of the globe? What ole fella needed cue cards to sing his signature song last time around at Radio City? What animal activist hypocritically uses dead cows in the form of leather and other s&m para-phernalia when he indulges in sex with young male hus-tlers? What r&b star/egomaniac is making unreasonable demands on his label in his quest to become bigger than Whitney Houston? What female newspaper writer's now seeing a younger woman, who's reportedly visible these days on a decisive cable channel? What same writer's ex considered moving back in with her mother, who wouldn't have it because "people would talk" about her way of life? What pretty face on the local news can be spotted hangin' with the homo boys at the Roxy?

What former children's icon married his grunge boyfriend at that socialite's mansion—unbeknownst to that socialite? What playwright/screenwriter hires female escorts, one of whom only talked him to a climax—fitting for one whose work is so verbose? What country good-looker gleefully tells racist jokes about how there are no blacks on *The Flintstones* because they were monkeys back then, ha ha? What married action star regales his buddies with one-liners about battered wives? What hip movie director just broke up with his teen boyfriend, who promptly found a girlfriend on the rebound? What youth-oriented magazine editor never paid for her table of six at that CRIA benefit, and, when asked, says she doesn't know what they're talking about? What indie director quickly found that his megastar can neither act nor take direction? What former club owner is so smacked out that he's living in Grand Central and hustling johns? Who would pay? What daytime TV window-dressing has had so much surgery that one of her eyes won't close and emits an unsightly ooze? What entrepreneur/club siren romance of the late '80s was never really consummated, as he couldn't get it up?

What drag star has an unrequited crush on that oily fashion editor? What large cabaret survivor, in a jealous, drunken rage, ripped down all the clippings about that other large cabaret survivor recently at a West Village nightclub? What D.C. bigwig found out she was going to be seated next to that AIDS activist at an event she was speaking at and decided that she couldn't possibly stay for dinner? What comic used to watch a certain star on video and comment about how fat, ugly, and untalented she was, shortly before they became good friends? What other comic is on the verge of publicly coming out, but her panic-stricken publicist is warning her not to and not returning calls from gay magazines seeking interviews? What TV teen is emerging so quickly as a daughter of Sappho that she recently bombarded a female barkeep she has a crush on with bouquets? What headline-grabbing young lady was recently heard in a deli saying of her older love object, "Well, he's not sexy!"?

What bubblegum star's recent comeback concert sold all of 125 tickets, an audience tally that was quickly enhanced by 300 comps? What quirky male film icon recently picked up a pair of lesbians in Miami, but only one of them would do the dirty deed? What songstress is entering Norma Desmond country so defiantly that she had the master tape of her latest song sent by Concorde from France and picked up at the airport by an employed henchman? What endlessly compelling personality is the subject of four of the above items? What's the capital of Ethiopia? Why do fools fall in love? Why is my life so empty?

Oh, no, they dih-int!

March 16, 1999

Gather 'round the campy fire and treat yourself to some tantalizing truths about the bald-faced liars and bare-assed hookers who compose our marvelous, much maligned mecca. To make things even more fun—well, less likely to attract spurious lawsuits—I've taken the names out.

And so: Which ambiguous matinee idol developed an obsession with that politico's son, a situation sonny became so nervous about that he promptly planted a gossip item in one of the dailies stating that he has a girlfriend? What rapidly aging screen ingenue's dad might as *well* have phoned the columns when he was seen holding hands in broad daylight with a broad who in any light is not his wife? What equally indiscreet famous relation accidentally kept a body mike on after she left a benefit, inadvertently allowing everyone inside the fundraiser to hear her mutterings—no doubt drug-related—for an uncomfortably long amount of time?

What family magazine that did a cover story on that much more guarded showbiz personality was terrified said star would come out in their interview? (Imagine a publication praying they *won't* get a hot scoop—now that's a twist.) She didn't. What *former* talk-show host hires prosties to sit on his knee, act girlish, and call him "Daddy"—though they probably would anyway? And speaking of girlish, which prepubescent nymphs in that arty theater project became so close—in showers and beyond—that they had to be broken up by disapproving spoilsports?

What auteur nutjob bad-mouthed his older costar, clearly irked that she dared to spurn his clumsy pass on the set? What titled person earned another title—*slut*—when he gainfully employed oodles of male hustlers while cavorting on the West Coast? What porn star is a part-time rent boy who's been hired by that movie mogul and that faded sitcom actor, just to name two illustrious checkbook carriers? What porn star *isn't* a part-time rent boy who's been hired by, etc.? What owner of a popular Chelsea restaurant self-loathingly enough tells friends, "I don't want this to be a place for queens"? What diva developed a black eye when the doctor administering her Botox shot accidentally hit an artery? (And we thought she only had nerves.)

What comic-film director used to get off on watching his famous wife do it with that female comedy legend, according to that still-living 1930s movie star? Why don't I believe that 1930s movie star? (Free answer: Because, while I'm sure the two women got it on, I sincerely doubt that the director got off on it.) What wildly successful daughter/actress is a devilish deadbeat who has to be coerced to pay her rent? What Christian recording artist/prick had a boyfriend he used to

beat up in a distinctly non-Christian fashion before he magically acquired a beard-slash-wifeypoo? What actor was
boyfriends until recently with that hotshot director who
helped guide him to Oscar? What internationally known
designer is gay, and his wife apparently knows it; she recently
told a handsome young 'un, "I'd better not leave you alone
with my husband. He *likes* cute boys like you"?

What tough-guy movie star started that ridiculous gerbil
rumor all those years ago because he fancied himself a
competitor with Richard Gere and figured it would be easier
to spread the gossip than simply learn how to act? What
hypnotist-magician is a sham who makes his TV subjects
sign releases saying they won't reveal all the pre-scripting?
What hypnotist-magician *isn't* a sham who, etc.? What glammy
new star has a not very glamorous little weenie? What gonzo
reporter is rumored to have made an unrequited play for
Andrew Sullivan at a party? (Sullivan spurned my request for
comment.) What blond actress has a prosthetic finger—not
as a result of fighting with that famed scion—that she lost
on a recent TV movie set, causing much hilarious havoc?
What awards show scene-stealer is a flamingly gay trophy
boy? What much acclaimed glossy style-mag editor is a fabulous lesbian with a baby?

What thirtyish heartthrob, a worldwide masturbatory fan-
tasy, is a walking testament to hair plugs? What lithe crossover
diva/cunt would stare straight ahead, reach out her hand,
and demand "Water!" during a recent video shoot, and, on a
separate occasion, alienated a major designer by ripping a
hole in the dress he'd made for her, because she thought it

looked better that way? What gimmicky '98 movie originally had characters sporting Nazi armbands, which had to be digitally altered at great expense when test audiences found it unsettling? What unkempt, druggy indie director made a play for a drag queen friend of mine?

What screen legend was approached last year by a fan who said, "You were robbed at the Oscars," to which she charmingly replied, "Was I speaking to you?" (Another freebie: Lauren Bacall.) What superstar—her again—was dining with one of her good-for-nothing but gorgeous ex-boyfriends when he murmured, "Can I have $10,000"? How smart was she that she said no? Why has the new Robin Byrd–presented CD of Latin love songs only been distributed to HMV? (I have no idea, but as Byrd exclaims, "They should be at Virgin! My Grammy dreams are lost!") Could that teenie group seem any gayer?

What's the most bizarre new porno video? (Answer: *Bend Over, Boyfriend*, an instructional tape about female-to-male anal penetration, for all those straight guys anxious to be plowed by ladies bearing strap-on dildos. Come on, try it, Kelly and John!) Which of Monica Lewinsky's remarks on 20/20 gets the "close but no cigar" award for not quite capturing why Bill was hot for her? ("Sometimes you just need a piece of . . . normalcy.")

What's with these Broadway "revivals"? (I don't know, but the folks bringing you the new, ill-conceived *Annie Get Your Gun* were clearly so uncomfortable with the source material that they rewrote it, added some winks, nudges, and a Lord of the Dance number, and presented it all as a play within a play.

The remaining joy is in the score and in the fact that when Bernadette Peters stops mugging for a second, she can remind us of her stature as a treasured musical presence. But just how pandering is this production? Well, a typical moment comes after the wonderful "An Old-Fashioned Wedding," when Peters turns to the audience and says, "You want [to hear] it again?"—though maybe she's doing so as the actress within the actress.) And what's with *new* musicals? (Beats me, but the affectionate if misguided *Band in Berlin*—about a sort of Weimar Manhattan of Transfer—manages to suck most of the drama out of the story in favor of providing a concert–slide show that should be relegated to high school auditoriums, but not that many of them.)

What did Joan Rivers tell me last week about Geena Davis's rival pre-Oscar show? (One last complimentary answer: "Geena said, 'I'm not gonna ask any shallow fashion questions.' Well, she has no *right* to! She came looking like a drunken dance-hall girl one year! I guess I'm gonna ask the shallow questions and she's going to ask about Bosnia.") How deep is your love? (I really need to learn.)

SURVIVING THE SURVIVING
OF 9-11

When did opening an envelope become a heroic feat?

December 4, 2001

Excuse me, but how are we supposed to find Bin Laden when we can't even track down Dick Cheney? That's been just one of the myriad of sick thoughts engulfing my mind during wartime, a situation that truly preys on my last nerve.

Of course things have started looking up—burkas already seem so last season—but even as the Taliban tumbles, anxiety continues to taint the everyday experience. Let me back up a little, to September 11, when New York became a stunned, alienated metropolis right out of a sci-fi movie, with an atmosphere of thick dust, a backdrop of overlapping flyers screaming out for missing people, and a populace of survivors walking in circles, some breaking into crying jags without warning, the rest stumbling about in an impenetrable daze. The downtown skyline, which was so majestic, suddenly looked a tad too similar to that of Pittsburgh or Milwaukee, the demolition reflecting our pain while threatening to make New York City second-rate and defeated. But then came the response: caring, dedication, restoration, and charity, all reminders of why this town is a kick-ass capital you can screw, but you can't fuck with!

Alas, since wartime brings out the best *and* worst in people, some truly rotten behavior was just around the (barricaded) corner. The most heinous offender may well have been me; I spent way too much time worrying about when my trivial lifestyle would resume (immediately, it turned out) and kvetching about how, when AIDS first came around, no one gave a shit about *that* devastation, since the victims were practically considered deserving! (But pitting tragedies against one another won't accomplish anything, I learned—just take each new horror afresh. Besides, I'm not that proud of my *own* initial response to AIDS.)

My runners-up in shame were the freaks who wanted to see no evil, hear no evil, speak no evil, and basically do nothing. You know, the righteous, flag-waving thought police who seriously said stuff like "Bill Maher and Susan Sontag should shut the fuck up. We've got to squelch any internal dissent so we can concentrate on fighting to preserve our democracy!" (And they said irony was dead.) Their brethren in ignominy were the folks obsessed with erasing problematic images from pop culture—you know, the worrywarts who snipped out representations of the towers and references to terrorism—absurdly discarding reminders of both good and evil, sort of the way Joan Crawford trimmed her exes out of photo albums. And alongside those denial queens were the worst-case scenarists who were even willing to take *themselves* out of the picture. These nervous nellies stayed home in fear during the Halloween parade, thereby sticking a razor blade in the

Apple—as if our spirits and economy weren't suffering enough! Again, the terrorists won big-time (though a well-meaning socialite did recently call around, trying to organize a visit to the hard-hit Chinatown, generously cooing, "After all, they're New Yorkers, too!").

And the zaniness kept on coming, as racial profiling became a popular response, especially at airports, where, if you have an olive complexion or a "funny" name, you can be taken into a private room and asked to drink from your water bottle. (Of course, if you're a kamikaze, you'd gladly do so anyway.)

Once the anthrax hit, fear truly divided us, and the country was awash in extra doses of panic and sensationalism; no doubt as Bin Laden sat back, laughing, and saying, "I can't even take credit for this one!" The government's blanket calmings on the subject only made us more frantic, especially since the cable channels were taking the opposite, screeching approach, and among all of them, no one could tell us just what to do about this unimaginable new horror. We were all learning along with Bush, though each new "Make no mistake about it . . ." failed to quell our misgivings, especially since we couldn't quite hear him in our gas masks and bodysuits!

The friendly neighborhood postman was suddenly in a Hefty bag and handing us our letters with ice tongs. And if you opened an envelope in public, people screamed and started running to the nearest shower stall. Their anxiety rubbed off more than any powder does, and gripped by contagious dread, I started wondering if it's really worth dying just to open some crappy press release for a celebrity photo op. (Answer: Yes. This is what I do, and I'll keep doing it, thank you, oh Taliban masters. Besides, when a paycheck arrives, you'd be amazed at how brave a person can become.)

But just open a *newspaper* and you felt assaulted anyway. Designer Wolfgang Joop made moronic remarks that implied we deserved the attack because the towers represented "capitalist arrogance"—this from a man who's made a fortune out of selling overpriced clothes and cologne—but again, such views are protected, as are Richard Gere's, as are those of the war protesters Chelsea Clinton yelled at, as are the opinions of Chelsea Clinton herself. But they're all dumb!

So let's just try to be rational (and stop rejoicing when a plane crash looks like it's only the result of mechanical failure). And while acknowledging their achievements, let's stop painting all men in uniform as impossibly superhuman—that won't even do *them* any good. But most of all, let's quit with all the irony funerals, since I have so many more examples of its renaissance that irony is clearly the new lambada. To wit: You can't bring tweezers aboard a plane, but just recently you could show up with knives and a loaded gun and be greeted with "Right this way, sir." Also, celebs got guided tours of Ground Zero (and Jack Nicholson even got to play with a crane), while victims' loved ones were only being shown red tape, hard luck, and the back of the bus. More irony? Reports that the beloved fire chaplain, Father Mychal Judge, was gay provoked outrage, but meanwhile, the Feds were awkwardly speculating as to whether demonic hijacker Mohamed Atta was a sister! And the same people who were angry at those gay Father Mychal reports ran around reminding everyone, "He was in AA!" And in perhaps the best example of irony's triumph, a gay guy heroically helped divert one of the hijacked planes, but if he'd lived, he wouldn't have been allowed to give blood!

Irony's even king on Broadway, where dark classics like *Hedda Gabler* and *Dance of Death* have survived largely because they're being played like sitcoms. And Hollywood power brokers anxiously started meeting with the government to forge a "patriotic" plan, forgetting once again that we're fighting for the right to have a free culture. Of course officials loudly insisted that they weren't asking for propaganda, but I'm sure that was just propaganda.

But what the heck, I'm thrilled to live in this great land of opportunity—even if I do get a little nervous when Bush malapropically says stuff like "nucular." (I guess grammar's not important when you're tearing new holes in the Taliban.) Don't be mad—my views are protected too. Make no mistake about it.

24-HOUR PARTY PEEPHOLE

Bosom buddies:
Who's the new it girl?

June 14, 1988

After many contenders, I think I finally stumbled on the worst party of this century so far—the postconcert soiree for Belinda Carlisle at the aptly named Heartbreak (as in "of psoriasis"). You crawled through the kitchen and down to a dank room that was all abuzz with 10 people and two bowls of pretzels. The plentiful drink tickets couldn't get you a Coke—only beer and whine. An aura of Forever Krystle—or cat pee—glamorously permeated the air. A limo stopped outside, then kept going—Belinda? Belinda come home! "Heaven is a place on earth," sings Ms. Carlisle. I'm still looking.

More fun—if not exactly sophisticated entertainment—was the night the Tunnel kids threw water balloons, pulled people into pools, and sprayed everyone with squirt guns, leaving the basement in Ranchipur-like shambles; oh well, Rudolf was on vacation. Meanwhile, at Boy Bar, drag queens dragged each other through the mud in their own pool, in which they wrestled viciously—a benefit for Gay Pride.

At that event was Sandra Bernhard, wryly claiming to be

a drag queen. This lippy lady has dropped from her show the line about Bruce Weber riding "the Hershey highway"—too much mud flung there?—but she's added a roasting of *VV*'s Laurie Stone, who trashed the show, then nervily left a message asking Bernhard for input on the Gay Pride issue. Bernhard, who feels the whole incident was "just beyond," now plays the message onstage. "I never dreamed my words would have such an impact on her," says Stone. "Maybe we should all leave messages for Sandra." Mud-wrestling anyone?

Wednesday at Bentley's, obese sadist Mistress Barbara forced her dildo on an ungainly slave with clothespins on his nips, and once again Lady Hennessy Brown lactated at the crowd, who held out glasses of Kahlua hoping to make White Russians. For a finale, she spread her legs wider than the Ganges as the M.C. said, "And you thought Mick Jagger had big lips." I just report these things.

Speaking of white Russians, club starlet Julie Jewels looks like Dianne Brill, also dated Rudolf, and has now decided to be a designer, too. "And I'm going to go out of business like Dianne," she laughs. Dianne's relatively low club profile lately (among other projects, she's playing a waitress at a mud-wrestling bar—a lot of that going around—in a film) has paved the way for the slinkier Julie and now and then, double-breasted Nanci Zipkin.

And wacky sparks are flying. In Queen Sheba's *Court* magazine—a club handout in which Julie usually columnizes about herself—Ms. Jewels called Dianne "yesterday's goddess." She also wrote that Dianne was recently mistaken for her. And then, in an otherwise glowing profile of Brill (Do we detect an obsession?), Julie wrote that Dianne sold designs to "Sacks" [sic]. Faux-Jewels recently won the World's "Bitch-Off" and was loudly told by Baby Gregor to use her cash prize on surgery so she wouldn't look like Dianne anymore. Or maybe she should give it to Dianne to not look like her anymore. Dianne, meanwhile, is taking all this in stride, offering Julie pointers over lunch—a big "hi-ski" conquers all. Are these taxing women or *shayna maidels?* To quote Joan Crawford, "You figure it out!"

The best party this week was Harvey Fierstein blowing in, monsoonlike, to shoot some of his *Torch Song Trilogy* movie, pausing only to schmooze me about the cast. Anne Bancroft, as his mom, is "a total pro—there's not a wasted lash." Ken Page does drag as Marcia Dimes; Charles Pierce is Bertha Vanation; hunky Brian Kerwin's the guy Harvey ends up with. And Matthew Broderick, who was the boy on Broadway, has graduated into the role of the lover (Brian and Matthew fighting over Harvey? Well, he wrote it).

"Matthew grew up," says Harvey. "What are you gonna do? It was a strange adjustment for us. All of a sudden I had to treat him with a different kind of respect." I know quite a few people who'd like to treat Matthew with whatever kind of respect he wants.

The play has been rethought, cinema-style, and cut to about two hours, but mercifully, the International Stud scene has not been axed (though there won't be actual penetration; I asked). "I will get fucked in a backroom bar," says Harvey, definitively. "We're filming that in L.A. Basically you need a black room with a couple of red lightbulbs. I mean we could film that in Peoria.

"I'm not ashamed of our past, or my past. I did go to backrooms and yes, if they want to say that it caused a lot of people to get sick because people were promiscuous, they're right—so what are you gonna do? We didn't do it to hurt anybody. We certainly didn't do it to commit suicide. And I think the people who'll criticize me for putting the scene in are the same ones who would call it a whitewash if I took it out."

The week *Torch Song* opens, *Legs Diamond*—for which he wrote the book—hits Broadway with "three times the sets and costumes as *La Cage*." *Torch Song*, the movie, is "five million times gayer than the play." Harvey—who recently called heterosexuals "pigs" and "the ungrateful children of the gay culture" to a *Times* reporter (who wasn't writing anything down)—is a zillion times more outspoken than anybody around. He's my favorite party line, better even than Dial-a-LOAD.

New clubs, same old people

December 15, 1992

New Year's Eve used to mean confetti and champagne and noisemakers, but now it means Chaka Khan at the Roxy screaming, "AIDS is a disease that has developed from germ warfare. It's a form of genocide. They're trying to kill off a type of people. It transcends racism . . . ," and so on, until our already feeble party spirit had waned into so many bent and soggy swizzle sticks.

That wasn't the only existential moment of this annual exercise in pathologically seeking release, then seeking help when it doesn't come. The place didn't feature any go-go boys, presumably so as not to offend the mixed crowd, which I think would have offended the go-go boys anyway. Plus there were only four drag queens dancing, as opposed to the usual army of tucked and plucked beauties. So while Roxy used to mean a colorful swirl of pecs and pearls and pretend-girls, this night it meant a little too much biologically correct big hair from New Jersey. As for Chaka, she sat in her limo outside for an hour before the show, "getting ready," and no doubt preparing her very festive speech. She's every woman.

At Club USA the same night, drag performer RuPaul—who's every man, too—faced a mostly straight audience who looked bewildered as he launched into his own pronouncement: "When Clinton gave his victory speech and he embraced Gore, it clicked in my mind—they're lovers. We're going to have a gay White House and I am going to the inauguration!" Jaws in the crowd dropped so low they're still leaving skidmarks. And they might *really* be agog if they learned that Ru's song "Supermodel" ("Sashay, shanté . . .") is climbing the dance and maxisingles charts, is in active rotation on MTV, and is No. 2 (right above Madonna) on the Telegenics club video chart.

At the Academy, Pearl Jam's grungy but brilliant Eddie Vedder had the audience chant along with the night's shortest sermon of all: "Fuck Marky Mark!" And the throng of queens over at the Tunnel's Saint party echoed his sentiments loudly when, after behaving like a testosterous Gypsy Rose Lee at the Palladium, the otherwise accommodating rapper/ecdysiast made a point of not even taking his rings off in a sudden fit of hypocritical demureness (this even though an alleged photo outtake of him, totally bare and erect, has been making the fax rounds). Of course the guy, who's painted himself into a corner by making seminudity his call to arms, has every right to try to change his image; it's just funny that he only chooses to do so on gay nights. And it's especially baffling since Marky's so insistently gay-positive in the press, going out of his way to relate how cool it is to "suck dick," even if he doesn't engage in that activity himself, tsk-tsk.

But the real Marky is another story entirely—a protectively sweatshirted creature who's apparently terrified either that gays are lechers who'll rape and "convert" him on the spot, or that playing to the gay crowd will somehow cheapen his already lower than lowbrow shtick. So he just takes the bookings, pockets the dough, and keeps his paranoid distance, while adding more layers of clothing and saying yet more gay-positive things to the press. Someone should sit the boy down and tell him that he's *already* playing to the gay crowd, so his imaginary line of demarcation—rapping, but not unwrapping—is rather idiotic. And that doing a shirtless, pantsless Calvin Klein ad campaign is playing to the gay crowd to the nth degree, honey. If he doesn't peel off his double standard soon, Marky will keep leaving gay audiences wet with hostility rather than delight, and those bookings will surely evaporate into so much hot air (at least one already has). I mean, does anyone really run to a Marky Mark concert exulting, "I can't wait to hear 'You Gotta Believe'!"?

Anyway, let me step off my high horse and go back to the solid ground of the cavernous Tunnel itself, which—like Marky's nerve—is somehow longer than ever, and still has that damned narrow railway that now provides a 20-minute push-and-shove to the cattle-car-like dance floor. But it is majestic in a raw, culty way and has an underground feeling that appeals to the kid in me. And by the March official opening, it'll be even bigger, and ready to challenge the

Roxy's long-standing Saturday night head on; you gotta believe *both* will have go-go boys up the wazoo.

Between Tunnel, USA's Thierry Mugler Room, and the 10th Street Lounge—a new boxlike hangout in the East Village—the raw, exposed-brick feeling of calculated decay is back (do I smell a seven-page *Times* style piece coming on?). There's a market for it; the 10th Street Lounge is so packed it's clearly for those who *fetishize* the old push-and-shove. In fact, when I went, the crowd seemed to consist mostly of preprofessional NYUers vastly suited to that concept, though I'm sure they'd rather go up than sideways.

But one doesn't need to know any of those people, actually. If one's interested in dance clubbing as a lifestyle, there are only three names that you need list in your Rolodex lately. If you happen to like these three folks and they like you, you're set for a rich and fulfilling lifetime of free admission, comp cocktails, and whatever house records you want to hear. But if you find them the least bit distasteful, or vice versa, promptly start preparing for another career (perhaps one of the ones Sally Struthers advertises in those correspondence school commercials—art appreciation, gun control, child care, dental hygiene, etc.). For the record, the trendy trilogy of terror is: club owner Peter Gatien (Limelight, Palladium, USA, Tunnel), gay party promoter/*Homo Xtra* honcho Marc Berkley (Limelight, USA, Tunnel), and DJ Merritt (Sugar Babies, Limelight, USA, Sound Factory Bar, Tunnel, and sometimes Roxy and Sound Factory). Monopoly, anyone?

It's amazing that I can form an opinion on this or anything, as a crumblet of New Year's Ecstasy found its way into my being and by 6 A.M. had me wielding a piece of peeled fruit and beaming at strangers, "Have you ever noticed how great orange rind smells? Isn't Mother Nature wonderful?" Help! Still, one's always coherent enough for gossip. Like: DJ Anita Sarko is producing demos for Mary McFadden's ex, Kohle Yohannan. . . . Katharine Hepburn is up against Drew Barrymore for a Golden Globe award. . . . Cable TV hostess Robin Byrd will soon be eligible for an Oscar, having just wrapped up a small part in *Life With Mikey* starring Michael J. Fox. "He came up to my breasts—just the right height," laughs Byrd. Even more amusingly, the talk-and-gawk diva's trailer had her character's name—Bambi—on it, prompting kids walking by to screech, "Look, ma—Bambi's in there!" Robin was tempted to step out in her skimpy costume and show them that, while this is also a Disney film, the Bambi in question was a go-go dancer, not a deer. But, like Marky Mark, she demurred. . . . In one more *Times*-ready coincidence, *Malcolm X* ends with children announcing, "I am Malcolm X" and *Lorenzo's Oil* concludes with real kids saying, "I take Lorenzo's oil." Some possible recent film endings that were mercifully averted: "I am Hoffa!"; "I am Bram Stoker's Dracula!"; "I take used people."

Heel, ball, toe, pivot, puke: when models attack

September 7, 1993

The unthinkable has happened, and models and model wannabes—who used to be the fringe element in nightlife that we all scoffed at—have somehow become the central crowd, the ones who dictate where we go and what we do. With clubs and restaurants becoming meat markets again, the focus has returned to superficiality and looks, a sad reality fueled by feverish fascination with Seventh Avenue to the point where someone who merely talks about wanting to assemble a portfolio suddenly assumes the massive importance of a demigod. It's a total warp on the creative aesthetics that clubs are supposed to be based on, and while it's the same situation in L.A., it's *always* been that way there (and anywhere sunny). Here, where the mythical melting pot has become a shiny copper bowl, it's far more frightening, and something must be done about it.

We, the uglies, must seize control back from these implant-laden pods and lock them up in jail cells without mirrors, visiting them only to taunt them with talk of potential go-sees. We must throw battery acid in their faces until their collagen dissolves; lobotomize them so the one thought lingering in their brains—whatever happened on *Beverly Hills, 90210* last week—will be eradicated and they can start afresh; make them scrub Zsa Zsa Gabor's floors until they know the true meaning of work, bitch, work. Join me, my brothers and sisters—let's take back the night from these vain and vapid pretties and restore it to the vain and vapid trolls, who at least have some character. Let's make the world safe for those who don't care about whether their tattooed eyeliner matches their fake Chanel handbags. And while we're at it, can we please banish that agent (Peter Pan or Pervert?) who chronically urges male models to stay over at his house—where there's only one bed, conveniently enough—and they generally awake to find him giving them a blow job (not the job they'd hoped for, alas)?

Until this crisis is resolved, I'm content to buck the trend and go anywhere models and their agents are not. That leaves a handful of frightening places. At Roxy, promoter/nonmodel David Leigh ended up naked (except for an ill-positioned belt) onstage, and while I found it kind of cute, someone else was heard to murmur to a friend, "If I ever get that desperate, promise you'll shoot me." . . . Gunning for revenge, USA/Limelight/(whatever happened to?) Tunnel owner Peter Gatien was irked about a recent daily columnist's item that suggested he may have called the fire trucks on a rival club (his flack denies the charge). Convinced it was promoter Kelly Cole who phoned in the item (though Cole denies *that* charge), he said Cole could come into his office on bended knee. "Get the fuck outta here," the promoter responded, defiantly. . . . That '80s den of non-Equity, the World, where we trolls enjoyed debauched nights that made Sodom and Gomorrah look like Minneapolis–St. Paul, is now a religious establishment called the Morning Star Tabernacle (their motto is "God is able"). God help them.

And back in the church of the poisoned mind, that whirlwind of Ronald McDonaldesque drag chic named Brandywine threw herself a model-free birthday dinner at Burrito Bar and managed to get throngs to come, pay, and pay *hommage* to her—an amazing feat considering that you can't even get anyone to come to comp dinners these days. As Brandywine videos played and "Brandy" (scrawled over the name "Barbie") streamers hit us on the head, the entrepreneur/cable host spent the entire party extorting the $11.50 prix fixe out of each person ("So you won't forget to pay later and get caught").

At the event, a new piece of Southern trade on the scene named Bubba admitted that Boy George had taken a liking to him and had been calling him with some frequency. "But he's very respectful of the situation," Bubba said, meaning that George knows Bubba has a boyfriend. Who's currently spending nine months in Ecuador.

Respectful of another situation—the appearance of Miramax cohead Harvey Weinstein at a screening of Richard Linklater's *Dazed and Confused*—the film's publicist was extraordinarily attentive to the guy. "Did you do drugs in high school?" the flack asked him. Nope, the mogul replied. "Well, you'll love the film anyway," grinned the flack. "Will you tell me what you thought of it tomorrow?" Sure thing, said Weinstein. But funny, I doubt that later exchange ever took place; smack dab in the middle of the flick, Weinstein raced out the door. Dazed and confused? "Knowing him, he's very busy," said a Miramax publicist the next day. "He probably had a business meeting."

Some more knowledge you won't garner from Mind Extension University: Isn't one of the male dancers for Madonna's "Girlie Show" tour a veritable impregnating machine, albeit one who can be bought for gay sex, to the tune of 200 smackers? Didn't the cute, youngish creator of that upcoming low-budget comedy used to be David Geffen's boyfriend? And wasn't it that multithreat quirky screenwriter who spent a week in a Royalton suite with something he dragged home from the Gaiety? Yes, yes, by all means yes—as surely as Hollywood Madam Heidi Fleiss gives new meaning to the expression "Heidi-ho."

And—if vampire talk isn't too much of a stretch here—am I nuts to feel that Tom Cruise, while seemingly a bad choice to star in *Interview with the Vampire*, should be allowed the chance to try, as long as he doesn't downplay the script's homo/androgynous elements? I'm sure he's as sated as we are of his playing the young schmuck who becomes enlightened by a best friend's brain tumor.

Wouldn't all the people pooh-poohing Cruise's casting have also told Phranc that she was all wrong to portray the great Neil Diamond? Undoubtedly. Yet, her tribute to Diamond at Dance Theater Workshop was the most amusing I've seen by a Jewish lesbian folksinger, or by anyone, for that matter. With hip-swiveling bravado, she presented a faux Diamond far finer than anything available on the Home Shopping Club. The audience went particularly berserk during "Longfellow Serenade," when Phranc/Neil suggestively gestured to her crotch on the word *Longfellow*. I also liked the bizarre passage from that classic work, "Sweet Caroline": "Warm . . . touching warm . . . reaching out . . . touching you, touching me," which Phranc somehow rendered both unsettling and heartfelt. An off moment, though, came during the opening act—Phranc as herself—when the singer lamented all her recently deceased friends and assured us that she won't be joining them any time soon. "I'm a life lover," she sang gleefully—as if anyone who's dropped dead wasn't.

The late International Chrysis certainly worshipped her life, and her joie de vivre is documented in *Split*, a revealing portrait of an insouciant drag siren, the Cyd Charisse of downtown. Another smallish film, *Sex Is . . .* , is an affecting peek at gay men's libidos and how you can embrace life even as it's taken from you. Both should be required viewing for models who feel combination skin is the most insurmountable problem goddess can deal you.

How Michael Alig deals with another kind of bars

June 24, 1997

As someone who's put out a lot of harsh commentary about club-kid-king-turned-accused-killer Michael Alig—I don't know, I just have a problem with dead bodies—I've been charged with sometimes going overboard in painting him as the devil's spawn (though I've *always* seen him as half genius, half nightmare). Having just come across a bunch of old invites for Alig's club debauches—many of which I was involved with—it reminded me that, before he totally lost control, a lot of Alig's career involved wildly liberating acts of outrage that were annoying in a *good* way. His glittering world of in-your-face mutants made hedonism commercial again— until its defining lack of boundaries proved to be its downfall.

Torn between affection and horror, I decided to give my old cohort a chance to speak for himself. I went to the Metropolitan Detention Center on White Street, where the waiting room is ominous, hot, and bleak, filled with adorable kids their mommies brought to see their serial-killer daddies. They're now joined by club kids. After being made to go through detectors, put all my belongings into a locker, and go through more detectors, I was finally escorted to the visiting area—actually an enclosed section of it designated the Children's Playroom. "It's the VIP room" said a voice, with a mild laugh. It was Alig. Instead of wearing his old French-maid-meets-space-age-Bozo chic, he was in de rigueur prison drab. He had a light beard and short hair and appeared calm, clear-eyed, and a bit pudgy; Alig's new sedentary lifestyle has caused him to gain 32 pounds.

Alig explained that he is getting VIP—as in Very Important Prisoner—treatment. He said the PCs (those in protective custody) like him don't mix with the GPs (General Population). They're often called "sir" by the guards. They have a gym, a TV area, and more to eat than they need ("It's a shame tax dollars are going to so much wasted food"). They even flaunt press clippings to prove who's more famous. But, while it's better than the seven other jails Alig's been in, this isn't the Limelight, by any means. It's punishingly alienating, I guess the way a prison's supposed to be.

One recent night, Alig said, he pulled his pants down and squatted in protest when an official wouldn't let him get to the bathroom. Later on, a vengeful captain made him strip again, sputtered some sexually threatened remarks, then threw Alig's belongings down and covered them with a garbage pail.

"I can't connect with anyone here," Alig told me, sounding miserable. "I miss just enjoying an orange or a movie. I'm a physical person. I miss the physical contact with friends."

Um, speaking of which, Alig and his cohort Freeze (who's in another clinic) are implicated in offing their pal, drug dealer Angel Melendez, supposedly in the middle of a tussle over money. Alig's lawyer has gotten the murder charge down to manslaughter and is pushing to go to trial to continue the battle. Right now they're dealing with a maximum sentence of 13 years, but if he gets five or more, Alig said, he'll kill himself by OD'ing. "I'm not saying that so people will feel sorry for me," he explained. "If I was in here a really long time, then they should feel sorry for me."

Ironically, now that he's drug free, Alig sometimes imagines that substances could be of use. "This is the worst place to be off drugs," he said. "My nerve endings are working again, but I'm in here! Heroin cures boredom. If I were on heroin, I could stare at that chair for eight hours and not need any other stimuli. But I'm adamant that once outside, I'm staying clean."

Even inside, when he starts entertaining druggie thoughts, Alig stops short. "I think of Angel and his family," he told me. In fact, hallucinogens clearly aren't needed because Alig said he regularly dreams of, and even has chats with, Angel. "We talk about what happened," Alig said, "and sometimes he tells me not to worry and sometimes he's coming at me to strangle me again. One time it was so real I woke up screaming."

Alig had another awakening when he saw Freeze at a court date a few weeks ago. Surprisingly, they didn't go at each other with hammers and Drano. "We hugged and cried," he said. "I thought he'd be mad at me, but he feels exactly the same as I do [that punishment is due]. Now that I'm reading *Crime and Punishment*, I know why I blabbed. I must have wanted to stop me. I was spinning out of control. It's like the old saying, 'What do you have to do to get attention around here—kill somebody?'"

These days, Alig can only kill time, mostly with regrets. For one thing, he wishes he hadn't done every drug known to man. "I was your total pill-popping, K-snorting mess," Alig admitted. "I'd do more than 15 hits of dope a day. I was shooting up five or six hits at once. It was always available to me—that was my problem. I was later told someone had brought 60 bags of dope to my place on credit, and I didn't even remember it. Sixty bags!" Will he take responsibility for what happened? "Not sole responsibility—not that I'm an angel." Embarrassed pause. "That night, we were on heroin, K, coke, Rohypinol, Ecstasy. . . ." He was so far gone, he said, "we thought everything was OK [with Angel]. We didn't even realize there was a problem." Can I get a "fucked up"?

As for more pertinent questions: Did Alig really get off on watching snuff films? "There was a movie called *Snuff*. It wasn't real. The subtitle was 'Made in New York, Where Life Is Cheap.'" How does he feel about his ex-boss, Peter Gatien? "I hold no grudge against Peter," he said, but wouldn't elaborate. And how about Alig's ex-boyfriend Keoki (who's paying his legal fees)? "We're closer than ever. When I get out, he wants me to be a housewife. That's what I wanted to be when I first met him, but he didn't ask me— he wanted to be a superstar—so I made myself a drug addict! Anyway, now the idea sort of appeals to me again.

He's been buying all this Lego, which I collect. It's good because it gives me something to look forward to." "What happened to Angel's legos?" I cracked, ghoulishly. To his credit, Alig didn't laugh.

Fascinatingly, the domestic dream isn't the only one captivating Alig. Like everyone else with any kind of name, he wants to—you're not going to believe this, but it sort of makes sense—direct. "I have all these million-dollar ideas in my head," he said. "I want to do a movie combining the nonediting of Warhol, the supernatural quality of David Lynch, and the campiness of John Waters." *Blue Flamingos?* Whatever the case, he wants to use his old posse as stars— "whoever's left of them when I get out."

Meanwhile, he's written a diary for *Paper* and is working on his memoirs, which he said World of Wonder's Fenton Bailey and Randy Barbato (who manage RuPaul and are doing a TV documentary about Alig called *Party Monster*) have bought. They've also procured the rights to eternal club kid James St. James's account.

Before Hollywood could call to ask if Alig wants Robert Downey Jr. or Andy Dick, it was time for us to go back to our respective cells. But first Alig gave me one more bit of self-reflection to chew on: "My mother said I always tried to push people for attention. I did it with Peter, I did it with everybody. She said, 'Maybe Angel was the last push.' "

Hair peace:
the Wigstock drag festival

September 16, 1997

I caught the first eight hours or so of Wigstock—held on the now ozone-depleted 15th Street Pier—and was delighted that the $10 admission seemed to weed out the types who generally come to laugh at, rather than with, the drag proceedings (I guess they'd rather do so gratis). The event created its own mockery-free zone, but, while there were some low points, it wasn't talent-free, by any means. Everyone turned it out, wore it upside down, and set it on fire—on heels yet.

The most common routine of the day was a number—any number—from that 'ho-down *The Life*, which has apparently become the drag inspiration of the '90s. The most frequent jokes were leveled at trannie-chaser Eddie Murphy, butch Rosie O'Donnell (who rails against Hollywood homophobia in the new *Us!*), and Mayor Giuliani, whom Wigstock's MC-organizer Lady Bunny said didn't return her calls inviting him to appear—"and you'd think he'd *want* to wear a wig with that sad comb-over job he's been sporting for years."

Bunny also got in a dig at the conspicuously absent RuPaul, saying, "Since Ru couldn't be here, I'll do her whole act: 'Everybody say *love*. This is the front. This is the back.' " At that point, she let out a loud farting noise and one sensed just a tiny hint of bitterness in the air.

But mostly things were upbeat—or at least up-tempo—and the occasional acts that mystified the audience at least couldn't be accused of pandering. Barbara Patterson Lloyd did a hilarious spoof of Riverdance, backed by a chorus of demented dervishes. Harmonica Sunbeam performed "Crazy" in a straitjacket. Sybil Barrington recited a list of "things that piss me off" (for example, "date rape with no money"). And the drag kings of Club Casanova did a Village People number that caught just the right textures inherent in gay women mock-embracing gay men's mock-embracing of straight male stereotypes (and afterward, Mo B. Dick told me she's playing a satanic lesbian stripper in John Waters's upcoming *Pecker*).

The only downers, as always, were the disco singers who have precious little to do with drag and who seem to view the event as a giant promotional blitz for their latest records. Ultra Naté was particularly offensive, berating the audience for not responding to her performance. She demanded, "You're gonna give me some energy! It's real easy to catch onto," and made us sing along with her tired song when we were really in the mood to *be* entertained. But, hey, it wouldn't be a Wigstock without some serious ugliness to help you appreciate all that unbelievable beauty on parade.

We kept the six-inch Pradas on for a whole mess of other

fashionable happenings, like the Marc Jacobs store opening in Soho, where Anthony Kiedis said his arm cast was the result of a motorcycle accident; Taylor Dayne told me, "Be nice, diva!" which suddenly made me feel very mischievous; and fabulous model Irina went on about how she'd seen my writing, and I was all thrilled until realizing she'd actually said, "I've seen you riding"—as in, on a bike! Real impressive stuff!

She got to see it again when I jumped on the nearest two-wheeler the second I spotted Sheryl Crow at the party. (I'd caught that *Strange Universe* segment about "The Curse of Sheryl Crow.") That took me to Balthazar's party for *The Game*, where a preggers Sean Young was radiating a sweet serenity that emboldened me to tell her I kept the Sean Young promotional panties they gave out for her movie *Fatal Instinct*. "You still have them?" she said. "I'm wearing them!" I exclaimed, as the entire room fell silent. "He's just like Theresa," Sean murmured suspiciously to her husband, and I didn't dare ask what that meant.

At this point, Sean spotted her old *Wall Street* buddy, the head *Game* player Michael Douglas, and she jumped up to greet him as hubby narrated, "Photo op! Photo op!" Or maybe not; two seconds later, Sean limped back to the table, quite defeated looking. "Wow! He ran right off," she said, no doubt reliving the horror of the days when her uppity, macho costars would pin four-letter words on her back. I asked Ms. *Fatal Instinct* why Mr. *Fatal Attraction* would dis her and she said, "I don't know. You ask him." I passed, since I was there to celebrate *The Game*, not play it.

After getting on that fucking bike one more time, I thought I'd found myself back at the Jacobs store, but it was actually Wax, a few doors down, where I was instantly handed a cardboard tiara to help celebrate the birthday of *Paper*'s David Hershkovits. Be nice, diva! In the tiara, panties, and heels, I looked extra fine at the MTV Video Music Awards the next night, joining in the mesmerizing parade of ritualized eccentricity. But when Madonna stopped rolling on her mother's grave long enough to tell us that we shouldn't pursue gossip or scandal, I wanted to turn to the Weather Channel to see if hell had just frozen over. Backstage, winners veered between mock-humility and scary megalomania, and I preferred the megalomania. Ginger Spice was handling recent tragic events with great Spice Girl dignity, blurting, "Prince Charles has got a nice bum." Chris Rock was similarly commenting about Mariah Carey's I'm-single-again outfit, "You can see the black in the ass." Martha Stewart was discussing her current musical faves and admitting, "I have a penchant for the Wallflowers" (she *would* go for a floral arrangement). And Jewel was being fairly realistic, enthusing, "I don't have to waitress ever again!" But don't forget the specials of the day just yet, honey. Then came a winners' wave of studied self-deprecation, with every celeb within miles trying to convince us of their heinously low worth, from Wu-Tang Clan's Method Man saying of his performance in *Cop Land*, "I need some lessons," to John Popper asking us if his onstage presentation with Dermot Mulroney "really sucked" (yeah, but not nearly as much as David Arquette's with Lisa Marie Presley's—will someone please take away whatever he's on and give it to her?). Fortunately, Puff Daddy managed to tie all the issues of the day together with élan, saying, "Diana made everybody feel good. You know she's in heaven with Biggie, Betty Shabazz, and Ennis." Yeah, I'm sure they're all doing a gigantic rap session in the sky right now—and I won't even get into how Billy Corgan almost joined them when Paul Sorvino threatened his life at Madonna's after-party.

By the way, having just gotten over being told that a GAY killed Versace, I'm now being fed how the PRESS murdered Lady Di. I'm feeling real popular. But whoever's responsible, the media circus around Di's death certainly reached its peak last week on the *Larry King Show* in which Fran Drescher—suddenly dropping her *Nanny* characterization—tangled with the editor of *The Globe* over media practices, and not only did Tom Selleck and Joan Lunden join the fray but Patsy Ramsey called in as a celebrity done wrong by the tabloids! The misbegotten matriarch voiced her objections to the autopsy shots the tabs ran of her darling JonBenet—as if the parentally approved ones of a bleached-blond, tarted-up three-year-old were the height of taste! Next time Patsy has a complaint, I wish she'd put it in writing so we can at least use it as evidence. Meanwhile, the Queen showed little evidence of any human emotion with her rather cold-fish tribute to Di, but the other queen, Elton John, keeps impressing with heartfelt musical tributes to his princess and designer friends. But how's he going to rewrite that Marilyn Monroe song one more time to make it about Mother Teresa?

A man, duh?

You can call me madam, but do not call Amanda Lepore a drag queen. The Downtown diva was labeled as such by one of the daily papers, so she promptly sent them a Polaroid of herself naked and giving them the finger. "I'm a transsexual!" she exclaims. "I have a vagina!"

And now that we know *what* Amanda Lepore is, it behooves me to explain just *who* she is. She's an omnipresent party girl with beet-red hair, bulbous lips, and the winningly woozy demeanor of an inflatable doll who only comes to life when a camera's in the room. Floating from soiree to soiree with a silicone smile, Amanda causes a stir without saying—or wearing—much, exuding a good-natured alien appeal, like a top-heavy escapee from a sci-fi porn comedy. As Amanda's mentor, photographer David LaChapelle, explains it, "She has no interest in being a girl. She wants to be a *drawing* of a girl, a cartoon like Jessica Rabbit. When I told her that silicone is dangerous, she said, 'I don't care, as long as I look beautiful in the coffin.' There's something kind of profound in that, that she's creating this moment of beauty for herself and is willing to make the ultimate sacrifice."

Now that concepts of beauty have been pushed to kooky new limits, the time seems right for Amanda's intergalactic glamour to catch on beyond 14th Street. LaChapelle recently used her in an Armani TV commercial, and when the designer sent the two of them to Milan, Amanda ate nothing but diet pills and was dubbed La Silicona by the press. On another jaunt, to L.A.'s Chateau Marmont, LaChapelle introduced her to a transfixed Quentin Tarantino, but the blank-faced Amanda had not one clue as to who the auteur director was. "She lives in a complete bubble," LaChapelle says. "Her whole day could be spent combing out hair weaves and massaging her silicone. She doesn't have time for anything else!"

Mercifully enough, she had time to tell me her rather vivid life story. Amanda grew up in Cedar Grove, New Jersey, quite possibly affixed with the name Manny (this is the only tidbit Amanda wouldn't confirm). "I was always really feminine, with the hands on the hips," she revealed. "My parents would say, 'Stop doing that,' and I'd do it more—and here I am!"

At 11, she saw a TV show about sex changes and woke up her horrified parents to tell them she wanted one. But she didn't sign up for the gender guillotine just yet. After unsuccessfully trying to pass as a boy, she went to school as a girl and that immediately won her the attention of a guidance counselor and a personal tutor. During this time, Amanda was getting hormones from an underage transsexual outcast friend, in exchange for outfits she'd make for the trannie. "All of a sudden, I had breasts," Amanda relates. "My mother noticed them, so I said, 'I don't know what happened, they just grew!' The tutor started noticing, too, and recommended I go to a psychiatrist. Well, the shrink diagnosed me as a transsexual, told my parents, and helped me get the hormones!" That's how things seem to happen for this little lady—she always manages to turn dogshit into champagne.

Fortune fell into her constantly morphing lap once again when she dated a plastic surgeon who gave her a free nose job. And later on, Amanda hooked up with a bookstore-owner beau, though she had to keep spurning his attempts to go all the way. "*The Jerry Springer Show* wasn't on then," says Amanda. "It was a lot easier to fool people." Finally, she told the guy her saucy secret, and he freaked—though, naturally, he eventually paid for the sex change and married her. Once again—champagne! (Though things turned shitty, Amanda says, when hubby wouldn't let her leave the house, and even *she* got bored, prompting a bitter breakup.)

But what *about* that operation—in Yonkers, by the way? Did she like her first glimpse of her spanking new vagina? "I didn't know what one looked like," she says. "I was just happy there wasn't anything down there. But at first, it looked pretty bad. It was swollen—like a cow pussy or something." Of course, the swelling eventually went down, and now Amanda says the change was the best thing she's ever done. She go-go dances at clubs, has modeled for CD covers and beer ads, and works the Patricia Field makeup counter, where her cute boyfriend, Victor, first spotted her (though he's yet to pay for any surgery). Amanda has it all. So everyone—chop off your dicks and become famous!

The party monster
I knew and loved

April 2, 2002

A movie about club-kid leader turned killer Michael Alig is starting to roll, but you know how movies about beautiful minds can be. So, as the only observer not on drugs at the time, let me uncork my own reminiscences of Alig in hopes of getting everyone out of a proverbial k-hole.

In his party days—the mid-'80s to mid-'90s—Alig was a charismatic presence with a naughty streak that made him simultaneously compelling and unnerving. He was a genius and the devil, and in '88, I wrote about his and the club kids' "cult of crazy fashion and petulance. They . . . are terminally superficial, have dubious aesthetic values, and are master manipulators, exploiters, and, thank God, partiers." I even compared Alig and company to the Manson family!

Alig and his then boyfriend, Keoki, were nuisances, but colorful ones, and suddenly, at Tunnel in '87, whenever I heard "Michael! Michael!" it was him everyone was calling for. A whole legion of fractured fairy-tale characters was begging for his attention, and if the new-style Mother Goose approved, he assigned them new names and personas and granted them a place in the commercial circus of clubland.

Aware of his rising stature, Alig threw a "Changing of the Guard" party at Red Zone, marking the transition from old school to nouvelle. But he knew how to cater to the dinosaurs, too, giving us titles at his King and Queen of New York pageants and trophies at the Glammies (his ragtag clubbie-awards ceremony). He also had me judge annual Filthy Mouth contests, at which people screamed obscenities for cash prizes, and I gladly contributed to the revelry, enjoying the nyah-nyah goofiness of it all. I even posed semi-nude for an Alig invite that had giant—well, medium-sized—cardboard lips covering my privates, next to the caption "The lips on my cock could be yours if you come to Michael's party!"

And his not-for-prime-time ideas kept coming—like an all-clubbie "Vogue" video he submitted to MTV and an air-tight "disco truck" packed with club kids who ended up, breathless, at one of his party sites. Zaniest of all were the outlaw bashes—illegal descents into subway stations and a McDonald's, which were left buried in sequins and drug dust. After one such blur, Alig ran from the police in a comical escape right out of the Keystone Cops. But he was more like Willy Wonka, giving the kids a factory of rambunctious thrills to play in, if only on his terms.

Disco 2000—his initially pre-Giuliani Wednesday night Limelight event—was a rude debauch with all sexualities blending under the great god Ecstasy. AIDS was other people's problem. Everything was other people's problem. Eventually, the weekly soiree became host to an *Unnatural Acts* revue, wherein an amputee danced until his wooden leg fell off, at which point a wasted girl from the audience humped both the stump and the prosthesis. Another enterprising young lady once took the stage to insert soda bottles into her various orifices—but she paled next to the guy who drank his own piss, ages before *Urinetown* made wee-wee theater legit.

Drunk with power, Alig promoted Julie Jewels, a wan teen with a fake Russian accent, and against all odds he got her to be "it girl" for a few minutes. Mostly, Alig pushed himself and even agreed to get a "downtown makedown" in the *Voice* in '91, letting us make him over into a conservative door-to-door salesman. "The bad seed in cha-cha heels," I wrote, "Alig will do anything to get a response, even if that response is the deafening sound that accompanies projectile vomiting. He's an arrested child who should be arrested . . . a cute little dolly that ends up biting your head off." But obviously, I was still attracted to his moxie and his frenzied, correctness-hating attempts to kill boredom and stir up some fun.

And oh, the memories. Once, Alig—wearing a ski mask—kept trying to unzip my pants and go down on me in a limo. I knew he wasn't turned on—it was just one more *Unnatural Acts* routine, another lips-on-my-cock shtick—and I pushed him away in bemused horror. Hardly anybody else put boundaries on him, though he was definitely screaming out for some. He'd probably ignore them anyway; I once saw him try to push pills into an unamused friend's mouth— and if that failed, honey, he'd just spike the punch bowl.

As the years passed, he wore ass-exposing rag-doll/clown

outfits, also revealing more menace behind the glee. One night, when I caught him mocking me to a friend, he grinned and said, "How do you know we're making fun of you?" Another time, he called me to gloat that shock rocker GG Allin had OD'd and died. (Alig claimed he'd just taped a talk show with Allin, on which the performer had vowed to commit suicide. Now Alig was sure the show would get lots of publicity!) By the time Alig sold a German kid as an indentured sex slave to another promoter, his marketing concepts had become beyond twisted (and I hear it wasn't just *one* kid he pimped).

In December '95, I agreed to go to Alig's apartment to plan some historical club society he'd cooked up. He was practically incoherent, talking even faster than usual and running into the bathroom with a stream of boys that kept arriving without introduction. In late March '96, he called me to plant the item that he'd been fired from the Limelight, but he gave trumped-up reasons, saying owner Peter Gatien's jealous girlfriend had the cops padlock his apartment and he was now homeless and suicidal. A source claimed Alig had busted out of an imposed rehab stint and was still drug ridden. And club kids were murmuring darker secrets—that Alig and roommate Freeze had supposedly killed drug dealer Angel Melendez in a money scuffle—but they'd add, "You didn't hear it from me." He still held power over them, and though I railed against them for this unspeakable outrage, I forgot that he'd long had power over me, too.

By the time Alig sent out a party invite joking about the murder, a lot of people wanted to kill *him* (especially since a source was floating a more premeditated version of the killing). Meanwhile, the cops were lying low since there wasn't a body—and besides, if there was, it would be that of a gay Hispanic club-kid druggie. When they finally found their hacked-up evidence, Alig was on the guest list for lockup and didn't care for the non-VIP treatment (though in later setups, he boasted to friends about all the sex and other privileges). He wrote me a 10-page letter asking for a reference, to help with his sentencing, but I was too busy on the phone with his mother, who cried about prison injustice, calling again the very next day to ask, "What have you done for Michael?"

In '98, Alig wrote a pal that he meditates in jail and "everyone thinks I worship the devil." But his religion was still marketing; from his cell, he asked me for photos for a memoir (then called *Pleasure Junkie: The Last Straw*) and casting advice for his movie. Even more hilariously, he said he wanted to direct! In retrospect, Alig felt he was a shy boy who overcompensated—a lot—and in '99, he more specifically blamed gayness for his ruin. He wrote in his hometown Indiana paper that the urban gay lifestyle is out of control and, self-destructively, "I dealt with that by medicating myself with drugs." Oh well, I still had my sweeter memories, like him trying to pull me into a pool at Tunnel or running a *Project X* chart of all the clubbies he thought had gotten hepatitis from each other. Those were the days—no, really. Now Hollywood?

County bears jamboree

May 31, 2005

As the strictures on nightlife get tighter than a tit clamp, the gay-bar scene goes further out on a ledge of tawdry yet exciting indiscretion. The specialty "flu shot" at the Slide allegedly has customers slurping a hit of booze out of the foreskin of a go-go boy. (Alas, I'm on a no-alcohol, no-cheese diet.) And now there's another vivacious genital beverage to be had—at the Man Party, which caters to gay skinheads with a follicularly challenged attitude, on the second and fourth Fridays of the month at Octagon. The bash has all the expected dart games, boxing, and head-shaving rituals you get with any Disney-esque macho emporium. But for the extra spunky, they've instituted a sperm contest, whereby attendees' spooge samples are judged based on their visual personality, if not their actual flavor. (It all tastes the same anyway—like chicken.)

On the party's opening night, Dr. Spunk, a friendly man in a lab coat, presided over a table loaded with plastic cups, which clubbies were urged to take home and fill with their viscous emissions. But not just at any old time. You were instructed to shoot your seed into the receptacle sometime between 10 and 11 P.M. on the night of the contest, May 27, then rush the specimen into the club before midnight (which admittedly could lead to a poignant party full of already spent gays.) Alas, none of the clientele—all of whom looked like slightly less butch versions of *Star Trek*'s Persis Khambatta—seemed to be going for this incredible opportunity, though a couple of lesbians were lurking around, probably trying to figure how they could eventually nab some of the stuff to make babies with. Not me—I was running for the exit, uncharacteristically declining the offer to be a "celebrity judge."

The Night of the Grizzly

A quick chubby-chasing stop at the Bear County Fair a couple of days later might have given potential jizz contestants the rise they needed; the LGBT Center event had plus-size gays and their admirers paying festive homage to love handles and back hair over heaping portions of ribs and brownies. And there were games galore—like a cock-ring toss and a cardboard Glory Hole Bear (you threw balls through . . . never mind)—though the real game-playing was in seeing which Smokey would put out your fire or why a certain Winnie wanted your poo. The fair—a benefit for Bear Café New York, Inc.—was such a hit it even drew a backlash in the form of a guy who showed up accessorized by a snout and a "Pig in Protest" sign. Every party has a Pooh-per.

But total pigs are more than welcome practically every-where else in gayland after dark. Boysroom has a check-your-clothes "Dirty Dirty" contest on Hustler Thursdays, oink oink, and Michael Wakefield and RED's monthly "SPAM" parties in the basement of a Park Slope residential building provide "mandatory pants check" shenanigans for the whole LGBT community. (Check out worldofwakefield. com for details.) Queers of all genders are welcome, and guess what, Mary? Not only aren't all the gay men spewing buckets of repulsion vomit over that, but some of them even let lesbians strap one on and ride their high horse, as it were. I love community diversity in action.

As Wakefield told me, "There's a real fluidity of sexuality that expresses itself at the party." Yeah—and with real fluids, too. "You see interesting combinations of gay guys, lesbians, and transsexuals," he went on, soberly. "I've met a lot of female-to-male transsexuals or bois that look like young boys. Some of them wear a softie—a fake penis that's com-pletely flaccid—in their underwear. Once, I started to suck someone's softie and people gathered to watch." Honey, that was no tranny with a softie—that was the best blowjob I ever got!

Disgusting!
A sex club without sex!

December 13, 2005

I finally cranked up the cojones to go to El Mirage, the gay sex club on East Houston Street, where love is just 43 bucks and a leather harness away. Crawling into the unremarkable-looking entrance while covering my face, I found an eager line of wannabe wankers, which I joined for the 10 longest, most brightly lit minutes of my life. Eventually it was my turn to check in, which involved being shown the rules—"Be courteous," etc.—and signing something that said, among other things, "I was born a male with male genitalia and chosen to retain such." (I guess that weeds out all those irksome transsexuals, if not the illiterates.) After forking over the 40-buck initiation fee and swearing I wasn't a cop, I was not only named a throbbing member, I was given a "frequent fucker's card," which guarantees that after only 18 visits, you get one whole entry, as it were, for free.

Alas, I won't even make it for a second time. The place is just too humiliating—in different ways than one had hoped. At the checkroom, I was ordered to hand over all my clothes except either my T-shirt or my underwear—plus three more dollars! This became like a gay Sophie's choice, as I anxiously stood there deciding which body part should be exposed, my doughy boobies or floor-scraping scrotum. Under pressure, I cooked up a plan, shrewdly telling them I'd wear just my T-shirt, while slipping my undies in my bag so I could sneak them on again in the club and cover my male genitalia. Practically everyone else chose to wear *neither* option, so I ended up as overdressed as Bette Davis in *Jezebel*—the only person to ever sport a cluttered look in a sex club.

But however you dress, the place turned out to be surprisingly lovely—let's be courteous—with fenced-off or netted areas studded with trees and awash in soft lighting and low-playing Brazilian music. It's all very Chelsea Market meets *On Golden Pond* en route to the Ramble. Too bad what's missing is any palpable sense of sex appeal. Every single guy there seems to be a five—not good looking, not bad looking; not young, not old; not to die for, not to die from. They're all about the same! It's totally tragic tuna! If a six ever wandered into the mix, he'd be mass-eaten alive before even getting to the clothes check. What's worse, though they've got it all hanging out, a lot of the guys act so skittish and tentative that the mood hardly ever becomes charged, and the paper towels available on tables (along with lube and condoms) seem to only get used for flop sweat. There's an occasional sex tableau on a sling or herky-jerky scene in a corner—with hungry faces pressed against the fence to watch—but I barely noticed them since I was busy dodging all the customers blankly roaming the joint, self-consciously waiting for Godot to come and pinch their nipples.

I had to applaud the more proactive types, like the two gentlemen lying on their stomachs with synchronized butts perched in the air—but they had to stay frozen in that pose for hours, devoid of any available frequent fuckers. Imagine the discipline that takes! "It's dangerous in here," one guy murmured to his friend outside the supposed orgy room. "I almost poked my eye out on a tree." Oh, *that's* what that was. Well, my bag must have been a hazard, too, because an employee eventually tracked me down and demanded I check it, no doubt for three more dollars. Instead, I took my male genitalia, along with my street clothes, and went to a tranny bar for free.